The Library
IN EAST AYRSHIRE

East Ayrshire
COUNCIL

Please return item by last date shown,
or contact library to renew

POISONED LIVES

Poisoned Lives

English Poisoners and their Victims

Katherine Watson

Hambledon and London
London and New York

Hambledon and London

102 Gloucester Avenue
London, NW1 8HX

175 Fifth Avenue
New York, NY 10010
USA

First Published 2004

ISBN 1 85285 379 4

A description of this book is available from the
British Library and from the Library of Congress.

Typeset by Carnegie Publishing, Lancaster,
and printed in Great Britain by Cambridge University Press.

Distributed in the United States and Canada
exclusively by Palgrave Macmillan,
a division of St Martin's Press.

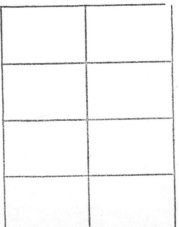

Contents

Illustrations

In memory of those who
were given no opportunity to choose

Acknowledgements

I would like to thank the following for reading and commenting on various chapters: Dr Adam Fox, Alberto Giannetto, Giles Hudson, Dr Eileen Magnello, June Nagai and Dr John C. Wood. Special thanks go to Dr Jonathan Andrews, who helped place things in perspective, Dr Viviane Quirke, for solving a tricky problem, and Martin Sheppard, sympathetic and supportive editor. Dr Bob Flanagan has long been the generous source of invaluable information on toxicology and cases of poisoning, while the friendly and efficient staff of the Public Record Office helped speed my research. Other friends (who will know who they are), and my family, have offered constant encouragement. Finally, I would like to acknowledge the support of the Wellcome Trust: the archive work for this book was begun while I held a postdoctoral fellowship at the then Wellcome Institute for the History of Medicine.

Introduction

A woman came to the shop about ten minutes after and applied
for a pennyworth of arsenic ... I asked her what she wanted it for,
and she said it was to destroy rats as they could not lay in bed
quietly for them. She said they had torn her husband's shirt to
pieces in bed and showed me two places on her hand that she said
had been bit by the rats when in bed.

George Gorell, 1837 [1]

Poisons were readily available in eighteenth- and nineteenth-century
England, and the would-be poisoner was spoilt for choice: over fifty
different substances appear in 540 cases over this period. By and large,
however, poisoners relied on what was easily to hand. For the majority,
this meant either some form of rat poison or the more expensive opium
and its derivatives. Thus, when Rebecca Stevenson bought one ounce
of white arsenic from druggist's apprentice George Gorell in March
1837, he believed her claim that her house was so infested with rats that
she and her husband had been attacked in their bed. It was only after
the death by arsenic of Ruth Watkin, the following day, that this story
was questioned. When her young son denied that there were any rats
in the house, Rebecca was forced to admit that the shirt-eating episode
had occurred years before. Her husband Joseph was of little help:
although he regularly used arsenic to kill the parasites that burrowed
under his horse's skin, he had not taken the packet that his wife brought
home. It looked suspiciously as though Rebecca had murdered Watkin,
but her death was in fact the result of an attempted self-abortion. Five
months pregnant and abandoned days earlier by her lover, Rebecca's
half cousin Robert Lunn, Watkin had threatened to abort the child, saying
that she could not tolerate the scandal of becoming an unwed mother.[2]

The question was whether Rebecca had knowingly supplied the poison, thus committing murder. At her trial, in July 1837, a jury decided that she had not.

Rebecca Stevenson's brush with the law offers a useful opening to this study of English poisoners of the eighteenth and nineteenth centuries, as many features of the case provide typical examples of their kind. Foremost among these was the poison that she bought, together with the excuse that she gave for wanting it. White arsenic had for centuries enjoyed a reputation as the poisoner's weapon of choice, but by the eighteenth century it had found many other legitimate uses, mainly in agriculture, manufacturing, medicine and vermin control. Affordable to even the poorest, arsenic accounted for about 45 per cent of known poison-related crimes between 1750 and 1914. At the time of Ruth Watkin's death this figure was even higher: a survey of inquests held in 1837–38 showed that, of seven deaths caused by the deliberate administration of poison, five were due to arsenic and two to laudanum, a solution of opium in alcohol.[3] Moreover, poisoning was at this time a crime found principally among the working classes, although, as employees of a paper mill, Watkin and the Stevensons were slightly better off than many other alleged poisoners and their victims. In addition, the relationship between Watkin and Rebecca was significant. They were not only neighbours but, through the absent Lunn, shared a moral bond of kinship. In many respects they could be considered to be part of the same extended family, and it was within families that the vast majority of poisoning crimes occurred.

Poisoned Lives will describe how and why poison appeared in people's lives. The motives that drove poisoners were always variants on the same themes: poverty and greed, love and hate – often exacerbated by a lack of choice and seething desperation. Spousal murder resulted from the inability of all but the wealthy to extricate themselves legally from unhappy unions. Child victims were once widespread: little valued by society, their parents found it remarkably easy to kill them, to save money or to profit by small sums. The first female serial killers poisoned family members for the same reason. The rise of the insurance industry led to a motive for murder that is today associated with large cash amounts, but which began among the local burial clubs of the north west. Domestic servants, once the second largest occupational group in

the country, had no recourse when frustrated or abused by their employers. Poisoning was thus primarily a crime of the poor and
underprivileged, a fact that has previously been consistently overlooked:
studies have focused on a few cases that became notorious because the
perpetrators were unusual – their gender or social status set them apart.
Historians have tended to scrutinise the cases of female and medical
poisoners, the former because women who kill (particularly middle-class
women) have long been seen as freaks of nature, the latter because
doctors who betray their oath to do no harm are little better. Most
people today automatically assume that the typical English poisoner was
a woman, or perhaps a doctor. This was not the case.

This study challenges old assumptions and breaks new ground by
examining several hundred cases of criminal poisoning that occurred
all over England during a period of nearly two centuries; it looks at the
majority, rather than a small minority, of poisoners. In this way, changes
in the crime and in the methods, motives and profile of its perpetrators
can be traced and linked to the changes that took place in society at
large. Such a widespread view of the crime has been achieved mainly
through accounts of the crimes themselves. A few of the more infamous
cases generated books and pamphlets, while many others received detailed newspaper coverage. But the main sources of information on
lesser-known cases are the legal records that they generated, principally
witness statements (depositions) taken by the coroner or magistrate who
investigated the case. Such statements were later used in court to prosecute the alleged poisoner, and are now part of the nation's archives.
As such, they are stored at the Public Record Office in Kew, classified
according to the region in which the case was tried. These documents
have made possible a more comprehensive study of poisoners than has
hitherto been feasible, but they restrict the study of most cases to
'snapshots in time': it is usually impossible to follow individuals once
they have emerged from the legal process. Nonetheless, the fact that
they give a voice to those who would otherwise remain unknown to
history – the poor and illiterate – offers a significant expansion of our
knowledge of the history of criminal poisoning in England. The very
few Welsh cases identified (only fifteen) have been included as further
examples of the type, but from a part of the British Isles which, though
governed by the same laws, was known for being the least criminal and

most orderly part of the country. Nevertheless, Welsh poisoners clearly suffered the same fears and privations as their English brethren.

This study of English poisoners will be unique in another way. Rather than concentrating on wide-ranging concerns such as the cultural meanings of poison, or issues of social deviance, moral panic, or medico-legal uncertainty (all topics which, though related to the subject in hand, have been explored in depth elsewhere),[4] it will address the particular concerns that underlay the actions of the people involved. It will look at the society that these individuals lived in, and consider what it really meant to become a victim of poison, to enable readers to understand both the crime and the investigative efforts that went into proving that poisoning had occurred. It will focus mainly on the period between 1750 and the First World War: scientific evidence of poisoning was presented in court for the first time in 1752, while the outbreak of war in 1914 marked the beginning of unprecedented changes in English society, and thus in the profile of the English poisoner. This book will, above all, focus on people: on associated actors such as coroners, police officers, doctors and chemists, but most especially on poisoners and their victims. We begin with the victim's experience.

1

Victims

Besides these appearances, I observed that he had a low, trembling, intermitting pulse; a difficult, unequal respiration; a yellowish complexion; a difficulty in the utterance of his words; and an inability of swallowing even a teaspoonful of the thinnest liquor at a time. As I suspected that these appearances and symptoms were the effect of poison, I asked Miss Blandy whether Mr Blandy had lately given offence to either of his servants or clients, or any other person.

Dr Anthony Addington, 1752 [1]

Imagine stomach pains so sharp that it seems like rats are gnawing at your insides. The pain is accompanied by a thirst almost impossible to quench, with loss of bowel control and a violent vomiting and retching. Vomit and faeces stain you, your bed, and the floor around you; your family cannot wash the linen quickly enough to keep it clean. The air in the room in which you lie is utterly foul. You have a few hours to live, perhaps a few days: despite the best efforts of your doctor, you will die. Opium may dull the pain a little, but you will be alert enough to wonder what has happened. If your doctor has had some prior experience, he will realise what he is facing and take samples of your vomit and faeces. At autopsy, he will find telltale signs: a red and inflamed alimentary tract, perhaps eaten through in small patches. A chemist will test the samples, in order to confirm the diagnosis. As a consequence, the legal system will take over. The local coroner or magistrate will order that someone to whom you are closely related – perhaps your spouse, or your parent – should be tried for your murder. You are a victim of arsenic poisoning, unwittingly ingested in a meal that probably tasted a little odd. If justice is to be done, the cause of your death has to be proved in a court of law.

Given our modern, media-inspired understanding of the effects of a drug overdose, it is perhaps unsurprising that the realities of death from one of the poisons common in the eighteenth and nineteenth centuries should be so little known. As regular viewers of TV medical dramas, we tend to think of death by poison as something that happens quietly at home or painlessly in a hospital, the suicidal result of alcohol mixed with prescription tablets. Poison seems the easy way out, far less traumatic and bloody than any other unnatural cause of death. But few people, even those who have survived a suicide attempt or accidental poisoning, have any idea of what it was like to perish by poison a hundred and fifty years ago, when the most common poisons operated in a manner that was anything but gentle. Probably the closest modern analogy is the stereotypical image of the heroin addict, found dead from an overdose in squalid circumstances, a needle protruding from his or her arm. But not even this horrific end is comparable to the sufferings of the typical Georgian or Victorian victim of poison. In order to understand the experience of poisoning from the victim's point of view – a subject that most works on the history of crime and forensic science tend to overlook – we need to know how poisons acted on the human body. Once they had done their terrible work, doctors and chemists had to learn how to read and correctly interpret the clues that they left to their presence.

Though sometimes quick and painless, death by poison was more frequently an excruciating and lengthy process that usually took place within the victim's home. Relatives, friends and servants could do little but act as nurses. Medical practitioners too were often baffled, as the effects of poison could be mistaken for those of disease. The appearance of Asiatic cholera in England in 1831 contributed significantly to this confusion, since it produced symptoms similar to those caused by arsenic (also known as white arsenic), the poisoner's weapon of choice. By the early 1840s chemists had developed two tests for arsenic, the Marsh and Reinsch tests, which played a central role in resolving this problem. Strychnine, another substance known for its lethal properties, was usually unmistakable in its violent symptoms and, after a somewhat shaky start, chemists developed tests that could be relied upon to detect it in the bodies of suspected victims. Opium poisoning was also relatively easy to recognise but more difficult to prove. Poisoning cases stimulated the development of the new medical and chemical approaches that were needed to meet the challenges posed by the increasingly sophisticated demands of the legal system.

When Mary Blandy, aged thirty-one, was tried at Oxford in March 1752 for the murder of her father, the case became the first in which convincing scientific proof of poisoning was given; if such a death had occurred prior to this date, it went unrecorded.[2] Before the trial, which aroused a great deal of public interest because of Blandy's position as the attractive and accomplished daughter of a local worthy, medical witnesses in murder cases were not uncommon,[3] but trials for poisoning were. This was almost certainly due to two reasons: a large proportion of deaths from poison were never recognised as such, and the overall incidence of such deaths was actually very small – the factors that led to the later widespread availability of poison were not yet of significant concern. At the Old Bailey, London's Central Criminal Court, where trials for London, Middlesex, and parts of Essex, Kent and Surrey were held, only four poisoning cases were heard between 1729 and 1768, out of a total of well over 300 trials for murder and manslaughter.[4] Convictions seem to have rested primarily on confessions, or on the scantiest of evidence that the victim had actually died from poison, which evidence was likely to be both circumstantial and hard to come by.[5] The principal signs thought to indicate a death from poison were external: bodies marked by blisters and decay, or which putrefied rapidly, might have been poisoned. Arsenic was long thought to preserve a corpse for an unnatural length of time after death.[6] During an era when rigorous autopsies and chemical tests were infrequent, it was as likely that an innocent person would be convicted and executed as that a guilty party would go free.

There is, however, little doubt that Mary Blandy was guilty of the crime of which she was accused, and her story has passed into legend. Unmarried at the age of thirty, she became attracted to a Scottish army officer named William Cranstoun, who had arrived at Henley-on-Thames, where the Blandy family lived, on recruiting service. They soon began a liaison, but he already had a wife. When this was discovered, her father, Francis Blandy, forbade them to see each other. Believing that Mary was to inherit £10,000, Cranstoun refused to give her up, and hatched a plot to remove the old man. After returning to Scotland, he sent arsenic to Mary: he did not tell her what it was, only that it would help to persuade her father to allow them to marry. She administered it to him in food and drink on several occasions between November 1750 and 14 August 1751, causing a severe and debilitating illness in Blandy and lesser symptoms in two maids who, towards the end of this period, ate some of the same food. These young women noticed a white powder at the bottom of a pot of gruel (a thin porridge), and gave it to the local apothecary.[7]

There is no record of what, if any, medical advice was given to the sick man before August 1751, when Dr Anthony Addington, of Reading, was called in; he was to become a principal witness for the prosecution. He told the court what Francis Blandy had told him: that after drinking some gruel on 5 August, he had noticed an extraordinary grittiness in his mouth, a very painful burning and pricking in his tongue, throat, stomach and bowels, as well as fits of vomiting and purging (diarrhoea). As a result of the purging, the area around Blandy's anus had begun to ulcerate. Addington quickly connected these symptoms with poisoning, and he was confirmed in his suspicion after he examined the white powder that the maids had given the apothecary: it was white ar-senic.[8] At last moved to pity by her father's sufferings, Mary Blandy admitted that she had given him some powder, thinking it would make him fond of Cranstoun.

It was too late to save Francis Blandy, who died on 14 August 1751, aged sixty-two. An autopsy was performed the following day, showing that his body was livid and shrivelled, and that his eyes had bled. The internal organs were discoloured, darker than normal, and stained with bruise-like spots. The inner surface of the stomach and intestines was 'prodigiously inflamed and excoriated'.[9] There was no trace of natural decay, a reference to the supposed preservative effects of arsenic. A second physician agreed that the signs were indicative of poison. Neither the organs nor stomach contents were analysed, but chemical tests were made on the powder scraped from the gruel pan. These were remarkably non-specific. Addington and an experienced chemist from Reading, a Mr King, concluded that the powder was arsenic because it was white, gritty and insoluble in cold water, and released thick white fumes and a smell of garlic when thrown on to hot iron, as did arsenic. Additionally,

it reacted in the same way as a known sample of arsenic did to five
different precipitate tests (chemical reactions forming identifiable solid
substances). A later commentator noted that it was lucky that the
accused woman confessed, as, with hindsight, the precipitate tests
seemed rather to indicate the presence of some lead compound than
arsenic.[10]

This evidence, together with Mary Blandy's own confession and the
testimony of servants who had heard her predict her father's death and
seen her put powder into his food, comprised the case for the prosecution. Defence witnesses spoke mainly of the good relations that had
always existed between father and daughter, and denied that Mary had
attempted to flee after his death. In his detailed summary to the jury,
the judge observed that Blandy had certainly died by poison administered to him by his daughter. The only question to consider was whether
she knew that what she gave him was a poison.[11] The answer to this
seemed obviously to be 'yes': after conferring for five minutes the jury
returned a guilty verdict. Mary Blandy was hanged a month later. The
instigator of the crime, William Cranstoun, escaped to France, where
he died soon after.

The painful and prolonged death of Francis Blandy was typical of the
classic arsenic murder. As late as 1936, a textbook of forensic medicine
warned that, when symptoms of gastroenteritis (inflammation of the
stomach and bowels) and failing health appeared in a patient, doctors
ought to consider the possibility of arsenical poisoning, which could be
acute or chronic.[12] Chronic poisoning developed after repeated but
minor exposure to a toxic agent. Symptoms emerged gradually, often
with remissions and recurrences, as the poison accumulated in the body.
Chronic poisoning was (and still is) often associated with occupational
hazards, but could occur by design, particularly in the case of arsenic.
In small doses it causes gastroenteritis, loss of appetite, nausea, occasional vomiting and general malaise. Diarrhoea can occur, but
sometimes constipation results. The body's mucous membranes become
inflamed, causing conjunctivitis, coughing and hoarseness. An abnormal
amount of fluid accumulates under the skin, the face and eyelids being
particularly affected. Over an extended period of time, the skin becomes
damaged because arsenic causes blood vessels to dilate: this can lead to

dermatitis and hair loss.[13] These symptoms of general ill health tended to allay suspicion when the patient died, as Blandy did, from a larger final dose,[14] and death was often ascribed to organ failure: arsenic affects the normal functioning of the kidneys and liver. In such cases, the time it took the victim to die was largely in the hands of the poisoner, who could complete his task in as little as a week or as long as several weeks or months.

In contrast, acute poisoning usually followed a single large dose, being characterised by the sudden onset of symptoms that ran a short course but did not necessarily lead to death. This is because individual responses to poison vary enormously: it is possible for one person to recover from what might be a fatal dose to another. Where arsenic was concerned, the first indication that a sufferer had consumed something unusual came almost immediately: despite the fact that arsenic has no taste, many people noted the fact that food or drink tasted 'hot'. What victims variously described as 'hot like pepper' (or cayenne pepper, or tobacco), was due to the burning sensation caused by arsenic's acidic properties.

Following ingestion of a large dose (about a grain, 65 milligrams), symptoms could appear within minutes, but more commonly within an hour. They began with nausea, burning in the throat, and pain in the stomach. Sufferers were known to report an almost instant feeling of pressure and swelling in the stomach, so forceful that they feared they would burst.[15] Uncontrollable vomiting and diarrhoea soon followed, and these were affected by the patient's intense thirst: the stools became thin and watery, and they eventually started to vomit up all the water that they consumed. As a result of dehydration, painful cramps could develop in the legs. A feeling of general weakness often abated during short periods of remission, but improvements were usually short-lived. The mind remained clear until close to the end, which was often preceded by delirium, convulsions or coma.[16] The time between the onset of symptoms and death varied, depending on the size of the dose and how much of the poison was absorbed, but was usually between a few hours and two or three days.

Absorption depended upon how the arsenic was administered. If it was in solution, it was absorbed very rapidly. If it was in the solid form, the more coarsely it was powdered, the more readily it was passed out of the body in the faeces. What remained in the stomach and intestines quite literally scoured the internal membranes, causing redness and, if many hours elapsed, ulceration to the point that holes could develop. These effects on the stomach appeared no matter what form the arsenic had been in when taken. If and when an autopsy was performed, it was this appearance that was instantly obvious to the medical practitioner, who often found tiny white particles of arsenic adhering to the membrane surface. If a post-mortem was performed some days after death, perhaps following exhumation, it was common to find yellow patches on both the inner and outer surfaces of the stomach and bowels. This yellow substance was orpiment, arsenic trisulphide, formed by a chemical reaction between white arsenic and hydrogen sulphide produced by the decaying body. On those occasions when an exhumed corpse was found to be unusually fresh looking, laymen and doctors alike long tended to attribute it to the supposed preservative effects of arsenic,[17] even though English forensic experts denied that it either hastened or retarded putrefaction.[18] In fact, this effect occurred as a result of dehydration suffered during life.

The relative paucity of poisoning trials during the eighteenth century may in part be explained by the similarity between the symptoms of acute arsenic poisoning and those caused by three bowel diseases once common in England: English cholera, dysentery and diarrhoea. To those well acquainted with them, and also with cases of poisoning, the differences would have been obvious. But most medical men lacked the relevant experience: by about 1800 the incidence of English cholera and dysentery had declined markedly, perhaps as a result of improved living conditions, better nutrition and hygiene, and efforts made to ease urban congestion.[19] Diarrhoea, a bacterial infection characterised by a constant flow of liquid but otherwise natural stools, remained a widespread illness that often proved fatal to infants and the elderly. Dysentery and English cholera were far more extreme in their effects. The former was marked by bloody stools caused by the sloughing of the mucous lining of the large intestine, as well as fever and abdominal pain. Severe dehydration and poisoning by bacterial toxins could kill a victim within two to fifteen days. English cholera was often preceded by mild diarrhoea, which gave way to frequent and violent vomiting and purging accompanied by abdominal cramps; bile produced by the liver to aid digestion was mixed with the excretions, giving them a distinctive yellowish colour. Death could occur in as little as two or three days.[20] Both diseases resulted from bacterial infection, though there was also a form of dysentery caused by amoeba, the symptoms of which were identical to those caused by bacteria.

It might thus have been possible to confuse the vomiting and purging caused by arsenic poisoning with the effects of disease. This became all the more likely with the advent in England of Asiatic cholera, a highly fatal bacterial gut disease endemic in India. Transmitted mainly by contaminated drinking water, the world experienced successive pandemics from 1817. The disease reached England from Europe for the first time in October 1831, and thereafter the country suffered epidemics in 1832, 1848, 1854 and 1866.[21] Characterised by violent vomiting and purging, Asiatic cholera received its name because of its similarity to English cholera, but the two diseases were distinct; the most obvious sign of this fact being the absence of bile in the excretions of patients suffering from the Asiatic type. Instead, the matter ejected from the bowels, which might at the beginning of an attack appear natural, eventually assumed the appearance of thin gruel, gaining the name of 'rice-water stools'. Victims also suffered considerable thirst, pain in the throat and stomach, feeble pulse and cold skin. But the most dramatic effects of the disease lay in its transformation of the facial features of sufferers, which became pinched and of a bluish colour, the eyes sunken and glassy, the bones prominent, the voice faint. Indeed, noted one observer, 'the whole aspect is that of a being who is about to become the tenant of the grave'.[22]

Superficially, then, Asiatic cholera closely mimicked the symptoms of arsenic poisoning, so much so that medical experts began to fear that suspected poisoners had found a ready-made defence. As the epidemic of 1848 raged, Henry Letheby, a well-known toxicologist based at the London Hospital, published a list of the symptoms caused by the two conditions, pointing out where they differed. Most notably, the symptoms occurred in a different order. In arsenic poisoning, there was first a feeling of heat and pain, followed by vomiting, then diarrhoea. The faeces were often dark and streaked with blood, a feature never seen in cases of cholera, where pain tended to follow a sudden attack of vomiting and purging. Patients who had been poisoned did not suffer cold or bluish skin, or the sunken features indicative of cholera; rather, the eyes were often bulging and bloodshot. In poisoning cases thirst usually preceded purging; in cholera cases it followed it. For medical men aware of these differences, it was possible to ensure that cases of arsenical poisoning did not go unnoticed. But in order to be absolutely certain of a diagnosis, a chemical analysis of the urine, faeces and vomit was necessary.[23] Not only would this distinguish cases of poisoning from those of cholera or other disease, it would separate arsenic from other mineral poisons with which it could sometimes be confused.

Among the inorganic (mineral-based) poisons most frequently encountered in English criminal cases, salts of mercury, lead and antimony ran a poor second behind arsenic. Of these, the symptoms of acute poisoning by tartar emetic (antimony potassium tartrate) were most similar to those caused by arsenic: severe vomiting and purging, and depression of the nervous system. If anything, they occurred even more strongly than in cases of arsenic poisoning. But a marked difference lay in the fact that the onset of symptoms was generally immediate (with arsenic they were delayed for up to an hour), and that they were accompanied by a distinct metallic taste in the mouth of the victim. After death, which usually occurred following an illness of a day or two, the post-mortem appearances were also similar to those caused by arsenic: gastric intestinal irritation, and orange stains of antimony sulphide as a result of putrefaction. Chronic poisoning caused nausea, vomiting, purging, loss of appetite leading to emaciation and, finally, death from exhaustion. Like arsenic, antimony poisoning caused dehydration, and thus had a preserving effect on bodies after death.[24]

Deaths caused by salts of mercury were rather more common than those caused by antimony, but were much easier to identify and distinguish from cases of arsenical poisoning. In all the forms in which it was most commonly found – red and white precipitate (mercuric oxide and mercuric ammonium chloride), calomel and corrosive sublimate (compounds of mercury and chlorine) – the general mercurial symptoms were the same: salivation, swollen gums and loosened teeth, foul breath and kidney damage. Only corrosive sublimate – as its name would suggest – caused violent symptoms, which usually appeared within five minutes in acute cases. These developed into gastroenteritis, nausea and vomiting, profuse diarrhoea (often blood-stained), and general depression. A clear distinction between this and arsenic poisoning lay in the strong metallic taste associated with corrosive sublimate, which could frustrate the efforts of would-be poisoners. Death usually occurred after several days, a much longer period than normally seen in acute arsenic cases. At autopsy, the mouth and oesophagus appeared whitened and corroded in places, the large intestine more inflamed and ulcerated than the stomach, the kidneys congested with blood. These effects were produced even if the poison had been absorbed through the skin, rather than swallowed.[25] Chronic mercurial poisoning, which was common in industrial settings, is not known to have occurred as a result of criminal intent. Symptoms included ulceration and gangrene of the mouth and jaw, anemia, emaciation and tremors known as mercurial palsy. Mania could follow, and it was from this that the term 'mad as a hatter' derived: mercurous nitrate was used in the making of felt hats.

Of the salts of lead, only lead acetate (sugar of lead) was soluble enough to cause a significant number of acute poisonings; lead carbonate and lead oxide more often caused chronic cases. Acute symptoms included a burning sensation in the mouth and throat, followed by vomiting and pains in the abdomen; the most obvious indication that the case was one of lead poisoning was the fact that these pains were relieved by firm pressure. There was usually a tendency to constipation, but any faeces that were produced were black in colour, due to the formation of lead sulphide. There was thirst, and the muscles of the legs became painfully cramped. Death from a large dose (at least an ounce was required to produce toxic effects) could occur in about three days, from general collapse. Sometimes acute cases survived long enough to develop some or all of the symptoms of chronic poisoning: exhaustion, loss of appetite and emaciation, nausea, foul breath, anaemia, paralysis of the nerves of the forearm, and a blue line on the gums formed by deposition of lead sulphide. The post-mortem effects of lead salts on humans were mostly unknown, but medical practitioners could expect to find the mucous membranes of the stomach and intestines inflamed, or occasionally eroded.[26]

If the effects of certain metallic salts could be confused for those of arsenic, this was never the case where the mineral acids were concerned. Their burning and corrosive action left such telltale signs on the bodies of victims that medical men could be left in no doubt as to the cause; it remained only to determine which of the three acids (nitric, sulphuric, hydrochloric) had been to blame. As little as a teaspoon of each, when concentrated, was sufficient to cause death from corrosion of soft tissue and internal organs, or from suffocation caused by damage to the airways; victims also succumbed to shock and haemorrhage. Because of their immediately destructive action, there was rarely enough time for mineral acids to act as true poisons, though it was possible for victims to die months or years later from secondary effects such as organ damage. Primary effects included burnt patches on skin and lips, intense thirst and pain, and vomiting of bloody matter; death normally occurred within twenty-four hours, the mind remaining clear until near the end. The burns and stains caused by nitric acid were usually bright yellow, those by sulphuric acid were brown, while hydrochloric did not usually produce any on the mouth and throat. The stomach was blackened, except in cases of nitric acid poisoning where it was yellow (caused by the action of the acid on proteins).[27] As one surgeon remarked of death from a mineral acid, 'it is the most agonising thing that can happen'.[28]

Of the signs and symptoms caused by the inorganic poisons most commonly encountered in criminal cases, many could, if a doctor were unwary, be confused with those caused by the poisoner's weapon of choice, arsenic. It was thus imperative that reliable chemical tests were developed for all mineral poisons, and such tests soon became the ultimate recourse of any prosecutor who had to provide sure evidence of poisoning. By the middle of the nineteenth century, the methods employed to gather this proof were far more advanced than those in use at the time of Francis Blandy's death.

On 14 September 1849, at a house in Chapel Street, Cheltenham, seven people sat down to a lunch of bread and cucumbers, boiled meat and apple dumplings. Within minutes, siblings Caroline (aged twenty-two), Elizabeth (twenty-one) and Samuel Gregory (fourteen) had become ill. Their mother Diana, a widow, suspected that the cucumber was at fault and so failed to heed Caroline's warning not to give the remaining dumplings to the lodger, Emanuel Barnett, until the doctor had come. Both Barnett and Diana Gregory's brother, James Keylock, ate a small portion of one; the complaints of Elizabeth and Samuel prevented them from eating any more, and Diana from eating any at all. Only she and her small grandson remained free of the vomiting and stomach pains that the others suffered, as neither tasted the dumplings.[29]

Recovering sufficiently to leave the house, Caroline Gregory went to fetch her uncle, a surgeon, at three o'clock, but he was out and his young assistant, William Hatch, came instead. He found Caroline and Samuel Gregory prostrate and vomiting a green fluid. Although he could 'find no smell of poison' on their breath, he nonetheless treated the case as one of poisoning, not disease, probably alerted by the intense burning pains in the stomach and throat that both patients were experiencing. He prescribed an emetic, and opium for the pain.[30] While he returned to the surgery to prepare the medicines, a neighbour's child was sent for a more experienced medical man, Dr William Brookes. She told him that five people were ill with cholera at the Gregory house, and that one was dying.

Arriving in Chapel Street at about half past seven, Brookes found the three Gregory siblings in an upstairs bedroom, Caroline and Elizabeth in one bed, Samuel in another. The odour in the room was terrible, from the diarrhoea and vomiting that none of them could control. All three craved cold water. Keylock and Barnett were downstairs, and had obviously been vomiting. But of all the victims, it was Elizabeth who was clearly suffering the most. In an effort to determine the cause of the illness, Brookes asked Diana Gregory about the state of the local drainage system, and about the food they'd been eating. She told him there were no drains or cesspools open nearby – thus ruling out Asiatic cholera – but that they had eaten three cucumbers and one and a half dumplings. The little boy had eaten some of the meat, but was perfectly well.

Brookes shared Gregory's suspicions about the vegetables, especially after he discovered that the one remaining cucumber was rotten. Deciding that it was a case of food poisoning, he prescribed opium and a chalk mixture to calm the vomiting. In addition, Elizabeth was to have a mustard poultice placed on her stomach, a common remedy for severe abdominal pains. He then left, telling Gregory to send for him again if the girl got worse. At 10 that night a boy came to his door to tell him that Elizabeth had just died and that the others were dying.

When Brookes returned to Chapel Street he found William Hatch already there. Caroline was still vomiting, as was Samuel. Their mother was, too, but knew that it was due to the stress of the situation: Elizabeth was dead, and Samuel seemed to be getting worse. Mercifully, Caroline appeared to have turned a corner, and was able to speak to the doctor, telling him that she had eaten less of the dumpling than her sister had because she'd thought it tasted 'hot like cayenne pepper'.[31] When the coroner was informed of the death, he sent a policeman to collect some of the remaining dumplings, which Barnett had cut up and thrown down the privy, as well as a sample of vomit and any flour or sugar in the house.

The inquest into Elizabeth Gregory's death was held the following day, at the Hole in the Wall Inn in Cheltenham. Diana Gregory testified that it had been Barnett who had suggested that Elizabeth make the dumplings, for which he had provided the flour and apples. Knowing what Barnett had done with the dumplings, the coroner felt it necessary to caution him, telling him that what he said might be given in evidence against him and that he did not have to answer. But Barnett wanted to tell his side of the story. He said that he could not remember where he had bought the flour, but that he had had it for two months. He had eaten a quarter of a dumpling, which had not tasted odd, but had been warned by Caroline not to eat more. He had then disposed of the remainder so that no animals could get at them. Within two hours he had become ill.[32] Though still very weak, Caroline Gregory was able to give evidence, stating that she had noticed an oddly hot taste to the small portion of dumpling that she had eaten, and that she had become ill about two hours after her siblings had.[33]

By now it was evident that this was neither a case of food poisoning nor of cholera, and the coroner adjourned the inquest for a week, to allow time for an autopsy and for the samples collected from the Gregory house to be analysed. It is not clear whether it was Dr Brookes or the coroner who suggested the name of William Herapath (1796–1868), but the choice was unsurprising: he was then the most famous analytical chemist in the west of England. Herapath, who lived in Bristol, had made a name for himself fifteen years earlier when his testimony had helped to convict Mary Ann Burdock of the arsenic murder of her lodger, fourteen months after the crime had occurred. This had been the first occasion on which an exhumation had taken place in England for the purpose of chemical analysis, and Burdock's execution in April 1835 did much to promote the usefulness of science to the law. It has been suggested that the publicity the case attracted started a wave of arsenic poisonings,[34] but it would be more accurate to view it as the first in a rapidly increasing series of prosecutions facilitated by the legal system's mounting reliance on improved methods of chemical analysis.

Brookes made a post-mortem examination of Elizabeth Gregory about twenty-four hours after her death. There were no external marks of violence on the body, in which 'adipose tissue was very abundant' – she had been a fat girl. All of the internal organs were healthy, with the exception of the stomach, which was inflamed in two patches on its inner surface. It contained about twelve ounces of a gruelly-looking fluid, which was removed and bottled. The intestines looked a normal pale pink colour. On the following morning, Sunday 16 September, Samuel Gregory died, and Brookes returned to Chapel Street to carry out another post-mortem. In death, Samuel looked as 'fat and healthy' as his sister had, but his internal organs showed the signs of the trauma that the boy suffered before his death. His brain and lungs were filled with fluid, his heart contained a blood clot, the gall bladder was distended with bile, and the entire surface of the mucous membrane that coated the inner stomach and intestines was red and inflamed. His liver, stomach and its contents, together with Elizabeth's stomach and stomach contents, were packaged and sealed with Brookes's personal seal, before being sent to Herapath for analysis.[35]

Police sergeant John Nightingale collected the samples and sent them to Herapath by railway; he took the dumpling and organs to Bristol himself. On opening the parcel, Herapath found that Elizabeth Gregory's stomach had been wrapped in a piece of white cloth, apparently part of a shirtsleeve. Examining it with a microscope, he found three tiny crystals that proved to be white arsenic. Samuel Gregory's stomach was nearly ulcerated in one patch; it contained arsenic, as did his liver. There was some flour in a paper bag (which Caroline Gregory said that she had bought), bread in a cigar box, the faded handkerchief in which Barnett had kept his flour, and some uncooked dumpling dough. Chemical tests showed that there was 'a large proportion' of arsenic in everything except the bread and the flour. A sample of matter that Nightingale had seen Samuel vomit up contained traces of arsenic, as did the stomach contents of both victims. At the adjourned inquest on

21 September Herapath produced the physical results of his experiments. These included black metallic arsenic deposited on a piece of copper (known as a Reinsch test); crystalline white arsenic formed by subliming the metal; and the three coloured precipitates that white arsenic forms on combination with silver nitrate (yellow), hydrogen sulphide (yellow) and copper sulphate (green). On the basis of these tests, he was able to state that he had no doubt that the stomachs were those of persons who had died from arsenic poisoning. Furthermore, that 'any person who had eaten even a small quantity of the dumpling ... would have been poisoned, the arsenic being in such considerable quantities therein'. He estimated that a piece the size of a walnut could kill.[36] In order to make such a statement he must have calculated the approximate amount of arsenic found in the samples he examined but, unusually for the time, he expressed this not as a mass, in grains or ounces, but in purely visual terms that non-experts could quickly and easily appreciate.

By 21 September, when the inquest was resumed, both Barnett and his wife Deborah were in custody, suspected of involvement in the two deaths. Barnett, a shepherd, and his fifteen-year-old son George had lodged in the Gregory's home for two years, while Deborah lived and worked at a nearby school. Local gossip suggested that she had mixed the poison for him, but there was no real evidence against her and she was soon released. The case against her husband was, however, stronger, especially after Caroline Gregory took the witness stand once again. Having had a week in which to ponder the sudden deaths of her siblings, Caroline appears to have convinced herself that Barnett was responsible. She now raised the fact that he had had a dispute with Keylock a year ago, and that he had once threatened to 'double him up like a nutshell', but she had to admit that they had not recently appeared to be on bad terms. More damning, though, was the fact that Barnett had once used something that he said was poison to cure a wound on Samuel's leg, and that he had also used it on sheep. It would have been common knowledge that arsenic was used to dip sheep and to cure skin complaints. As a parting shot, Caroline stated that it was her belief that Barnett had never intended to eat much of the dumpling: he had eaten more slowly than usual, and had put much less sugar on it than he normally would have done.[37]

Despite Dr Brookes's claim that Barnett had appeared to him to be as ill as Caroline had been (both had weak pulses, vomiting, and the same strange appearance of their eyes), there seemed to be a case against him. His claim that he did not know what arsenic was sounded unlikely, given his occupation, and the inquest jury brought in a verdict of wilful murder. In early October the evidence was heard by two magistrates, who ordered Barnett to stand trial on two charges of murder. Tried at Gloucester in April 1850, he was acquitted, the jury having accepted the defence claim that the deaths must have been the result of an accidental contamination of the flour by arsenic. There was no way to link Barnett to the contamination, or to prove that he had been aware of it, a fact that can have been of little comfort to the remaining members of the Gregory family. In this case, science and medicine were able to explain what had happened to the victims, but no one could explain why it had happened. It was, in all probability, just another in a series of fatal accidents caused by the ubiquitous presence of arsenic in mid nineteenth-century England.

Several chemical tests for arsenic were in common use between 1750 and 1850. By the later date, what had formerly been rather unspecific and vague methods had been improved and supplemented by more systematic and precise procedures designed to distinguish arsenic from other mineral poisons with which it could most easily be confused, namely antimony and mercury. With the occasional modification, the following remained standard until the twentieth century: the reduction test; the three precipitate tests; the Marsh test; and the Reinsch test. Only the Marsh test, with some modifications, was truly quantitative; that is, it could be used to measure the exact amount of arsenic in a given sample. The reduction test had to be carried out on a dry sample, while the others required the arsenic to be dissolved in aqueous solution, preferably free from organic matter such as human tissue.

Of these methods, the reduction test was the simplest and oldest, relying on the fact that white arsenic, when heated to redness, loses oxygen (in chemical terms, it is reduced). In the eighteenth century this was done in open vessels,[38] but by the second decade of the nineteenth century, toxicologists and medical jurists were recommending the use of glass tubes.[39] If the process was carried out inside an open-ended tube, the oxygen was driven off but metallic arsenic remained, clinging to the glass in the form of a mirror, a brownish-black deposit with a dull metallic lustre. If the mirror was then gently heated, a reverse process occurred: the metallic arsenic was oxidised, and crystals of white arsenious oxide were deposited in the tube above. This could then be shown to be normal arsenic by dissolving it in distilled water and applying the three precipitate tests, all of which were recommended in a textbook published in 1816.[40] A solution of silver nitrate in ammonium hydroxide, when added to a neutral solution of white arsenic, produced a yellow precipitate of what chemists of the period termed silver arsenite; in acidic solutions, the same reagent produced a red-brown precipitate of silver arsenate. In modern chemical terms, these were compounds of arsenic in two different oxidation states, +3 (arsenite) and +5 (arsenate). If hydrogen sulphide gas was bubbled through a solution of white arsenic, yellow arsenic sulphide was formed. Lastly, when a basic solution of copper sulphate was mixed with arsenic it produced a green precipitate of copper arsenite, the pigment known as Scheele's green.[41]

As characteristic as these tests may have been, they did not provide conclusive evidence of the presence of arsenic in cases of suspected poisoning. This was nowhere more obvious than during the trial of John Bodle, who, at the age of twenty, stood accused of murdering his grandfather with arsenic at Plumstead, Kent, in November 1833. James Marsh (1794–1846), who was employed at the Royal Arsenal in Woolwich, was the only competent chemist in the area, and as such was called in to test both the coffee that the dead man had drunk and his stomach contents. Marsh was able to show that arsenic was present in the coffee (which had made four other people in the Bodle household ill), but was unable to demonstrate its presence in the stomach contents. The jury was reluctant to accept evidence of poisoning in which the poison itself could not be produced from the body of the deceased, and acquitted the accused youth. Eleven years later, however, having been convicted of fraud and blackmail and under sentence to be transported to the colonies, John Bodle confessed that he had indeed poisoned his grandfather with arsenic.[42]

Stung by the acquittal, Marsh set out to develop a test for arsenic that would detect even the tiniest amounts in organic samples, and by 1836 he had succeeded.[43] Basing his method on the production of arsine, a gaseous compound of arsenic and hydrogen that, when burned, gives a deposit of metallic arsenic, what became known as the Marsh test was quickly established as the most delicate and reliable of all the tests for arsenic. When it was first introduced into analytical practice, it was able to detect one grain of arsenic in four pints of water; by the eve of the First World War, its sensitivity had been increased by successive improvements to over one hundred thousandth of a grain. By this date, however, nothing of Marsh's original process remained but the theory behind it: the decomposition of arsine.[44]

In order to use the Marsh test, organic samples (such as stomach contents, human organs) had to be boiled. The resulting solution, which contained any arsenic present in the sample, was then acidified and a piece of zinc added; the reaction between the acid and the zinc led to the formation of hydrogen, which then reacted with any arsenical compound to form arsine. The arsine escaped through a U-shaped tube and was then ignited (for this step of the process, Marsh recommended the assistance of a second person). Metallic arsenic was deposited on a glass or porcelain plate held over the end of the tube. With a slight modification, the escaping gas could be oxidised to white arsenic. To prove that the product was arsenic, the usual precipitate tests were applied. This was an important step in the process, since antimony could form a very similar kind of mirror, though usually of a more silvery appearance.

This method gave only qualitative results, but in 1837 the Swedish chemist Jöns Jacob Berzelius (1779–1848) devised a quantitative version. He constructed an apparatus in which the gaseous arsine was passed through a glass tube that was heated in the middle. The gas was then ignited as it escaped from the reaction solution, and the metallic arsenic so formed was deposited inside the glass tube, which could then be weighed. The modified form became known as the Marsh-Berzelius apparatus. But, in any form, the Marsh test required a great deal of skill on the part of the person who performed it, and was thus subject to errors and misleading results. Moreover, each test took several hours to perform. It achieved notoriety in 1840 during the trial of Marie Lafarge in France, who was first declared innocent of the murder of her husband when the Marsh test failed to reveal arsenic in his corpse, but then convicted when the same test performed on a new sample proved positive.[45] Legal records show, however, that, regardless of such birth pains, provincial medical practitioners and chemists in England were using the Marsh test during the early 1840s.[46] There was, however, a clear need for a simpler but similarly sensitive test.

In 1841 the German chemist Hugo Reinsch (1809–84) published a description of a method whereby metallic arsenic was deposited on copper foil from hydrochloric acid solutions.[47] The test was quicker than that of Marsh, since it could be applied to a liquid containing organic matter and could be completed in a few minutes. It could be used to test for both mercury and antimony, which also formed stains on copper foil; to distinguish them from those of arsenic, the foil had to be heated in a glass tube to volatilise the deposit. Mercury produced globules of the pure metal, arsenic crystals of the white oxide, and antimony an amorphous mass of its oxide, which was also white but usually clearly different from that of arsenic. The main defect in the test lay in the fact that both hydrochloric acid and copper could often contain arsenical impurities; this meant that a blank test always had to be carried out. Famously, in 1859 Thomas Smethurst, a London physician who had been convicted of poisoning a young woman whom he had bigamously married, was pardoned, largely as a result of the confusion that surrounded the medical and chemical evidence in the case. This confusion was in part due to an error made by the toxicologist Alfred Swaine Taylor, who failed to note that certain positive tests for arsenic had been due to impurities in the reagents he had used when performing the Reinsch test.[48] Despite this drawback, and its slightly lesser sensitivity (it would not show less than one two hundredth of a grain), the Reinsch was easier to use than the Marsh and thus became the favoured test for arsenic; today it remains useful in the preliminary diagnosis of poisoning.[49]

Much of the value of the Marsh and Reinsch tests lay in the fact that they gave chemists and toxicologists physical proof of poison which could then be presented to a jury. It quickly became common practice for expert witnesses at both inquests and trials to arrive with glass tubes containing arsenical mirrors, slips of copper stained with metallic arsenic, and samples of the coloured precipitates known to be formed by arsenic and other metallic poisons. Such visible evidence of poison obtained from the bodies of victims did much to sway jurors, who might previously have entertained the same doubts as those who had deliberated the Bodle case. It was this factor, combined with the publicity given to the trial of Mary Ann Burdock, which led to the marked increase in the number of poisoning trials after 1835. Medical and scientific witnesses were better able to provide proof of poisoning, making detection and trial a far more likely prospect than had once been the case.

Chemical tests for the other common inorganic poisons developed alongside those for arsenic, but were rarely as potentially controversial. A simple litmus test was sufficient to prove the presence of a mineral acid, while the characteristic stains that each formed on cloth were a helpful distinguishing feature: yellow by nitric acid, red-brown by sulphuric, reddish by hydrochloric. Two straightforward precipitate tests designed to further identify each acid were suggested in the medical literature very early in the nineteenth century, and remained standard for well over a hundred years. A solution of barium chloride added to sulphuric acid produced a white precipitate insoluble in hydrochloric acid. Silver nitrate added to hydrochloric acid gave a white precipitate insoluble in nitric acid but soluble in ammonia.[50] No precipitate tests were developed specifically for nitric acid, but the fumes produced when the acid was decomposed in the presence of copper and sulphuric acid was long considered a sufficiently unique indicator.[51] In the twentieth century, colour reactions superseded this test.

The first qualitative tests for common inorganic poisons were described by the French toxicologist M. J. B. Orfila (1787–1853) in his *General System of Toxicology*, an English translation of which appeared in 1816–17.[52] If a sample of the poison was boiled in distilled water and filtered, the addition of potassium hydroxide or hydrogen sulphide gas gave a variety of coloured precipitates that could be used to distinguish salts of antimony, copper, lead, mercury and zinc, as well as arsenic.[53] These were superseded as preliminary diagnostics by the advent of the Marsh and Reinsch tests, but remained among the supplementary tests recommended to medical students in the 1920s.[54]

The inorganic poisons accounted for about two thirds of criminal poisonings. Their counterparts, the organic poisons, also exercised both the diagnostic skills of doctors and the analytical abilities of chemists, though not until some years following the isolation of morphine (1805) from opium, and strychnine (1819) from the seeds of the nux vomica plant. These, together with other alkaloids (particularly aconitine and atropine) and prussic acid, entered the pharmacopoeia in the early nineteenth century (prussic acid was first used in medicine in 1804), thus becoming easier to obtain. The wide use of strychnine in rat poison was, of course, an invitation to murder.

When grocery shop manager William Mabbott, aged thirty-seven, arrived at work on Monday morning, 14 June 1886, he cannot have known that the day was to be his last. By all accounts an honest and trustworthy employee, he had for four years divided his time between branches of the shop located in Shropshire and just across the Welsh border in Welshpool, Montgomeryshire. He was at the latter shop every Saturday and Monday, a fact well known to William Samuel, a twenty-five-year-old business colleague who was in debt to Mabbott's employer, Joshua Judge, for the small sum of 16 shillings. As a consequence, Judge had earlier warned Mabbott not to supply goods to Samuel on credit; he had also asked him to collect the money owed. Eyewitnesses testified to the events that ensued.

Samuel was seen at Mabbott's shop twice that day. During the first visit, in the late afternoon, some altercation took place, making Samuel so angry that he went out and borrowed a jug from a neighbour. This he took to the local pub, where he paid to have it filled with ale. He offered a drink from it to two men who happened to be nearby, and then took it to Mabbott, who drank a little from it. No one saw this, or saw Samuel put anything into the jug but beer, but shop boy Thomas Morris, ten, returned to find Mabbott lying on the floor and exclaiming that Samuel had 'dosed him in porter', a statement that he made repeatedly in the presence of witnesses. As Mabbott began to twitch and complain of pains, other neighbours arrived and a doctor was sent for.

Two doctors arrived at about half past six, surgeon Herbert Hawksworth and general practitioner Francis Marston. By then Mabbott was suffering extreme pain and thirst, and Marston sent for a stomach pump and a strong emetic. They saw him suffer a convulsive spasm, upon which they both remarked 'strychnine'.[55] The emetic worked a little, then the victim had another spasm, worse than the first. The stomach pump was used and another doctor arrived. But the efforts of the medical men were to no avail: Mabbott died during a third violent spasm, half an hour after young Morris discovered him on the shop floor.

While this drama was being played out, William Samuel returned to the shop with the jug in question. Alerted by Mabbott's declarations, someone took the jug from Samuel and Marston looked into it. Seeing some white crystals clinging to its sides, he tasted a few of them. They were intensely bitter, and caused such unpleasant symptoms that he had to have an emetic. Hawksworth applied a chemical test to them on the spot, and both were satisfied that they were crystals of strychnine. For his part, Marston felt it unnecessary to have a chemical analysis of the victim's organs in order to state what the cause of death had been, so certain was he of the diagnosis. But the local magistrates ordered a formal analysis, which was made by the county analyst, Thomas Blunt. He found one tenth of a grain of strychnine in Mabbott's stomach contents, the excess over what had killed him, as there would be no absorption after death.[56]

The other facts of the case were easily ascertained by police enquiries. On 3 June Samuel had asked an old friend to buy him some strychnine, saying that he had the permission of the local ratcatcher but asking him to tell the druggist that it was for a railway employee. Two druggists refused to accept this story. Samuel then asked his friend to go to a third druggist, whose young apprentice, being inexperienced, would probably oblige; but this too failed. Four days later Samuel asked another man to buy strychnine for him, but to say it was for someone else. This man, John Pugh, was sold phosphorus paste, which Samuel demanded that he return and replace with strychnine. Later the druggist explained that he had only sold it because he knew the man for whom it was supposedly bought; he had mentioned a rat problem.[57] Although the law required a formal record of his purchase, Samuel was in this way able to procure six pence worth of pure strychnine, a packet weighing thirty grains (enough to kill up to sixty people), without having to sign a poison register.

Samuel's trial in July 1886 lasted a day and a half, at the end of which he was convicted and sentenced to death. The minutes recording the trial list the names of the jurors, the costs paid to the analyst (£8 8s. od.) and a marginal note: 'Executed July 26th'.[58]

The horrifyingly painful and speedy death suffered by William Mabbott was entirely typical of strychnine poisoning, so much so that it took his doctors only minutes to make a diagnosis. The alkaloid acted on the nerves of the spinal cord, increasing their sensitivity to the slightest sensory stimuli; this led to general convulsions, the most unmistakable symptom caused by strychnine. In fatal cases, death usually occurred within one hour, following a predictable pattern. Symptoms began when the patient noticed the extremely bitter taste of the poison, which was also considered diagnostic; even in the 1930s taste was recommended as one of the main tests for strychnine.[59] Then, within fifteen minutes, the muscles began to twitch, followed by violent and painful convulsions. During these, the body could be bent so far backwards that the patient rested solely on his head and heels; breathing was impaired by constriction of the airway. As the spasm gradually faded away, the patient resumed breathing, and was conscious and able to speak. After the first convulsion, others occurred; death usually came at the fourth or fifth, due either to heart failure (between spasms) or asphyxia during a spasm.[60]

The only natural disease that strychnine poisoning resembled was tetanus, but it was always easy to distinguish the two. Tetanus cases invariably resulted from some wound or trauma, and progressed over several days. Strychnine cases developed very suddenly after the ingestion of some bitter substance and terminated almost as rapidly. In the unlikely event that a patient died during a single convulsion, the case might be mistaken for one of epilepsy, but a chemical analysis could soon put the question to rest. Given that there were no characteristic post-mortem appearances, analysis was all the more necessary to provide the proof of poisoning required by a court of law.[61] One of the most famous trials of the nineteenth century revolved around just this point.

In May 1856 Dr William Palmer was tried for the strychnine murder of his gambling companion, John Parsons Cook, marking the first time that such a case had been heard in an English court. As there was then only a small literature on cases of death from strychnine, medical witnesses were divided as to the actual cause of death. Those retained by the defence contended that the symptoms did not match what they knew from their clinical and experimental experience, and could have been due to some natural disease, such as epilepsy, angina pectoris, or spinal cord irritation of undetermined cause. To further complicate matters, a chemical analysis made by Alfred Swaine Taylor, England's most famous toxicologist, failed to detect strychnine in the body. Palmer was convicted, nonetheless, the medical and circumstantial evidence being seen by the jury as sufficient proof of his guilt. This verdict exposed the gap between public expectation and legal and scientific practice: there was no rule of evidence that required the discovery of poison in a victim's body in order to prove that death had been due to poison.[62] Where medical experts, including Taylor, had before stressed the import- ance of successful chemical analysis, they afterward tended to use the Palmer case to show that analysis was not always necessary to secure con- viction on a poisoning charge. Few of the murder trials that came after Palmer failed, however, to include an analysis. In the less than ten cases where it is clear that no analysis was done, yet someone was tried for murder, the poison in question was opium or laudanum. Only one case involved a different poison, carbon monoxide, where the characteristic pink colour of the blood – caused by the effect of the gas on haemoglobin – seems to have been considered sufficient evidence.[63]

What was it about opium and laudanum that allowed this apparent certainty in diagnosis? Opium and opium-derivatives were, throughout the nineteenth century, the leading cause of accidental and suicidal poisonings, accounting for about 35 to 40 per cent of such deaths.[64] Their general use among all segments of society meant that they were familiar to medical practitioners, who were easily able to recognise the characteristic symptoms of stupor, slow pulse, contracted pupils, noisy breathing and flushed face. Death occurred usually within six to twelve hours, from asphyxia. Other poisons (notably carbolic acid, alcohol and belladonna) produced coma before death – but, where there was any doubt, the odour of opium frequently served as an important diagnostic. This scent, now completely unfamiliar to doctors and laymen alike, used to be well known; once smelled, it was not easily forgotten. As one witness put it, 'I cannot say that I know the smell of laudanum, but it had a wild, fierce smell, something I cannot describe'.[65]

It was because the symptoms and smell were so characteristic that chemical analysis was sometimes deemed unnecessary. This was despite the fact that post-mortem appearances were not particularly reliable indicators: although the brain was often found suffused with blood, this was a result of asphyxia, not the direct action of the poison. Furthermore, since many of the victims were children overdosed by their carers, there was not much mystery surrounding such cases; the prosecution had little difficulty in proving them. The situation was only somewhat different in cases where death was due to morphine, the principal active constituent alkaloid in opium. The symptoms and post-mortem appearances caused by morphine were the same as those caused by opium and laudanum, but there were almost no cases of homicide by morphine in England before 1914. Where such deaths did occur, however, chemical tests were unavoidable, since pure morphine has no smell.

With the exception of strychnine and morphine, the vegetable alkaloids did not account for a significant number of criminal poisonings: most prosecutions involved druggists who had filled prescriptions carelessly, not cases of murder. Atropine (from deadly nightshade) and aconitine (from monkshood) were widely employed in medicine, the former mainly in eye drops, the latter in liniments used for the relief of neuralgia. The minimum known fatal dose of each was less than a grain, but aconitine was much more poisonous and killed more quickly, within five hours rather than the twenty-four hours typically associated with atropine.

The symptoms of atropine poisoning developed within half an hour to three hours, and were characterised by dryness of the mouth and throat, widely dilated pupils (which made vision difficult and caused the patient to stagger as if drunk), flushed skin, rapid pulse, incoherence and, occasionally, vomiting. Stupor and depression gradually came on, leading to slowing of the heart rate and respiration. Death occurred from asphyxia. The main characteristic feature of aconitine poisoning was a severe tingling in the mouth, felt within minutes of taking a dangerous dose, followed by salivation and burning pain in the throat. In about half an hour abdominal pains and vomiting began, while the tingling sensation spread over the entire skin. Cramps and convulsions could occur, and cardiac and respiratory functions were slowed. The pupils tended to dilate but then to contract, sometimes several times in succession. The victim usually remained conscious throughout, until death from heart failure or asphyxia occurred.[66]

At autopsy the internal signs were minimal, particularly in cases where the poisons were taken as medicines. Where a victim had died from eating the plant, its leaves, berries or seeds were usually found in the alimentary tract, and were easily identified. Otherwise, in cases of atropine poisoning the signs were those of asphyxia: unusually dark and

fluid blood saturated with carbon dioxide, and small haemorrhages in
the membranes surrounding the lungs and heart. The same could be
the case where death had been caused by aconitine, but was by no means
characteristic. In neither case were chemical tests reliable. Instead, forensic experts had to rely on the effects caused by samples extracted from
the victims and tested on living subjects, mainly animals, but sometimes
humans – usually self-experiments. Atropine was known by its ability
to dilate the pupils of humans and animals; aconitine by the tingling
and numbness of the tongue that it caused.[67] When surgeon George
Lamson poisoned his nephew with aconitine in 1880, the only evidence
that toxicologist Thomas Stevenson was able to offer in relation to the
cause of death was that of the effects of an extract of the suspected
material on his own tongue, and on a mouse. In his experience, no
other alkaloid produced such symptoms. Defence counsel argued that
this was hardly evidence on which to hang a man, but the jury, guided
by the fact that Lamson was known to have bought aconitine, found
him guilty.[68]

Stevenson's tests were made after the suspected poison was extracted
from the victim's body by means of a method introduced in 1851 by the
Belgian chemist Jean Servais Stas (1813–1891).[69] The process was based
upon the fact that all alkaloids were basic and thus soluble in organic
solvents and, as bases, were likely to combine with acids to form
crystalline salts, which were soluble in water. The bodies of humans and
animals are made up of substances that dissolve either in water or
alcohol, or are insoluble in both. If a body organ in which an alkaloid
was present was mashed up, stirred in a mixture of alcohol and acid,
and filtered, the alkaloid would be dissolved out of the organ into the
alcoholic filtrate. After several repetitions, the pure alkaloid could be
isolated in solution in an organic solvent like ether, and obtained in
crystal form by evaporation. The solid could then be tested by chemical
or physiological means. In the Palmer case the chemical tests failed
because, although the analyst, Taylor, had extracted the poison using
the Stas method, he had not done so carefully enough to obtain a sample
large enough to test by the precipitate reactions then in use. His problems were compounded by the loss of the stomach contents, and by the
testing of the viscera some days after death. It was because strychnine
deaths were so unusual in 1856 that the Palmer trial led to such acrimony

amongst the medical and toxicological witnesses. Lessons were learnt, however, and strychnine soon became one of the easiest of the alkaloids to detect, since it caused death in such a short time that the poison had little chance to be entirely eliminated from the body.

Chemical tests for the alkaloids fell into a single main category: colour reactions, first introduced during the 1860s. When an analyst had managed to isolate a sample of the suspected material, a preliminary determination – as was done while William Mabbott was dying – could be quickly made if the appropriate reagents were at hand. To test for strychnine, the solid sample was mixed with a little sulphuric acid and potassium dichromate or manganese dioxide; if present, strychnine produced a vivid purple colour that faded gradually to red. This ruled out brucine, an alkaloid often found as an impurity in commercial strychnine and which produced similar symptoms. Solid morphine could be tested in a similar way. If it was moistened with sulphuric acid and a drop of formaldehyde, an intense purple-red colour that changed to blue and violet was obtained. To make absolutely certain, another sample could be tested with ferric chloride, which gave a blue colour; or strong nitric acid, which gave an orange colour.

Prior to the advent of colour tests for alkaloids, analysis rested on precipitation tests: most alkaloids could be precipitated in crystalline form by adding them to an aqueous mixture of mercuric chloride and potassium iodide. The crystals could then be checked under a microscope, or administered to animals. Such physiological tests, long abandoned in cases of poisoning by inorganic compounds, remained standard throughout the nineteenth century and into the twentieth. The most famous of these was the use of a frog to test for strychnine. Developed by the physiologist Marshall Hall (1790–1857) amidst the furore surrounding the Palmer case, a live frog exhibited the characteristic spasms when placed in solutions containing as little as one five-thousandth of a grain of strychnine.[70]

The use of animal testing in cases where the presence of a vegetable alkaloid was suspected was both a matter of necessity (the chemical tests were not reliable for all alkaloids) and choice (the physiological reactions caused by some of them were truly unique). But for the other common poisons, both organic and inorganic, animal testing (dogs, cats, mice, rabbits, chickens and pigs were all typical experimental victims, because of their widespread availability) was abandoned as soon as reliable chemical tests became available. In practice, this meant that animal evidence began to disappear from poison trials following the introduction of the Marsh and Reinsch tests. Forensic experts accepted that animal evidence could supply proof of poisoning, even if no poison was found in the corpse, when food that the victim had eaten killed an animal in which poison was detected. In the eighteenth century the standards were somewhat slacker: if food that was suspected of killing a person also killed an animal, or if the stomach contents of a suspected victim of poison killed an animal, that was evidence that the person had been poisoned. The Blandy case was unusual in its reliance on chemical to the exclusion of animal evidence; the reverse was more usually the case until the 1820s, when the first English-language textbooks of forensic medicine, advocating chemical tests, had been in circulation for a few years. Animals subsequently remained indicators that a poisoning might have occurred, but only in conjunction with chemical tests.

Among the common organic poisons, only prussic acid could kill more rapidly than strychnine and aconitine, and as painlessly as opiates. The free acid (a compound of cyanide and hydrogen) was used in solutions of varying strengths as a medicine, as it was thought to relieve heartburn, pulmonary and other inflammations, and some skin complaints. The famous almond-like odour associated with prussic acid was due to benzoic aldehyde, formed by the decomposition of an organic compound called amygdalin; the other decomposition products included prussic acid and glucose. The aldehyde was frequently used as a flavouring matter; where purification was incomplete, free prussic acid could form from 2 to 14 per cent of the solution. The salts of prussic acid, particularly the potassium and silver salts, found widespread use in photography, electroplating and gilding, and were easily available. The minimum lethal dose was about five grains of the cyanide salts, one teaspoonful of oil of bitter almonds containing 3 to 4 per cent of prussic acid, or thirty drops of the medicinal acid (about 2 per cent). Suicides and accidental deaths were therefore common. Homicides were relatively infrequent, possibly because cyanides had a pronounced taste and odour and thus could not be completely disguised.[71] Also, they were far more expensive than arsenic- or strychnine-containing vermin killers and, after 1868, had to be signed for in a poison register.

Cyanide is toxic to all forms of life. In mammals, it can act in four ways, by affecting the blood, the metabolism, the central nervous system, and the heart. The poison inhibits the body's ability to use oxygen, and death usually occurs when the tissues of the central nervous system become so starved of oxygen that respiration and/or heart action ceases. Following ingestion of a large dose, the victim would become unconscious almost immediately; death usually followed within minutes, sometimes preceded by convulsions. The process was delayed by up to several hours if a small dose was taken, and the victim could experience nausea and vomiting, loss of muscle control and dizziness. He or she would then become paralysed, comatose and cyanotic (the face and lips taking on a blue colour due to lack of oxygen in the blood), before dying from respiratory and heart failure. As prussic acid was rapidly metabolised to harmless products in the body tissues, it was possible to recover from cyanide poisoning, particularly if it did not prove fatal within the first few minutes. But most victims would probably have echoed the sentiments of a surgeon who mistakenly swallowed a large dose of the medicinal acid in 1876: 'If that is prussic acid, I am a dead man.'[72]

The post-mortem appearance of the face was the most characteristic sign of cyanide poisoning, as it usually presented the peculiar bluish colour associated with cyanosis. The blood, internal organs and brain tissue often smelled of almonds; but, as only about 50 per cent of the population was able to detect the odour, it was (unbeknownst to doctors in the nineteenth century) not always a reliable indicator. Internal signs were often lacking or inconsistent: the blood could be bright red, from the formation of a compound of cyanide and haemoglobin, or dark when death resulted from asphyxia. When potassium cyanide had been taken, the mucous membrane of the stomach was sometimes inflamed or eroded.

Chemical testing had to be done quickly, since prussic acid was volatile and could disappear completely within days, or convert into a different substance during putrefaction. Tests usually involved the stomach contents, blood and brain, and relied on certain precipitates formed by the pure acid; where a cyanide salt was tested for, it had first to be converted into prussic acid by the addition of sulphuric acid. The most distinctive test involved hydrochloric acid and ferric chloride: the resulting precipitate of Prussian blue, a compound long used as a dye, was instantly recognisable.

Throughout the eighteenth and nineteenth centuries the experience of poisoning was one that few people today can imagine without returning to the victims of the time, to try to comprehend a little of their painful, dirty and undignified deaths. Poison was as terrible a form of violent death as any other, distinguished only by the once very real possibility that the crime might be wholly undetected, or impossible to prove. The best analytical and diagnostic efforts of chemists and medical practitioners were vital to the successful identification and prosecution of such crimes, and, as such, play a fundamental role in the stories of English poisoners and their victims.

2

Poisons and Poisoners

The ease with which poison can be procured, and the perfect facility
with which it can be administered in small doses, so as frequently
almost to defy detection ... ought to awaken the public to a demand
for the absolute enforcement of legislative regulations for the sale
of all such drugs and deadly ingredients.

Household Words, 1851 [1]

Almost any substance, taken in large enough quantity, can be harmful
– the dose makes the poison – but most English men and women of
the past were well aware that some substances were more harmful than
others.[2] The poisoner's task was made easier by the fact that there were
few controls on the sale of even the most dangerous poisons, which
were commonly stocked together with medicines in druggist's shops.
What regulatory measures were taken during the nineteenth century
actually resulted in a shift of emphasis away from the chief homicidal
poison, arsenic, onto a range of alternatives rather more difficult to
obtain and administer. In so doing, however, nineteenth-century legislators took the first steps on a path that led to the strict legal controls
on poisons and drugs that we know today. This, together with the
methods of detection developed by analytical chemists and toxicologists,
led ultimately to a significant reduction in the incidence of criminal
poisoning in England.

Considered in terms of their source of origin, most poisons used with
criminal intent fall into one of two broad categories: mineral-based and
plant-based. The first group includes those poisons derived from non-
living (inorganic) things, such as metals and ores, and comprises mainly
strong acids and metal salts. Plant-based poisons, on the other hand, are
organic in nature (that is, they are compounds of carbon). They include

alkaloids (mainly from flowering plants) and organic acids (from fruits and leaves). A small number of organic poisons are produced by animal life, mainly fungi and beetles; these should not be confused with bacterial toxins, which have little role to play in the history of criminal poisoning. The poisons that were most often employed in criminal cases, in order of decreasing frequency, were arsenic; narcotics (opium and laudanum); strychnine; cyanide and organic acids; compounds of mercury; mineral acids (hydrochloric, nitric, sulphuric); other plant alkaloids; and compounds of lead, antimony, copper, potassium, iron and zinc. This excludes cases in which two different poisons were used or where no poison could be identified despite the initial suspicions of investigators, seventeen cases in which the records refer only to a 'deadly poison', and seven 'poisons' not absolutely identifiable as organic or inorganic. Table 1 shows that 61 per cent of all crimes (332 of 540 cases) were committed using a single inorganic poison. (Table 2 gives a summary of the principal uses for the most common poisons.) Although a slightly wider variety of organic than inorganic poisons were used in criminal cases, in absolute numbers the latter far exceeded the former. Furthermore, one substance dominated the group as a whole. The story of poisoning in England and Wales is in many ways a chronicle of the rise and fall of arsenic.

In most cases of criminal poisoning arsenic was used in one of three forms: the white oxide (in chemical terms, arsenic trioxide); or one of two coloured sulphides, yellow orpiment and red realgar (naturally occurring ores which are roasted in air to form white arsenic). Neither orpiment nor realgar is especially dangerous when pure, but both are frequently contaminated by white arsenic, which is highly poisonous: three grains, or about as much as will lie on the tip of a knife, can kill an adult. Small doses of this odourless and often tasteless substance are easily disguised in food: it can be powdered (and consequently mistaken for flour) or crystalline (occasionally mistaken for sugar or salt), and has therefore been the cause of more poison-related homicides than any other chemical in history. Most people knew it simply as arsenic, but in some areas – mainly Yorkshire and Lincolnshire – it was, rather confusingly, called mercury or white mercury. It was cheap and, before the introduction of controls in 1851, could be bought or sold by virtually anyone.

The price of arsenic (here this term will be used to refer to the white

Table 1

Poisons Used in English Criminal Cases, 1750–1914

Inorganic Poisons	
Arsenic (oxide, sulphides)	237
Mercury (ammonium, chlorides, oxide)	32
Acids (hydrochloric, nitric, sulphuric)	24
Lead (acetate, carbonate, oxide)	11
Antimony (tartar emetic)	7
Copper (sulphate)	4
Potassium (dichromate, carbonate, sulphate)	4
Ammonia	2
Iron (chloride, sulphate)	3
Phosphorus	3
Zinc (chloride, sulphate)	4
Other (calcium chloride)	1
	332

Organic Poisons	
Narcotics 1. Opium and laudanum	52
Plant alkaloids 1. Strychnine and nux vomica	41
Acids (acetic, carbolic, oxalic, tartaric, prussic (including cyanides)	34
Plant alkaloids 2. Aconitine, aloes, atropine, colchicum, croton oil, hyoscine, lobelia, morphine, mandrake	19
Savin	6
Narcotics 2. Chlorodyne, chloroform, chloral hydrate, other	9
Organic poisons of animal origin (ergot, cantharides)	5
Carbon monoxide	4
Alcohol	2
	172

oxide only) varied little between 1755 and 1905, never rising above 6d. per ounce.[3] In Yorkshire the price fell dramatically between the end of the eighteenth century and the early 1820s, so that an ounce cost less than 2d. Elsewhere, prices were even lower: in parts of Cheshire, Lancashire and Warwickshire arsenic was sold for less than a penny per ounce.[4] This was still considerably more expensive than popular foodstuffs like sugar, the price of which fell from 6d. to 2d. per pound between 1760 and 1900. Crucially, however, until the early twentieth century arsenic was much cheaper than other poisons of similar toxicity. Mercuric chloride (known popularly as corrosive sublimate), with which arsenic was sometimes confused, was the sole member of the inorganic family of poisons that was, ounce for ounce, as or more toxic. But at six times the price of arsenic, vendors who were asked for 'mercury' rarely assumed that this meant corrosive sublimate. Among the organic poisons, only strychnine was both more poisonous than arsenic (the minimum dose known to have proved lethal is a mere half grain) and almost as easily available, being widely used as an animal poison. The retail price of pure strychnine was far higher than that of arsenic, but its use in ready-made vermin killers meant that in small quantities it was affordable: a packet containing about one and a half grains could be purchased for 3d.[5] This was at a time when the average weekly wage of skilled and unskilled male workers ranged between 35s. (engine drivers) and 12s. (soldiers). Women and children were paid far less. The average annual income per household was about £32.[6]

Strychnine, the most murderous of the many alkaloids extracted from plants during the first few decades of the nineteenth century, was isolated in 1819 from the dried ripe seeds of the tree *Strychnos nux vomica*, which is found in India. Prior to the isolation of morphine from opium in 1805, the known vegetable poisons comprised a tiny group, some of the members of which found legitimate uses in medicine and all of which were dangerous if eaten accidentally. Among British plants, the alkaloids extracted from deadly nightshade or belladonna (atropine), henbane (atropine and hyoscine) and monkshood (aconitine), were found to be both useful drugs and highly effective poisons. Croton oil, savin (both British) and aloes (of African origin) were violent laxatives frequently used to produce abortion, though when they actually worked it was not due to a specific action on the womb but to the general severity of the

Table 2

Common Uses of Poisons Encountered in Criminal Cases

Common Use	Poison(s)	Comments
Abortion	Arsenic, savin, ergot, iron (III) chloride, potassium carbonate, potassium sulphate, strychnine, aloes	Iron and potassium compounds not particularly toxic in small doses, but can cause abortion if injected into womb.
Vermin control	Arsenic, corrosive sublimate, cantharides, strychnine, nux vomica, phosphorus	Cantharides more commonly used to excite sexual impulses.
Medicine	Arsenic, alkaloids, opiates, mercury compounds, tartar emetic, prussic acid, chloral hydrate, chloroform, chlorodyne, sulphates of iron, potassium and zinc, nitric acid, lead acetate	Pure prussic (hydrocyanic) acid is found in the seeds and leaves of some fruits, including plums, cherries, peaches and apples. Mercury compounds were used to treat venereal disease and ringworm. All alkaloids act on the nervous system.
Disinfectant	Zinc chloride, carbolic acid	First accidental death from carbolic acid 1864; favoured by suicides.
Dyeing; leather, straw and brass working	Oxalic acid	Potassium salt used to remove stains from linen; pure acid easily mistaken for Epsom salts.
Gas lighting	Carbon monoxide	10 per cent of coal gas by volume.
Manufacturing, heavy industry	Inorganic acids: hydrochloric, sulphuric, nitric	Most deaths due to accident or suicide; homicides usually involve children, as their struggles are easily subdued.
Colorants, paints	Compounds of arsenic and lead; copper sulphate	Arsenic used to produce yellow, green and red pigments; lead for yellow, orange and white.
Photography; electroplating, metal polishing	Potassium cyanide	The characteristic almond-like odour of cyanide is perceptible to only 50 per cent of the population (genetically determined).
Agriculture	Arsenic, sulphuric acid	Pesticide, weed killer; acid used to make fertiliser.

symptoms they caused. Colchicum was helpful in the treatment of gout, opium relieved pain, and lobelia was used as an emetic. Nux vomica was ground to a brown powder and used as rat poison, but pure strychnine entered medicine as a nerve stimulant.[7]

Arsenic too had medicinal uses, most notably in so-called cancer cures and in Fowler's solution, a potassium compound of white arsenic considered beneficial in the treatment of conditions including skin disorders, anemia, malarial fevers and cardiac pain.[8] Its association with the treatment of skin diseases led to its use as an ointment for the relief of sores and abscesses and, in the form of a thick paste, as a topical 'cure' for cancerous tumours. Unfortunately for some patients – often women suffering from breast cancer – arsenic can cause death by absorption through the skin. At least one victim, seemingly oblivious to the risk he was taking, used pure arsenic as a remedy for toothache: in 1860 in Lincolnshire, Elizabeth Dodds was acquitted of the murder of her husband when it emerged that he had been seen to rub the poison onto his gums.[9] Women used arsenic as a cosmetic, as it was thought to improve the complexion and to act as a depilatory, and men used it as a tonic. When Florence Maybrick was convicted of the murder of her husband in 1889, her death sentence was commuted to life imprisonment partly on the grounds that he had for years taken daily doses of arsenic as a strengthening stimulant.[10]

Arsenic and strychnine may have been of dubious use to medicine, but they remained effective in the constant battle that humankind wages against rodents and other pests. As Rebecca Stevenson well knew, most small purchases of arsenic (an ounce or two) were made for the purpose of controlling household vermin: mice, rats, beetles, fleas, flies, lice and bed bugs. To kill rats and mice, it was mixed with flour or oatmeal and put down near their holes. For crawling insects, it was mixed with lard or soft soap and rubbed on to furniture, or with water to wash floors and walls. Even in the early twentieth century, it was not considered unusual to add arsenic to whitewash as a defence against wood-boring insects.[11] Until the invention of arsenic-coated fly-papers in the 1860s, flies were lured to their deaths by strong solutions of arsenic set in dishes around the home; accidental deaths from this, particularly of children, were not uncommon. As Joseph Stevenson could attest, arsenic was also regularly used to kill animal parasites like warble flies, and huge amounts were used for dipping sheep – four pounds per hundred animals.[12] Entire flocks were poisoned by dips that were too concentrated, or after rain washed the dip off their fleece into the grass on which they grazed. As an effective insecticide, farmers used arsenic to steep grain before planting (normally one or two ounces per bushel), a practice that could and did have serious consequences for humans and wildlife. By the mid nineteenth century so many deaths from arsenic had occurred that the ease with which people could obtain it was emphasised in *Punch* as a 'fatal facility'.[13]

There were, of course, other ways to kill rats and mice: wooden and steel traps and cats were widely used, and preferred by many people. In 1784 Ellen Bayston claimed that mice had got into her cupboards and eaten her clothes, and that she needed to buy arsenic to deal with the problem. A friend recommended a trap as a safer option, and in the end Ellen gave the arsenic to her husband instead.[14] Decades later a Lancashire housewife, Mary Hunter, was strongly suspected of having murdered her husband because she had purchased arsenic to kill the rats and black beetles in her house. The prosecution made much of the fact that there was little evidence of infestation: the neighbours had never seen any, and the police officer who searched the house could find no rodent holes. When buying the arsenic Mary was asked why she did not get a cat. Her reply, that she had an aversion to them after having fainted at the sight of one killing a rat, led to an unsuccessful attempt to show that she had once kept a cat to which she had never shown antipathy.[15]

Those who did not wish to engage directly with the rodent population could call upon the services of ratcatchers, who used ferrets, terriers and traps, as well as arsenic and, from the 1840s, strychnine. The members of this distasteful but time-honoured profession usually combined pest control with other jobs, the more careless among them being sometimes the cause of seemingly suspicious deaths. But so long as vermin control remained primarily the responsibility of individual householders, rather than city councils or professional exterminators, suspected poisoners could with good reason employ it as a standard excuse. The police investigated such claims with increasing diligence, so that by the late 1870s a sergeant in Lancashire had noted that 'examining for mice is a new occupation'.[16]

At the time of Mary Hunter's trial, in 1843, many supposed that it was mainly people 'in her rank of life' – the poor – who habitually bought pure arsenic to kill household rodents. There was some truth in this assumption, if only because one could poison more rats with a pennyworth of arsenic than with the ready-made rat and mouse poisons that began to appear around this time. Normally priced at between 2d. and 6d. for a packet containing from one to six grains of poison, these products were originally made and sold by local druggists. The active ingredient, normally arsenic or strychnine (sometimes both), or less frequently corrosive sublimate, was mixed with flour or starch powder, a colouring agent and a bit of liquorice flavouring to produce a powder that could as easily be added to someone's dinner as applied to a rat hole. Battle's, Craven's and Steiner's were among the best known strychnine-containing powders, of which there were at least ten different national and seven local brands available by the late 1880s.[17] There were fewer rat powders based on arsenic, Burton's and Harrison's being the most popular, plus a selection of anti-rat pastes made with phosphorus. The pastes were less useful to the prospective poisoner because they could not be easily mixed with food; rather, they had to be spread on, like jam, and were consequently easier to see.

Among the chief homicidal poisons, only opium was more widely available than arsenic or strychnine. A killing dose of it or of one of its derivatives – mainly laudanum plus a variety of 'soothing syrups' intended for infants – was, however, more expensive. Solid opium – the dried juice of the white poppy – retailed at over two shillings per ounce, a price beyond the means of many poor people. When Jane Torkington, suffering a fit of depression in 1861, decided to kill herself and her two children with opium, she was unable to afford to buy enough to achieve her aim and only the younger child died. The druggist's assistant who served her thought that she had the appearance of an opium addict, and would have sold her more had she had the money.[18] Used by doctors as a remedy for a variety of ailments, by patients who acted as their own doctors, and by anyone who craved the delirium that narcotics offer, opium played a central role in English society. With virtually no controls on its sale until the twentieth century, addiction was widespread.[19] Because considerable tolerance was acquired by regular use, the toxic dose was exceedingly variable: as little as five grains had been known to kill an adult, but recovery after much larger doses was not uncommon. This meant that its use for homicidal purposes did not guarantee success, a conclusion borne out by the fact that, of eleven opium-related cases, only four resulted in a charge of murder. Of those, all involved attempted murder-suicides or double suicides in which someone unintentionally survived to face charges, attempting suicide being a criminal offence in England and Wales until 1961. Opium proved an equally unreliable method of doping robbery victims, a practice known as 'hocussing', but that didn't stop thieves from trying.

Opium contains nearly twenty alkaloids, but the principal active ingredient is morphine, usually present as about 10 per cent of the dry weight. For those who found solid opium either too strong for their needs or too expensive, a variety of weaker liquid preparations was available. Chief among these was laudanum, which could vary in strength, depending on where it was made, but usually contained about thirty-two grains of solid opium per tablespoon (3.2 grains of morphine). The price, between 3d. and 6d. per fluid ounce, enough for a fatal dose, varied little during the nineteenth century. This was often cheaper than the narcotic syrups intended mainly for the use of babies, the most famous of which, Godfrey's cordial, enjoyed a long history of vigorous sales. Adults, particularly among the working classes, relied on such products to keep young children quiet, but accidental overdoses could easily occur, especially when laudanum was substituted for the more expensive patent mixtures such as Godfrey's. As little as two drops of laudanum could kill a baby, and many mothers were consequently charged with murder or manslaughter. A large proportion of similar tragedies never reached the criminal courts, however, as inquest juries acknowledged the ease with which overdoses could occur by finding verdicts of accidental death.

Alternatively, an inquest could find that, where there was blame, it lay with the person who had sold the drug rather than with the purchaser. In 1837 a grocer's wife, Elizabeth Pettit, was tried for the manslaughter death of a baby whose mother had wanted Godfrey's but to whom she had probably sold laudanum in mistake for child's cordial, not having any Godfrey's in stock. Pettit was acquitted because there was no evidence to establish that she had not sold cordial.[20] As the practice of giving infants such products declined with the growing

control of the medical profession over drugs, however, so did the
number of accidental deaths;[21] a textbook of the 1920s noted that there
had been none since 1903.[22]

There were in fact no legal restrictions on the sale of poisons until
1851, when the Arsenic Act came into force. Before then, anyone who
wished to buy or sell any poison or drug could do so; no special
precautions were required. In small towns and rural areas it was common for one shop to offer poisons along with a range of goods such as
foods and fabrics. In Cambridgeshire in 1811, Michael Whiting could
supply his customers with nux vomica (ground and whole), arsenic,
and blue, white and green vitriol (sulphates of copper, zinc and iron),
all of which were kept in paper parcels in a box. No one realised until
after he had attempted to poison his two young brothers-in-law that he
had also had access to corrosive sublimate, which had been included in
the stock he had taken on when he purchased his business three years
earlier.[23] For those who wanted to avoid shops altogether, there were
other options. When Lancashire weaver Henry Scholfield poisoned his
family in 1817, he did it with arsenic obtained from the local shoemaker,
who had been 'in the habit of selling it for twenty years'.[24]

Casual purchases of poison remained commonplace for a long time,
but even in Scholfield's day most people saw no need to go anywhere
other than the nearest druggist's shop. Such shops had begun to spring
up throughout England during the late eighteenth century. Forerunners
of the modern pharmacist (pharmaceutical chemist), druggists (also
known as 'chemists' or 'chemists and druggists') were originally the
unlicensed competitors of apothecaries, themselves once members of
the lowest tier of the traditional tripartite division of medical labour.
At the top of the pecking order stood the physicians, university-educated
men whose purview was mainly restricted to internal diseases. Occu-
pying the middle rank were surgeons: trained primarily by
apprenticeship, they focused on the treatment of external wounds and
the performance of invasive procedures. Apothecaries were in trade:
also trained by apprenticeship, they made up prescriptions and sold
compound remedies.[25]

In practice, however, these distinctions had become blurred from as
early as the sixteenth century, often for financial reasons: in all but the
largest towns there were too few customers to support large numbers

of apothecaries. Conversely, there were too few physicians for the population as a whole. Most patients were therefore treated either by a surgeon or by an apothecary, each of whom took on some of the duties of the physician as well. Under this stimulus, remaining lines of demarcation between the two groups faded, so that by the mid eighteenth century it had become common to find the two professions united. These surgeon-apothecaries, as they were styled, had taken a step toward the establishment of the general practitioner, or GP, that we know today. Their profits lay mainly in the medicines that they prescribed and sold to their patients, though some found that there was more money to be made by manufacturing medicines on a large scale for retail and wholesale purposes. Somewhere within this group lay the druggists. They had no formal medical qualifications (they were not licensed by the Royal Colleges of Physicians and Surgeons or by the Society of Apothecaries), but they dispensed prescriptions, offered a limited amount of medical advice, and prepared their own nostrums for sale.[26] In rural areas, which were poorly supplied with doctors, their services were widely used. Numbers increased rapidly as the industrial revolution created an urban consumer society which favoured retailers operating from fixed shops; in most towns the highest rates of shop growth occurred from the end of the eighteenth century to around 1820.[27]

The selling of drugs and poisons thus became a subject of concern on two related fronts. On one hand lay the much-publicised ease – alluded to by *Punch* – with which dangerous substances like arsenic could be obtained. Despite the fact that death by poison was relatively uncommon (569 reported in England in 1848, in a population of about fifteen million),[28] fears of secret poisoning – fuelled in part by a handful of notorious arsenic murders during the 1840s – began to gain a hold on the public imagination.[29] On the other hand lay the problems associated with lack of professional control over the business of making and selling drugs. For decades this had been the remit of persons of varying degrees of training, including doctors, druggists, and a large group of medical 'irregulars' identified by the *Pharmaceutical Journal* as 'grocers, oilmen, and hucksters ... drug brokers, drug grinders, and drysalters, patent medicine vendors, quacks, mountebanks, bone-setters, and medical herbalists, farriers, and cow doctors ...'[30] Members of all these groups were often perceived to hold a cavalier attitude to safety.

Upon its foundation in 1841, the Pharmaceutical Society began a campaign to restrict the retailing, dispensing and compounding of drugs and poisons to all but professional pharmacists.

Not every druggist was willing to sell poison to all comers: many required an adult witness to a sale, or refused to sell to someone whom they did not know or who could not give a satisfactory reason for wanting poison. But too many failed to take sufficient precautions until it was too late. When the teenager Jane Clarke poisoned her mother at Putney in 1831, she tried to buy arsenic from four different druggists. She was unknown to all of them, and was successful in making only one purchase; three refused to sell to her as 'she appeared much agitated'. The fourth felt so guilty about his part in the drama that he took half an ounce of arsenic himself, and was only just saved from death.[31] It was to be another twenty years before such variable standards of conduct were, in theory at least, abolished.

Agitation by the Pharmaceutical Society, which allied itself with the Provincial Medical and Surgical Association (the British Medical Association from 1856), culminated in two important Acts of Parliament in the early 1850s. The Arsenic Act of 1851 placed restrictions on the sale of arsenic, which thereafter was not to be sold to anyone under the age of twenty-one. Sales could be made only when the buyer was known to, or introduced by some person known to, the seller. Further, an entry of the sale had to be made in a Poison Book, and had to include the signature of the purchaser. The arsenic itself had to be coloured with soot or indigo, to make it easier to detect; this was usually done at the point of sale. But this rule did not apply to bulk sales of ten pounds or more, which were common among farmers, manufacturers and wholesalers. In 1852 the Pharmacy Act gave the Pharmaceutical Society the power to hold examinations and issue certificates, thereby restricting the professional title of 'pharmaceutical chemist' to members of the society. Until the Act was amended in July 1868, however, anyone could continue to call himself a chemist or druggist. To close this loophole, the new Pharmacy and Poisons Act further restricted the selling of poisons to doctors, pharmacists and registered druggists. The register, established and overseen by the society, was open to those who had passed its examinations; any druggist who had been in business before 1868 could be registered upon proof of satisfactory qualifications.

The Act of 1868 severely limited the number of people who could sell substances containing poisons, but its weakness lay in the fact that it specified the poisons so considered; anything not listed was not a poison and could continue to be sold by anyone. Of the two lists drawn up by parliamentarians under the advice of the Pharmaceutical Society – Parts One and Two – the substances on both had to be labelled with the name and address of the seller together with the word 'Poison'. The recording of sales in Poison Books was extended from arsenic to the subgroup of substances considered to be the most dangerous (Part One), including all known alkaloids, cantharides, corrosive sublimate, cyanides and prussic acid, ergot, savin and tartar emetic. Vermin killers were apparently intended to be included in this group, but many druggists failed to understand this until a succession of prosecutions in the early 1870s led to the issue of a fresh explanation of the Act in January 1873.[32] But infringements of its provisions continued throughout the 1880s. Part Two poisons, including opiates, oxalic acid, and patent medicines containing strychnine, morphine and mercury, did not require an entry to be made in a Poison Book. Most of the acids that together accounted for a large proportion of accidental and suicidal deaths did not appear in either part of the poison schedule. This unsatisfactory state of affairs was addressed when the Pharmacy Act was again revised in 1908: tighter controls on the sale of opiates and carbolic acid (a disinfectant favoured by suicides) were introduced. It was not until a series of Dangerous Drugs Acts was introduced in the 1920s and 1930s that control over opiates was placed solely in the hands of doctors and pharmacists – who thereafter featured disproportionately as opiate murderers.[33]

Despite its piecemeal implementation, legislation intended to control the sale of poisons was gradually effective in reducing poison-related crime, particularly that attributed to arsenic. Of the 237 cases noted in Table 1, 197 occurred before 1860, fifteen in the years 1860–67, but only twenty-five in the long period from 1868 to 1914. Notwithstanding the Act of 1851, uncoloured arsenic continued to be found in the stomachs of victims until at least the 1880s, by which time the zealous prosecution of druggists found to have made such illegal sales brought the practice more or less to an end. But arsenic murders could not be entirely eliminated so long as arsenic itself retained a central role in pest control and manufacturing. Barrels of uncoloured arsenic remained on the premises of dye-makers and wholesalers, in glass factories and on farms, open to the attentions of opportunistic poisoners. From the late 1880s, when commercial herbicides began appearing in poisoning deaths, it would have been a simple matter to feed weed killer to an intended victim. This is what Edith Bingham was suspected of doing in 1911, when gallon tins of Acme Weed Killer, containing over ninety grains of arsenic per fluid ounce, were found in the garden of the house in which three members of her family died. Ten drops of this pale straw-coloured solution represented a fatal dose,[34] but the case against Bingham was never proved.

The use of alkaloids for criminal purposes also declined in the last quarter of the nineteenth century, particularly after controls on vermin killers were tightened. The first successful prosecution of a strychnine murderer was in 1856, when Dr William Palmer was hanged for the murder of his gambling associate, John Parsons Cook. The case spawned a copycat crime: three months after Cook's death, William Dove killed his wife with strychnine stolen from a surgeon's office.[35] The next thirty years saw a steady succession of cases come before the courts, and in the early 1890s the serial killer Dr Thomas Neill Cream murdered four London prostitutes with strychnine-laced pills. Of the cases on which this book is based, the last strychnine crime occurred in 1901, when an elderly and near-blind druggist was convicted of the manslaughter of a child.[36] The other alkaloids were involved more infrequently in criminal cases, since they were readily available only to members of the medical profession. Two of the most infamous poisoners of the late Victorian and Edwardian periods were doctors who used alkaloids that the average person could not obtain: Dr George Lamson poisoned his nephew with aconitine in 1880; and Dr Hawley Crippen used hyoscine to murder his wife in 1910.

Poisoning crimes of the type so often seen during the nineteenth century are now a rarity, thanks in part to additional legislation and twentieth-century advances in forensic science. In 1933 a revamped Pharmacy and Poisons Act established the first fully comprehensive controls on the sale, supply, labelling, storage and transportation of poisons; these were further tightened by the Medicines Act 1968 and the Poisons Act 1972. It is now exceedingly difficult, though not impossible, to obtain the poisons formerly responsible for so many deaths, and poisonous drugs may only be obtained by prescription. New poisons have, however, taken their place, and despite the best efforts of law-makers to restrict access, and of manufacturers to preclude accidents, the determined poisoner usually finds a loophole.[37]

Contrary to popular opinion, not all poisoners were women or doctors. Of those poisoners caught or suspected, male and female perpetrators were in fact almost evenly divided: of 540 criminal cases, 48.7 per cent of accused poisoners were men and boys, while 51.3 per cent were women and girls. These figures correspond to the proportion of males and females in the nineteenth-century population of England and Wales.[38] But they should also be considered in relation to general statistics of violent crime, which show that during the early Victorian period females comprised about 40 per cent of all persons tried for murder. Later, Home Office statistics distinguished infanticide (the murder of one's own infant) from other homicides, so that by the end of the nineteenth century women accounted for less than one quarter of all those tried for murder. (In Victorian England the homicide rate hovered around 1.5 per 100,000, corresponding to about 400 reported murders per year in the period 1857–90.[39] On average, only one or two of these were attributable to poison. In Victorian Wales there were normally about twenty cases of homicide per year. Manslaughter was fives times as common as murder, and only a relatively small number of poisoning crimes were brought to light during the entire century.)[40] Roughly speaking, then, men were three times more likely than women to commit murder, but women who did so were far more likely than men to choose poison as their weapon.

This supports the stereotype of the physically weak woman who uses poison to avoid a direct confrontation with her victim, but it does not explain why men intent on murder might choose poison. The most obvious response is that all perpetrators, both male and female, thought that their crime might go undetected: no wound, no murder, no con-sequences. There is much truth to this statement, although we have seen that even if death by poison did not leave visible trauma, it could often mark the victim's body. Rather, to answer this question it will be necessary to look in more detail at the types of poisoning crimes with which men and women were charged (Table 3). The category 'Others' includes six men charged with unique offences such as assault, conspiracy to murder and throwing a corrosive fluid; one woman and two men who were not tried; and two men who were charged with 'poisoning'.

These statistics are based on the gender of the principal accused person, since approximately 13 per cent of all cases involved two or more people acting together. It is obvious, however, that a much larger proportion of women than men were charged with murder and attempted murder related to poisoning: 92 per cent compared with 62 per cent. This does not show that women usually turned to poison with the decided intention to murder, but that the criminal justice system assumed that they did. Men, on the other hand, used poison in a wider variety of situations, particularly those that resulted in charges of destroying animals and of manslaughter. The former was a crime almost always motivated by revenge, while the latter normally arose in cases of professional negligence. Given that most doctors and druggists were male, the figures are predictable. Finally, little should be read into the fact that six men were suspected of poisoning crimes but apparently never charged. For each of these cases, by chance preserved in the nation's legal records, a search of local newspapers would reveal many similar stories about both men and women.

Poisoning is largely a crime of opportunity: a poisoner has to get close enough to his or her victim to administer the poison, normally in food, drink or medicine. This is rarely difficult when the intended victim is an animal, but can be awkward with people. It is for this reason that a trusting relationship – most often a family or a professional connection – almost always existed between poisoner and victim. Where there was no close relationship, gifts of poisoned food purporting to come from friends were remarkably effective, as when a Cornish gunsmith, Richard Sargent, sent sugar laced with arsenic to the family of an excise man against whom he bore a grudge.[41] Where the victims were animals, the relationship existed between the poisoner and the animals' owner – the poisoner was normally a neighbour or an employee. Although exceedingly uncommon, random poisonings were not unheard of. In retrospect, most appear to be attributable to carelessness on the part of someone who was unwilling to acknowledge their role in a suspicious death; in such cases coroner's juries found verdicts of murder by person or persons unknown. The crimes of Neill Cream – who told his

Table 3

Main Charges Laid in Poisoning Crimes, 1750–1914

Charge	Female	Male	Total
Murder	210	132	342
Attempted Murder	44	32	76
Manslaughter	5	40	45
Administering Poison	14	21	35
Destroying Animals	0	14	14
Attempted Poisoning	3	8	11
Unknown	0	6	6
Others	1	10	11
Total	277	263	540

Table 4

Principal Relationships of Poisoner to Victim, 1750–1914

Relationship	Female	Male	Total
Mother or Stepmother	82	–	82
Father, Stepfather, Father-in-law	–	28	28
Wife	75	–	75
Husband	–	59	59
Daughter or Daughter-in-law	17	–	17
Son, Son-in-law, Stepson	–	22	22
Sister or Sister-in-law	10	–	10
Brother, Stepbrother, Brother-in-law	–	9	9
Other Family	11	7	18
Servant, Housekeeper	40	10	50
Lover or Fiancé(e)	2	27	29
Neighbour	3	13	16
Medical attendant*	2	32	34
Nurse or Nursemaid	6	–	6
Friend or Acquaintance	1	8	9
Abortionist	4	3	7
Colleague (work-related)	1	14	15
Unknown	4	7	11
Other	19	24	43
Total	277	263	540

* This includes medical practitioners, herbalists, druggists, pharmacists, grocers and healers: all those persons who were involved in the selling or prescribing of drugs.

prostitute victims that the pills he gave them would be good for their complexions – show, however, that it was possible for an individual to murder complete strangers with poison. Table 4 shows the principal relationships that existed between poisoners and their victims.

Most poisoning crimes, as most homicides generally, were family affairs.[42] Of the accused poisoners represented in Table 4, 60 per cent targeted members of their immediate family. If we add to that the crimes committed by servants (considered family members by law and custom), including nurses and nursemaids who lived in the home, the proportion rises to 70 per cent. Disgruntled lovers, neighbours, friends and colleagues together account for another 13 per cent. When medical attendants and 'professional' abortionists are taken jointly as another important type of relationship, we are left with the fact that a meagre 10 per cent of poisoners had a distant association with their victims. Some encountered them in lodging houses and pubs, or through mutual acquaintances. Anyone who was willing to consume food or drink provided by a poisoner was, potentially, at risk. In much the same way that so-called date rape drugs feature in modern society, nineteenth-century pub-goers fell victim to professional thieves who spiked their drinks with laudanum or chloral hydrate. Lodgers who were known to have saved a little money occasionally had cause to wonder whether their landlady might wish to get her hands on it, especially after Mary Ann Burdock very nearly got away with the murder of her elderly female tenant in the 1830s. Suspicious relatives finally urged the exhumation of the victim, and Burdock was convicted of murder.[43] Though notorious in its day, her case was probably unknown to Frederick Seddon, whose greed led him in 1911 to try a similar gambit; he too paid for his crime at the end of a hangman's rope.[44]

The relationships between poisoners and their victims were to some extent tied to established gender roles. Women poisoned those people for whose care they were primarily responsible, mainly husbands and children. An analogous point can be made in the case of servants, the vast majority of whom were female: they poisoned the people they were employed to look after. Men too poisoned family members, but to a lesser extent than women. Conversely, they were more likely to poison their lovers than were women, often in the course of attempting to cause a miscarriage, a fact related to financial motives: wives and children cost money, and some men preferred to avoid the responsibility. Those who were already married sought to hide illicit liaisons from their wives. Men seem to have been more likely to use poison as a means of settling scores, as indicated by the fact that no animal poisonings can be attributed to a woman; women were sometimes involved, but only as accomplices. These cases were often motivated by incidents related to work and professional self-esteem. Women, on the other hand, carried out revenge poisonings after suffering what they considered to be personal slights or rejections, and targeted either the object of their anger (usually a man) or someone close to them. Men, but not women, used poison to play what they considered to be practical jokes on friends and colleagues, though the victims probably found nothing funny in being taken suddenly and violently ill.

Male and female poisoners varied little in one respect: most were aged between twenty and fifty.[45] Significantly more children and teenagers than elderly people committed poisoning crimes; the youngest encountered in this study was just eleven years old, while the eldest was over ninety. Although the exact ages of only 60 per cent of all poisoners are known, the trend indicates that young women, perhaps being under greater strain as wives, mothers and junior domestic servants, took to poisoning at a slightly earlier age than young men. The situation was reversed in old age, when men featured more frequently as poisoners than women. This was possibly because men who lived long lives remained responsible for dependants and continued to work, while women often outlived family commitments, and thus the situations that might lead them to become poisoners. The fact that there were so few elderly poisoners is also a reflection of the age structure of the population. From the slow start seen in the period 1750 to 1850, life expectancy at birth in England and Wales began to rise steadily from the middle of the nineteenth century. The average man or woman born in 1750 could expect to live to the age of thirty-seven; if born in 1850, to forty. But by the end of the Edwardian period, the figure had risen to fifty-two years for men, and fifty-five for women. It has been estimated that in 1826 one person in fifteen was aged sixty or over, and that this figure increased steadily to one in thirteen by 1911. The proportion of elderly people remained small, however, at about 5 per cent of the population.[46]

The social status of poisoners was also evenly balanced between male and female, the vast majority being poor and, at best, semi-literate. Most were members of the lower classes (generally considered to be the dangerous classes),[47] who turned to poison as a means of escaping intolerable situations. Many could see no other viable option, particularly as they strove to maintain the veneer of respectability that was such an integral feature of Victorian society. Part of what the notion of respectability implied was behaviour appropriate to one's status; hence, standards differed for members of different classes.[48] This is why accused poisoners like Florence Maybrick and the medical murderers excited so much public revulsion. As members of the middle class who held respectable positions in society, their crimes were unexpected, and thus all the more shocking for their peers to contemplate. It is impossible to estimate the number of poisoning crimes that took place in middle-class households but which were never reported, or even suspected, because relatives and doctors could not accept that such behaviour might take place among their class. Those cases that were brought to light tended to involve two types of middle-class people: those who had abandoned their respectability by indulging in illicit affairs (like Maybrick); and the mentally unstable, whose actions were beyond their control.

Most poisoners acted alone, but approximately 13 per cent of cases involved two or more persons working together. It was most common to find a man and a woman jointly accused, usually of crimes involving the death of a spouse or child. But it was not always the case that both were charged, as it was sometimes impossible to prove anything against a lover who had clearly had something to gain but who had not actually given poison to the victim. Occasionally, lovers who had killed together were hanged together; the crowds drawn to such events, before the abolition of public executions in 1868, were enormous. Cases where couples poisoned more than one victim usually involved children, who were killed because they were in the way or because they were worth more dead than alive.[49] Of forty-one poisoning crimes committed by couples, nine involved multiple victims. The single case in which a couple accounted for more than four deaths is that of Thomas and Rebecca Mallett, who were acquitted of poisoning six bullocks in Suffolk in 1839.

It was less common for two men or two women to act together as poisoners.[50] Among women, the most common pairing was that of mother and daughter, the victim being the infant child of the daughter, usually a poor and unmarried girl living with her widowed mother. Occasionally siblings or friends found themselves accused of crimes against other family members or members of their household. Of the cases under study, the only one in which there was no obvious personal motive was that of the murder of her family's female lodger by teenager Mary Barnes and her friend Charlotte Barnacle.[51] Both were obsessed with poison, and the case appears to be one of what would in modern parlance be termed a 'thrill kill'. Far more vicious partnerships were infrequently formed for the purposes of financial gain, as when Scottish sisters Catherine Flanagan and Margaret Higgins murdered nine people in Liverpool in the early 1880s. Convicted of the murder of Margaret's husband Thomas, they were hanged together in March 1884. In London a few years later, a scheme of comparable scope was revealed. When Amelia Winters and her daughter, the aptly named Elizabeth Frost, were indicted for three murders, it transpired that they had insured over twenty people, five of whom had died between June 1886 and February 1889. Winters cheated justice by dying in gaol; tried alone for murder, Frost was convicted only of forgery, for falsifying information on the insurance documents.[52]

Men who committed poisoning crimes together were less likely to be related to each other; they were more usually friends or colleagues. The victims were often young women, drugged for the purposes of sexual conquest or simply as a professed practical joke. As many as three or four young men could be involved in such cases. Until the Offences Against the Person Act was passed in 1861, the law was powerless to punish such dangerous games unless the unfortunate victim died, as did Eleanor Turner after her beer was laced with cantharides by her brother, her suitor and a third man in 1830. In what seems a small price to pay for the death of a girl of nineteen, the brother and the suitor were found guilty of manslaughter and sentenced to one year's imprisonment in the county gaol.[53] Other victims were poisoned in incidents related to hocussing or revenge. It was less common to find serious attempts made by two men to murder someone, but it did happen. In 1859 a young woman named Honora Turner charged her estranged husband James and his friend Edward Keefe with attempting to murder her with lead acetate. At their trial at the Old Bailey, the jury accepted Keefe's claim that, although he had been present, he had not known what was going on, and acquitted him. Turner was convicted, his death sentence being later commuted to imprisonment.[54]

Only a little less common than the poisoners who worked in pairs were those who, acting alone, accounted for more than one victim. The members of this relatively small group (about 12 per cent of persons tried for poisoning crimes) divide themselves evenly into two rather different sets of criminals. One group may be most accurately described as multiple murderers: people who killed, or attempted to kill, more than one person in the same incident. This would include, for example, Michael Whiting and Henry Scholfield. The other group aroused terror in the minds of the Victorian public. These were the serial killers, people who murdered again and again, usually for profit, until they were caught and executed. In some cases suspicions were entertained at an early stage, limiting the number of victims to two or three. But other killers, mainly female, escaped detection for many years. Of these, the most prolific was Mary Ann Cotton, a poor woman from County Durham who is supposed to have murdered at least fourteen people, perhaps as many as seventeen, between 1860 and 1872. All but one was a relative: three husbands, numerous children and stepchildren, her mother, her sister-in-law, and a lodger who had been her lover.[55]

Women feature disproportionately (three to two) as multiple poisoners, and particularly as serial poisoners. Not only were there more of them, but they accounted for more victims than did their male counterparts (again, by about three to two).[56] It was in these remorseless killers that the stereotype of the female poisoner found its truest form: not only did they betray their natural role as wives and mothers, but they perverted the concept of medical assistance by posing as nurses to those whom they were slowly killing. In order to understand why these women did what they did, and how their motives may have differed from those of men – indeed, to explore criminal poisoning in all its guises – we must consider the poisoners themselves. What follows cannot refer to each of them individually, but presents a representative sample of the English poisoner, male and female, rich and – overwhelmingly – poor, young and old, in the period between 1750 and the First World War.

3

Reasons of the Heart

I said to her one day, 'Now young Spraggons is gone, you may
have John Foster'. And she answered, 'No, I won't have him. I hate
him bad enough to poison him'.

Maria Woodgate, 1846 [1]

The ideal marriage has long been considered one in which husband
and wife form a harmonious working partnership; friendship is at least
as important as love and sexual attraction. In earlier centuries, the one
unshakeable rule governing marriage was that couples must be able to
form an independent financial unit.[2] At all levels of society, women
were expected to uphold and enhance their husbands' position. Thus
women who were hard working and frugal, and who came from families
of good repute, made fine wives and mothers. A good husband was
sober, kind, dependable, and capable of supporting his wife and family.
The choice of whether or not to marry was usually straightforward:
men wanted to father a legitimate heir, while women found that their
greatest chance of economic and social survival was through marriage.
In a male-dominated society, more spinsters than bachelors ended their
days dependent on charity.[3] The proportion of each generation that
married remained remarkably stable, at about 87 per cent, between 1750
and 1950.[4] Most couples were content: a spouse offered companionship
and affection; children, though costly, could be a source of pride and
future support.

For those who could not live happily together the options were few.
Divorce was practically impossible for all but the wealthy. Before the
law was changed in 1857,[5] couples could divorce with the right to remarry
only by obtaining a private Act of Parliament, a process estimated to
cost upwards of £700. Thereafter, the newly created Court for Divorce

and Matrimonial Causes was empowered to grant divorce, but solely on the grounds of adultery – a limitation that remained in effect until 1937. Women were at a marked disadvantage: where men only had to prove adultery, until 1923 their wives had to prove both adultery and at least one act of desertion, cruelty, incest, rape, sodomy or bestiality. Those who were willing to air such unsavoury laundry in public had to do so in London, as local courts had no jurisdiction in marital matters. It soon became apparent that the change to the law had merely extended full divorce from the aristocracy to members of the growing upper middle class; it was cheaper, but still far too expensive for the working classes.[6]

This inequality was addressed by the Matrimonial Causes Act of 1878, which gave magistrates' courts the power to grant separation and main-tenance orders to the wives of persistent wife-beaters. This made it possible for poorer women to leave their husbands and set up inde-pendent households, and by the early twentieth century, about ten thousand mainly working-class women were obtaining orders for main-tenance in England and Wales each year.[7] Many women who lived apart from their husbands received no financial support. Regardless of the good intentions that underlay this law, it served merely to uphold the status quo: until the middle of the twentieth century, the poor were denied the convenience of divorce. From 1920, undefended divorce cases and those of poor people could be heard at the county assize courts, eliminating the cost of travel to London. But it was not until the institution of a full legal aid system in 1950 that poverty was finally removed as a barrier to divorce.[8]

The emotional and financial turmoil associated with separation and divorce was compounded by another hazard: all women who wished to leave their husbands faced the prospect of losing custody of their child-ren. A father was the sole legal parent of his legitimate offspring, though a mother was the sole parent of illegitimate children. In 1839 it became possible for mothers who lived apart from intolerable husbands to apply to the courts for custody of children under the age of seven; a later amendment raised the age to sixteen. By the late 1880s a father's assumed right to custody had been undermined by further legal reforms stipu-lating that the welfare of children had to be taken into full consideration.[9]

Despite the social stigma, a few brave members of the middle class, notably the novelists George Eliot and Mary Braddon, lived openly with their married lovers, but this was never an easy decision. Marriage was morally and socially the respectable – and thus the preferable – option. It is surely no coincidence that, of the small number of solidly middle-class poisoners of the nineteenth century, about half were accused of murdering a spouse for the sake of a lover. (For middle-class men, money seems to have been an equal or more powerful stimulus to murder.) [10] Many gained lasting notoriety: Florence Maybrick (innocent but condemned for her adultery); Adelaide Bartlett (probably guilty but given the benefit of the doubt); and Dr Hawley Crippen (guilty but still an object of pity). A great deal has been written about these three over the years, but it is unlikely they would have attracted so much attention had they been poor and uneducated. The Victorian cult of respectability touched everyone, but standards of behaviour differed according to status.

Among poorer people, common-law unions were a source of gossip but rarely resulted in ostracism. It was generally perceived that men behaved better towards women to whom they were not married, as they did not feel they 'owned' them, so many women preferred to live with a partner but remain unmarried.[11] When working-class marriages did break down, men could easily flee and begin a new life elsewhere. This often led to bigamy, usually conscious on the part of men but presumptive on the part of their deserted wives, who had no way of finding out what had happened to their husbands. Wives who left home usually did so to join another man, under whose protection they could hope for both happiness and economic security. Desertion was far less common among members of the middle class: even those who possessed only a little property could not so easily relocate their lives. Wife sales, immortalised in Hardy's *The Mayor of Casterbridge*, offered a way in which very poor couples could divorce themselves, but rarely took place without the agreement of both parties.[12] Modelled on cattle sales in order to appear legitimate and legally binding, the number of recorded cases began to grow rapidly at the end of the eighteenth century, reaching a high of some fifty sales per decade in the period from 1810 to 1840. The humiliation and ambiguous legality associated with the process, however, tended to discourage it. Although one or two cases occurred each year until the eve of the First World War, by the middle of the nineteenth century it had become a comparative rarity.[13] For most people, tied by family loyalty or economic necessity to one community, death was the only way to end a marriage.

Given the financial, legal and social constraints placed upon couples who experienced marital breakdown, it is easy to see why 25 per cent of poisoners were accused of murdering, or attempting to murder, a spouse: thwarted romantic aims and acute unhappiness can be powerful incentives. Faced with the realisation that they wished to be with a new lover or without an unloved spouse, and that there was no easy exit from an existing marriage, some individuals chose extreme measures. The chances of success were relatively good: at a time when the average life expectancy was less than fifty, early death was not uncommon. Of marriages made in the 1850s, death ended 19 per cent of them within ten years and 47 per cent within twenty-five years.[14] Historians estimate that, during the second half of the eighteenth century in England and Wales, between 15 and 20 per cent of all marriages were for the second time. Widowers and childless widows could expect to remarry; in the countryside, however, custom opposed the remarriage of widows who had children, since it might threaten their inheritance.[15] This is at least partly reflected in the fact that around 1850 about 14 per cent of men but only 9 per cent of women married for a second time. By the turn of the century, the figures had dropped to 9 and 7 per cent respectively. The decrease in the overall number of second marriages was a feature of increased life expectancy, since divorce statistics did not rise significantly until after the Second World War.[16]

Widowers who had children usually sought to remarry quickly; they needed a woman to look after their household. In contrast, women left in an economically sound position, free of male domination, might be happier on their own – the stereotypical merry widow. But those who needed the emotional or financial support of a man and who did choose to remarry could easily become an object of local gossip if they did so too speedily. Tongues began to wag whenever a bereaved woman was known to have taken a fancy to someone else or married again with unseemly haste – within a few months. In small towns and villages neighbourhood rumours quickly reached the ears of the local police constable or coroner, setting in motion an investigation that might bring to light an unnatural death. This is what happened when Hannah

Harris, middle-aged and twice-widowed, married Edmund Curtis within three weeks of her second husband's funeral. Thomas Harris was buried on 5 May 1850, at Frampton Cotterell in Gloucestershire, but the body was exhumed on 29 June because of stories that he had been poisoned. These proved to be true: his stomach was coated with arsenic sulphide. If his widow had waited a decent interval to remarry the crime would never have been discovered; he had taken five days to die, and a doctor had ascribed death to general weakness and too much beer. Hannah had a narrow escape: her death sentence was commuted to transportation.[17]

Between 1750 and 1914, a slightly higher number of women than men were charged with poisoning (but not necessarily murdering) a spouse, seventy-five as opposed to fifty-nine. Of that total, very few were suspected of having poisoned more than one spouse, and equally few poisoned both a spouse and one or more of their own children. Most of these were crimes related to money. The numbers do not include people convicted of having murdered someone else but suspected of having poisoned a spouse, crimes that were, again, prompted mainly by financial motives. The five women and two men who poisoned the partner of someone they were in love with form a distinct but related group, as do the twenty-seven (often married) men and two women who poisoned their lovers. Finally, one unusual case defies easy classification. When a young married couple, Eliza and Henry Foxall, were unable to resolve their love-hate relationship, she turned to a soothsayer for advice. Mary Ann Scrafton told her that Henry could not live long, and that she had only married him as an act of revenge against a former admirer. Thus were the seeds sown: from then on, Eliza regularly bought love charms from Scrafton (one cost as much as five shillings), and eventually began dosing her husband's food with a powder – arsenic – that Scrafton posted to Bishopwearmouth from her home in Lancashire. Henry Foxall, who seems to have been as gullible and foolish as his wife, suffered months of chronic poisoning before he finally realised that all was not well and the scheme was exposed. Tried at Durham in November 1887, Eliza and Scrafton were sentenced to prison terms of five and seven years respectively. The latter, having clearly masterminded the plan, was, at the age of forty-six, perhaps trying to create a name for herself as a remover of unwanted husbands: she claimed to have killed a man in Durham.[18] In a mark of how times had changed, the local authorities failed to take her seriously.

The incidence of husband poisoning reached what seemed to be epidemic proportions in the late 1840s and early 1850s. Nearly as many crimes came to light between 1845 and 1853 – twenty-three – as had done in the entire century before or the half century after. In Essex in 1848, it was feared that an entire nest of poisoners had been uncovered in the villages around Tendring, supposedly led by a middle-aged woman named Mary May. She had been hanged in August 1848 for the murder of her brother, and when a neighbour, Hannah Southgate, was arrested for poisoning her husband, a connection was inferred. Despite claims that all recently deceased husbands would have to be exhumed, only one body was, and no evidence of poison was found.[19] Southgate was acquitted, as were half the women tried during that period. It is difficult to avoid the conclusion that a certain amount of hysteria – often whipped up by the media – prompted many prosecutions, but a few guilty women undoubtedly went free. These crimes were part of a wider trend: in England and Wales, between 1840 and 1850, a total of eighty-seven women and seventy-seven men were tried for murder or attempted murder by poison.[20] This decade was one when poverty was widespread and child victims became increasingly numerous as a result of the rise of the insurance industry. The Arsenic Act of 1851, which imposed stricter controls on the sale of arsenic, helped to bring these figures down.

Unlike husband poisonings, there was no obvious cluster of wife poisonings in the period. Rather, wife poisoners were exposed at a consistent rate of one or two per decade until 1830, about one per year between the late 1830s and 1880, then dropping to one every three years thereafter. These figures stand in stark contrast to the general statistics of spousal murder. Between 1830 and 1900 about one thousand men and women in England were convicted of killing their spouses; of these, female poisoners numbered about forty and males twenty.[21] Most of those who murdered a spouse were men: killings of wives by husbands reported in the *Times* between 1820 and 1900 outnumbered reports of killings of husbands by wives by nine to one.[22] The typical assailant in all varieties of assault was in fact male, fuelled by alcohol, suffering the stresses associated with earning a living and providing for dependants, and showing the physically aggressive behaviour regarded and accepted as typically masculine.[23] Unhappy women were clearly less likely to become homicidal than unhappy men, but, when they did, their chosen weapon was likely to be poison; men tended to engage in a more direct, impulsive, violent confrontation.

The traditional view of husband murder holds that women, being oppressed in practice and law, and physically weaker than men, sought a means of escape that was guaranteed to be effective. No one would dispute the fact that women who wanted to escape abuse or replace their husbands probably used poison more widely than we know.[24] But we must also accept that proportionally as many wife poisoners may have gone undiscovered. It is clear that men did poison their wives and lovers; the question is whether their motives differed significantly from those of female poisoners. Love, hate and sexual desire accounted for the majority of such crimes; where love triangles formed, jealousy could lead to the death of one of the persons concerned. The marital discord that could develop as a result of financial difficulties, or from a basic inability to get along, sometimes led to violence, bolstered by a strong contempt and anger felt by one partner for the other. Regardless of motive, however, to dig deeply into these crimes is to discover at their root a graveyard of hopes and shattered dreams. The relatively few cases of poisoning among the frequent beatings, kickings and stabbings that constituted the bulk of spousal assaults stand as much in tribute to human self-control as in indictment of nineteenth-century crime statistics.

When John Foster married Catherine Morley in October 1846, he clearly had in mind the Victorian ideal of marriage, one in which both partners shared a mutual love and worked together in harmonious partnership. He was known to be deeply in love with his seventeen-year-old bride, whom he had known since their childhood in the Suffolk village of Acton. Although she preferred 'young Spraggons', in Spraggons's absence Foster, a farm labourer aged twenty-four, talked her into marriage. This proved to be a mistake: three weeks to the day after the wedding, he died from what the local surgeon, Robert Jones, assumed was English cholera.[25]

The events that culminated in Foster's death began with his new wife's visit to an aunt who lived a few miles from Bury St Edmunds. Catherine, who had worked as a servant before her marriage, had never travelled beyond Acton. The sights of Bury, a large market town and county centre, made a strong impression on her during the ten days she was away. Shortly after her return she met a friend and fellow servant, Maria Woodgate, to whom a year earlier she had sworn a murderous hatred of John Foster. Asked how she liked her married life, she told Woodgate 'Not at all'.[26]

On 17 November Catherine Foster prepared a meal of dumplings and potatoes, which she ate with her husband and eight-year-old brother Thomas. John Foster began to vomit after eating the dumplings, and his mother-in-law, in whose house they were living, emptied it into a ditch that bordered their neighbours' property. The next day, these neighbours found nine of their thirteen chickens dead, and the other four died early the following morning. Foster died during the afternoon of 18 November, and an autopsy was performed two days later. This revealed nothing unusual to Jones, but news of the dead chickens aroused suspicion and the stomach was sent to William Edmund Image (1807–1903), a surgeon at the Suffolk General Infirmary who was beginning to gain a name in forensic analysis. His findings led to the exhumation of the body and further tests, which showed the presence of large amounts of arsenic in both Foster and the fowls.[27]

At the inquest young Thomas Morley admitted that he had seen his sister make two dumplings, into one of which she had put a white powder. After her husband's death Catherine Foster had been heard to say, 'I wish I had gone to Bury before I was married, for then I shouldn't have married at all and would have got a good place'.[28] Her fate sealed, she was tried and sentenced to death. She eventually confessed, but did not explain why she had done it. From her comments before and after the trial, however, the motive seems obvious. She had lost the man she loved, because she chose the better off Foster; or, more likely, because Spraggons had left and she had been drawn into marriage by a man who had a long-standing passion for her.[29] Added to this was the discovery that there was a world beyond Acton, to which, as a wife, she now seemed irrevocably bound. To a girl barely seventeen and poorly educated, widowhood seemed the best way to regain lost opportunities.

It was a little unusual for a woman so young to be married in nineteenth-century England: around 1850, the average age of a man who married for the first time was twenty-four, while women were just a year younger. Most couples had to delay marriage in order to save enough money to set up their own household. The fact that John Foster moved into the Morley family home suggests that he could not quite afford a wife; his ardour must have made him persuasive. Realising her mistake almost immediately, his wife may have considered murder even before she went to Bury: her mother claimed that Catherine had been complaining of Foster's health for three weeks before his death, though he was known to be a healthy man.[30]

Catherine Foster was not the only woman to realise soon after her wedding that she had made an error that she now wished to escape. In July 1784 a middle-aged widow married widower John Bayston, a farm labourer whom she poisoned two months later. In her confession, Ellen Bayston claimed that she had not meant to kill him, only to 'shorten his days', but admitted that she had many times thought of giving him poison during the preceding weeks; an argument finally drove her to it. Her motive was desire for one Richard Brown, to whom she had been betrothed until another man (possibly her adult son) in the town of Easingwold, in north Yorkshire, had managed to force her to marry Bayston. How exactly this came about is not revealed in the case depositions, but her hope that it was not too late to have Brown is clear. As with the Foster case, the story seems more poignant because Bayston loved his wife and tried to make her happy.[31] At her trial Ellen Bayston was found guilty but insane, thus avoiding the hangman's noose.

Men too found themselves married to one person while longing for another. If Cumberland labourer John Graham poisoned his pregnant schoolmistress wife Jane in 1839, he was almost certainly motivated by lust for the thirteen-year-old granddaughter of a neighbour. Both in their thirties, he and his wife had only been married for ten months, but she had already complained of his violence – he had kicked her several times. The girl in question, Ann Bell, denied that Graham had ever been seen to take improper liberties with her, a comment that cleverly avoided revealing the exact nature of their relationship. He was acquitted because no one could show that he had purchased arsenic; and, despite vigorous denials on the part of the local druggist, the jury was prepared to believe that a prescription error had been to blame.[32] Perhaps this really was the more logical explanation, but Graham could certainly have hoped to marry the child after his wife's death. Until 1929, the age of consent for a marriage was twelve years for girls and fourteen for boys, though in practice marriage at these ages had been almost unheard of for centuries. Local feeling would probably have prevented such a union between Graham and Bell.[33] (The low minimum age fostered not early marriage but the widespread exploitation of children within the Victorian sex industry.)

Despite these and a few similar cases (including May-December marriages where the young wife quickly grew to hate her aged spouse), it was relatively unusual to find husbands and wives poisoning their partners within months of marriage. On those occasions when a relationship broke down very soon after the wedding, men tended to use poison as a form of revenge, not as a means of freeing themselves to go to another woman. Honora Turner left her husband James within weeks of their wedding in February 1859; thereafter he saw her occasionally, the last time in August of that year. They had an argument about money, during which Honora pushed him against a wall and threatened to strike him. The next day he returned with a friend, Edward Keefe, and a pot of poisoned beer. He had added lead acetate to it, a substance commonly believed to be more poisonous than it was, and Honora suffered nothing worse than a bout of vomiting. Both men were tried for attempted murder: Keefe was acquitted, but Turner was convicted and received a suspended death sentence. His actions were born of anger, sparked by her refusal to give him money and by her aggressive stance;[34] it was a calculated response to a woman who had affronted his masculinity. Many other men would have resorted to physical violence, but either it was not in his nature, or Turner felt that he could not have won such a confrontation.

Most husband- and wife-poisonings took place after several years of marriage, usually sparked by the appearance of a third party, a man or woman who became an object of desire and the unwitting – or sometimes fully cognisant – stimulus to murder. For many women, this person was a neighbour or lodger; for men, a servant, a woman to whom they were related or one they had met locally. Perhaps the classic example lies in the case of the still notorious Dr Crippen, who, in 1910, poisoned his drunken and adulterous wife, whom he could have divorced, for love of his secretary.

The Crippen story has been told again and again, much of its appeal lying in the grainy black and white photographs and film footage of the principal characters: the mild-mannered murderer, his mousy mistress and slatternly wife, and the dogged police detective who exposed their secrets. The case had all the elements of a modern blockbuster, highlighted by a dramatic flight from justice and arrest at sea, a five-day trial dominated by forensic experts, and, inevitably, an execution. The public remain fascinated by the gory details of the murder, the illicit sexual affair that precipitated it and, especially, the pathos of the man himself. Even the pathologist who contributed to Crippen's downfall felt the spell.[35]

Hawley Harvey Crippen was born in Michigan in 1862, and followed what was then a fairly normal course of medical studies in the United States. He obtained a diploma from the Homeopathic Hospital in Cleveland, Ohio, which was endorsed by the Faculty of the Medical College of Philadelphia, and in 1885 he qualified as an eye and ear specialist at the Ophthalmic Hospital in New York. In 1883 he spent a few months in England, studying medicine informally; on his return seventeen years later he was entitled to call himself a doctor but could not legally practise as one.[36]

During the intervening years he practised medicine in a number of American cities. He married and had a son, but his wife died around 1890 and he sent the boy to live with her mother in California. He then spent some time in New York, where he married again, a girl of seventeen called Cora Turner; it was she whom he eventually poisoned. Her real name was Kunigunde Mackamotski and, according to Crippen, she had been the mistress of another man. An attractive but coarse young woman, she lacked the talent necessary to achieve her dream of becoming an opera star. In 1894 Crippen took a job with Munyon's, a company that dealt in patent medicines, and six years later he was appointed to their London office. In 1902, however, he was recalled to the United States for six months. He left his wife in London, where she found work on the music-hall stage and began an affair – apparently the first of many – with a fellow performer.

Their married life thereafter seems to have been one of restrained passivity on his part, exuberant tyranny on hers. Cora, under the stage name Belle Elmore, failed to make a real career for herself, but her vanity never allowed her to acknowledge this and she immersed herself in the theatrical world. Nor was her husband very successful in the patent medicine business, having initiated a number of failed enterprises. Still, he managed to save about £600, and they lived in a large house, 39 Hilldrop Crescent, Camden Town; it was decorated in Cora's favourite colour, pink. They had no maid, and the house fell into a state of disgusting untidiness. Although he always indulged his wife, Crippen eventually began a relationship with his typist, Ethel le Neve, whom he had first met around 1902. By the beginning of 1910 she had been his lover for three years and he could not contemplate life without her. But Crippen's wife was aware of the affair, and wanted it to end.[37]

In January 1910 Cora Crippen issued an ultimatum to her husband: if he did not give up his mistress, she would leave him and take his savings. On the 15th she gave notice of withdrawal to the bank. As Crippen had unwisely placed his money in a joint account, his options were limited. He could not abandon Ethel le Neve, whom he loved passionately. Cora's prior adultery was grounds for divorce, and he would probably have faced the social stigma cheerfully, but it would have taken too long: she had immediate access to the bank account. So, a man who had endured much over the years finally snapped: he decided to murder his wife and dispose of the body. As a peripheral member of the medical profession, he was able to buy an unusual poison, hyoscine hydrobromide, which he brought home on 19 January 1910. In tiny amounts it was used as a cerebral sedative and sexual depressant, but the five grains that he gave his wife after a dinner party on 31 January must have been almost instantly fatal.

After Cora's death Crippen set about hiding the evidence of his crime. He cut up her body, removed the bones, limbs and some of the internal organs (which he probably burnt) and head (probably dropped overboard during a subsequent trip to France), and buried what remained beneath the floor of the coal cellar. He told her friends that she had returned to the United States to be with a sick relative, but had died in California. Then he made a mistake: Ethel le Neve moved into the house in Hilldrop Crescent on 12 March, and was seen wearing his wife's furs and jewellery. Cora's friends became suspicious, and finally went to the police on 30 June.

A week later Chief Inspector Walter Dew visited Crippen at his office to ask some questions, bringing a search warrant for the house. Dew spent the entire day with Crippen, had lunch with him, looked around his house, and was almost fully persuaded by the story that Cora had left him and he had lied to avoid the scandal. Had Crippen's nerve held, the crime would never have been discovered. But he was rattled, and the next day, 9 July, he and Ethel (disguised as a boy) fled to Antwerp, from where they embarked for Canada on the SS *Montrose*. When Dew returned two days later to verify a date and found them gone, an alarm was raised. The house and garden were searched thoroughly, and on the third day Cora's remains were found.

While a team of forensic experts were called in to make what they could of the bits of hair, skin and muscle found in the cellar, Dew set about tracking down Crippen and le Neve. An arrest warrant was issued on 16 July; the captain of the *Montrose* saw it before his ship sailed on the 20th. By the 22nd he had become suspicious of two of his passengers, Mr and Master Robinson. The boy's clothes fitted oddly, and the pair seemed unduly affectionate. Radio was then in its infancy, but the *Montrose* had one and the captain used it to send a message to London, becoming the first man to use the new invention to aid in the capture of a killer. On 23 July Dew sailed from Liverpool on a faster ship, and reached Quebec before his quarry. When the *Montrose* docked on 31 July, Dew was waiting for Crippen and le Neve.[38]

They were tried separately at the Old Bailey in October 1910, the doctor for murder and his mistress for being an accessory after the fact. In a masterful piece of forensic work, the prosecution's four principal experts, pathologists Augustus Pepper and Bernard Spilsbury, and toxicologists William Willcox and Arthur Luff, showed not only that the bodily remains discovered in Crippen's cellar were those of his wife (an old operation scar on the abdomen proved its identity), but that at least half a grain of hyoscine was present and must have been taken by mouth. A fatal dose was from a quarter to half a grain; a medicinal dose was not more than a hundredth of a grain; the accused had purchased five grains. Crippen remained calm under cross-examination, but the circumstantial evidence against him was strong and the jury did not take long to convict him. A week later, le Neve was acquitted.[39] Crippen remained devoted to her until the end, and his wish to be buried with some of her letters and a photograph was honoured by prison officials, who seem to have regarded him with both respect and affection. He was executed at Pentonville Prison on 23 November 1910, his case testifying to the fact that even people who had choices could be so blinded by passion or fearful of damaging their reputations that they failed to appreciate them. But most people found that they had no choice at all.

Before the spate of poisonings that led to the Arsenic Act, the most infamous English husband poisoner was Ann Barber, a forty-five-year-old Yorkshire woman. She and her husband James had been married for sixteen years and had two children when, in March 1821, she gave him a fatal dose of arsenic in warm ale. The motive for this crime was obvious: she had been having an affair with a younger man, the family's lodger William Thompson, and wanted to marry him. In December 1820 she and Thompson had run off with some of the furniture and moved into a rented cottage, but when the landlord discovered that they were not married he forced them out. James Barber, in an act that spoke volumes about his kindness (or perhaps his sanity), took them both back. But this ménage scandalised the neighbours and, about a month before the murder, they drove Thompson out of town. If she wanted to continue her affair with him, Ann Barber had to become a widow. The evidence against her was clear; she had confessed to the local druggist. Her end was a foregone conclusion, and her execution at York was notable for the size of the crowd it drew. Her pitiful shrieks and lamentations touched the hearts of many. For his part, Thompson almost certainly knew what she planned, as he had spoken about poison to at least one witness, but his denials were accepted and he escaped indictment.[40]

In the cases where a husband-poisoner had a lover, the man was often one who lived in her house as a lodger. Although on the whole lodgers are difficult to track through time, census data and other historical sources have allowed some trends to be identified. The typical lodger was a young, single or childless married person; two thirds were male.[41] During the eighteenth century, lodgers may have comprised up to 5 per cent of the urban population. As industrialisation led to increasing migration, the figures rose. In 1851, 12 per cent of all households included a lodger, of which over a quarter had one lodger only and just under a quarter had two. These households were concentrated within certain social groups. Hardly any lodgers lived in the homes of the middle classes, while one fifth of the households of semi-skilled workers and one ninth of those of skilled workers included a lodger.[42]

Lodgers had of necessity to live at close quarters with their host family: most shared a room with one or more members of the family, though some, like Emanuel Barnett, had a room to themselves, and they usually ate their meals with the family. The cottages of the poorest families were so small that there was little or no separation of the sexes at night, and opportunities for illicit sexual unions abounded. Though a greater proportion of lodgers lived within families headed by widows rather than married men, there was still ample opportunity for relationships to develop between married women and single young men. Similar prospects existed within families that could afford a servant: most domestics were single women, a fact of which many married men took advantage. And, at a time when everyone knew their neighbours, many ended up on very intimate terms indeed.

Of the seventy-five women accused of poisoning their husbands between 1750 and 1914, thirty-six had an acknowledged lover. It is not known how most of these couples met, but at least nine of the lovers were lodgers; the others included friends and neighbours, the odd servant and an employer's son. Twenty of the fifty-nine men accused of poisoning their wives admitted having a lover. Although these figures do not include every single case of spouse-poisoning, they are representative, suggesting that half of all husband-poisoners had a lover, but only a third of wife-poisoners did. Discontented husbands clearly had more options when they found a new lover: they could leave home, or throw their wife out onto the mercy of the local authorities. But the fact that relatively few had a lover is more interesting, as it gives us an insight into the motives that drove men to become poisoners. Where bigamy was not a satisfactory option (always the case when an individual wished to stay in the same area), some needed freedom to remarry; others did not want to leave their children; and quite a few simply wanted to hurt a wife that they could not otherwise subdue. Where lovers were involved, it was always difficult to prove how much they had known of the poisoner's intentions, and it was therefore rare for both to be tried, let alone convicted. But there were exceptions.

In April 1850 a large crowd gathered at Cambridge to watch the double execution of Elias Lucas, aged twenty-four, and Mary Reeder, twenty, a pair of dim-witted lovers who had been condemned for the arsenic murder of Reeder's elder sister, Susan, to whom Lucas had been married for four years. He had begun an affair with his sister-in-law during the winter of 1849–50, while they were both working for the same employer, a farmer who gave him a pound of arsenic to dispose of following the winter wheat sowing. Instead, he had brought it home to use on garden slugs. It had been less than three years since Catherine Foster had been hanged in the neighbouring county of Suffolk, and it eventually occurred to Mary Reeder to wonder whether it was so wrong to poison for love, as Foster had. Deciding that it was not, she took her opportunity in February 1850, shortly after her sister had given birth to a baby that did not live long, and dosed Susan's evening meal with arsenic. This was easily accomplished, since she was living in the Lucases' cottage at Castle Camps, a small village six miles due south of Newmarket.

The unfortunate Susan died the next day, an apparent victim of the hazards of childbirth. The doctor called in had reached this conclusion before he was asked to look at the corpse by Henry Reeder, the sisters' father. Its appearance – clenched fingers and probably covered in vomit and faeces – necessitated a change of opinion: death was due either to cholera or poisoning. The doctor tended more toward the latter diagnosis, especially after he noticed that the family cat was perfectly well, even though Mary had claimed that both the cat and her sister had become ill from eating the same food. An autopsy revealed two ounces of arsenic in Susan's stomach. In the days immediately following, Lucas spoke frequently about his wife's death, making no secret of the fact that he wanted to marry Mary; he had said much the same thing to several witnesses before the murder. With means, motive and opportunity so transparent, it was inevitable that Lucas and Reeder would face the gallows together, and both confessed before they died.[43]

There are a few other cases where men became embroiled in affairs with their own sisters-in-law and a death ensued. In 1822 a young man named William Barnett was executed at Leicester for the murder of his wife, whom he had poisoned because he desired her sister.[44] Fifty-five years later, Samuel Shotliffe, a railway signalman, was prosecuted at Cambridge for the murder of his sister-in-law, a twenty-one-year-old woman who had one child by him and was four months pregnant with another. After two years, the shame of the affair had become too much and Shotliffe wanted a way out. Although he had bought ten grains of strychnine and signed the poison register with a false name, the jury was prepared to believe his claim that the dead woman had taken the poison herself.[45]

Others poisoned their lover rather than their spouse. This was an almost exclusively male crime, and often resulted not from a desire to kill but from a botched attempt to bring on a miscarriage (something married men also did). Of those men who clearly planned to murder their lovers, fear of exposure as an adulterer was a strong motive, sometimes allied with a wish to save the money it cost to keep a mistress (sometimes a whole second family). In 1845, respectable Quaker elder John Tawell found himself under pressure on both accounts, and so decided to murder his mistress, Sarah Hart. He poisoned her with prussic acid at Salt Hill, near Windsor, but was seen leaving her house just before she was found dying. He boarded a train for London, but his distinctive dress and a message sent by the newly invented electric telegraph made it possible for a London policeman to identify him as he alighted at Paddington. The case aroused a great deal of publicity as a result of Tawell's social status and the unusual poison used – a chemist came forward to say that he had sold prussic acid to him on the day of the murder. Convicted and sentenced to death, Tawell made a full confession before he died. Although he had once been transported for forgery, he had since become a prosperous and charitable businessman, married to a Quaker wife and highly respected within the Society of Friends. Sarah Hart was his son's widow, but she had been having an affair with John Tawell for about six years, and had borne him two children. He had become increasingly worried that his wife and friends would discover the arrangement, and the expense of keeping Hart was beginning to bite. Thus he determined upon murder, neither the first man nor the last to make this decision.[46] Women, on the other hand, rarely poisoned the man with whom they were having an affair; they had more to gain by remaining in the relationship or by leaving. That isn't to say, however, that troubled partnerships didn't sometimes lead women to perpetrate violence upon men, just that the violence seems rarely to have taken the form of poisoning.

While men like Elias Lucas and William Barnett poisoned their wives for the sake of a woman with whom they were having an affair, other men did so in the hope that widowerhood might attract the object of their affections. In a case that proves there really is no fool like an old fool, fifty-two-year-old gardener Thomas Duke attempted to murder his wife – a bed-ridden invalid – by placing a strychnine vermin killer in her breakfast. He had begun a relationship with a much younger woman (the *Times* described her as a girl, while Duke was 'elderly'), a domestic servant in Nottingham; letters proved the strength of his feelings for her. In April 1878 he decided to be rid of his wife, but cannot have been thinking too clearly: all vermin killers were coloured, and his wife noticed that her food was blue. For his passion-inspired folly, Duke was sentenced to twenty years in prison.[47]

Extra-marital affairs occasionally inspired one of the lovers to plan the death of the other's spouse. These poisonings were usually triggered by a specific event: the discovery that a child was expected, or the realisation (like Ann Barber) that the affair could not continue while a spouse remained alive. The ease with which this type of crime could be committed depended upon living arrangements: if the lover was a family member or neighbour, access to the intended victim was straightforward. It was thus quite simple for Frances Billing to murder Mary Taylor, with whose husband she had been having an affair for two years. All aged around fifty, James and Frances Billing lived next door to Peter and Mary Taylor, each couple in half of a semi-detached cottage in Burnham Westgate, Norfolk. This proximity first fostered the affair, and then the murder, which took place in March 1835 at the suggestion of Catherine Frarey, a woman who also had a lover and who had poisoned her own husband, Robert, two weeks earlier (slowly, so no doubts were aroused). James Billing, who had long known of the affair and had consequently taken to beating his wife, was marked out as the next victim, but survived the attempt. His son made it known that he had refused to eat the dinner his mother made for him, fearing for his life. Hearing this, the local grocer thought it his duty to call in a surgeon to test the suspect food, and the coroner was informed of their suspicions. Robert Frarey was exhumed, and arsenic was found in both his stomach and that of Mary Taylor. The link between Billing and Frarey was easily uncovered, and Billing explained what they had done. Practising a kind of folk magic, they had burned salt and arsenic as a means of keeping their lovers keen, before poisoning their victims. They were executed together in August; Peter Taylor, convicted as an accessory to his wife's murder, followed them to the scaffold eight months later.[48]

Blacksmith John Stratford, aged forty-two, had preceded these three to the Norwich gallows in August 1829, convicted of murdering a man he had never met. His trouble began when he discovered that his lover, Jane Briggs, was pregnant. A widower who already had four or five young children, Stratford – previously of exemplary character – decided to murder Thomas Briggs, Jane's husband, so that he and his mistress could marry. This required complex planning: Briggs, who was suffering from a facial cancer and could not have lived much longer, resided in the Norwich workhouse, where he was difficult to reach. In a plan used by others with varying degrees of success, Stratford decided to send his victim an anonymous gift of poisoned food; in this case, flour laced with arsenic. As such things are wont to do, the plan went awry: the flour was left in Briggs's room, and John Burgess, who was paid to look after him, used it to make dumplings; but it was Burgess – who ate the most – not Briggs, who perished. Stratford had himself brought the bag of flour to the workhouse, and had not bothered to disguise his handwriting on the parcel's label; but it still took a jury over four hours to decide that he was guilty.[49]

Even when accused poisoners were not known to have a lover, suspicion fell upon them because their marriages had been unhappy; rumour could transform a suicide or accidental death into murder. This is what happened when Judith Holdsworth, the wife of a Yorkshire farmer and blacksmith, died from arsenic poisoning in December 1848. James Holdsworth was sixty and said to be of 'crabbed temper and miserly habits'; his wife was half his age and of a 'vagrant disposition'. Such a conflict of personalities was bound to cause unhappiness, and, after five or six years of marriage, they did not live 'on terms of affection or kindness'. Just before her death, Judith made a sworn statement in which she accused her husband of poisoning her, though he claimed she had taken it herself. The suicide theory was supported by a scene that, the following year, was to be taken as proof of murder in the Lucas case: a cat Judith claimed had eaten the poisoned food was alive and well. Although the only evidence against him was his wife's testimony, word spread that Holdsworth's two previous wives had died as a result of foul play. At the inquest, the jurymen were unable to agree: five were for an open verdict, and seven for one of murder. When the coroner refused their request to have dinner brought to them, they hastily decided to err on the side of caution and brought in a verdict of murder; but their indecision was indicative of things to come and, at his trial at York in March 1849, Holdsworth was acquitted.[50]

A similar situation arose in July 1860. When labourer John Dodds died suddenly at Wrangle, Lincolnshire, his wife Elizabeth was charged with murder. Not only had she bought a quarter pound of arsenic, but witnesses at the inquest swore that the couple 'had not lived comfortably together, and that Mrs Dodds was jealous of her husband being too intimate with her mother'. Whatever the truth of this shocking state-ment, the point was a moot one when it was proved that the dead man had used the arsenic to relieve toothache.[51] She was acquitted, though rumour had it that Elizabeth Dodds had claimed her husband would die soon, when 'the apple trees had come into bloom again'. We are consequently left to wonder whether she was a very clever murderess, or just an unhappy woman who benefited from her husband's timely act of folly.

If Dodds had cause to worry about her mother's relationship with her husband, her loyalty must in the end have rested with blood: a woman who felt her relationship under threat from a third person normally attempted to remove that individual from the scene. Where threats and warnings failed, violence might succeed. It was this thought that led Eliza Gooch, a forty-five-year-old char woman, to attempt – via the postal system – to poison Jane Walls, who lived in a neighbouring village in Suffolk. Gooch had lived for many years, unmarried, with John Malster, but at the beginning of 1835 he met Walls, a widow with whom he began an affair. By April Gooch's jealousy had become so great that she decided to eliminate her rival. She baked six plum cakes, five small ones and a larger one that she spiked with arsenic, and posted them to Walls who, with her children, ate all the small cakes. The large one looked so odd, however, that she gave it to the village doctor to test; he found it contained enough arsenic to kill three or four people. When it was discovered that Gooch had sent the parcel, she was con-victed of attempted murder. A legal technicality led to the commutation of her death sentence to transportation for life.[52]

In Kent over thirty years later, a middle-aged widow, Susannah Seaman, found herself in an even more difficult situation. Where Gooch had faced the prospect of losing her man and her financial security, Seaman had actually lost both. Having lived with William Glover for six years, she suddenly found herself replaced in his affections, and his house, by her own niece, a much younger woman. Homeless and alone, Seaman returned sporadically to Glover's home, where it was alleged that she poisoned his food on each visit, just enough to make him ill. On the last occasion, she put white precipitate (a mercury compound) into the tea that his new mistress had prepared. This time it was clear what had happened, and, like Gooch, she was tried for attempted murder. Seaman received a much lighter sentence, however, ten years in prison (half that meted out to Thomas Duke nine years later), a reflection of the fact that her earlier attempts were unproven and, though she had meant to kill, she had not actually used enough poison to do so.[53]

Seaman's actions – prompted both by desire for revenge against Glover and longing for the resumption of her relationship with him – stemmed from extreme emotional distress. Other women who had suffered poor treatment at the hands of a man decided that they would be better off without him; for those already married, this meant disposing of an unwanted husband. In later years this type of crime was sometimes motivated solely by the prospect of financial gain, but before the rise of the insurance industry, a lack of money could lead to the same outcome.

Take, for example, the case of Cecilia Collier. At the time that she poisoned her husband with arsenic, Collier was fifty-two, a home weaver in Barton upon Irwell, Lancashire. John Collier had been ill for some time, suffering from an asthmatic complaint, and was incapable of working. Cecilia was therefore the family's only earner; added to this, she had several children to look after, the youngest just six years old. To make ends meet, the couple had a lodger, a female weaver. Crisis point came in December 1812, when John Collier sold part of the family's loom. According to Cecilia, he used the money to buy puff cakes and butter (other witnesses claimed it was meat), but the point was clear: 'I cannot spend my days any longer with him, and am determined to be without him.' She bought arsenic the next time she went to Manchester, and poisoned his evening mug of warm milk. The crime would have gone undetected had not the lodger, Elizabeth Oxenbould, decided to make a statement, seven weeks after the funeral. The body was exhumed and, despite an obvious lack of experience, a surgeon stated that death had been due to poison. Cecilia was arrested and, in an unguarded moment, confessed her guilt to the local constable. But, as a consequence of two important factors, she was acquitted: no arsenic was found in the body; and Oxenbould had threatened revenge following a quarrel with one of the elder Collier daughters.[54]

Sometimes the only explanation advanced for a poisoning was the fact that a couple had been on bad terms. This is entirely believable where the intention was not to kill but to injure, but it may or may not have been the whole story where murder was done. It may be that 'bad terms' was a euphemism, and that these were abused wives who had finally snapped – wife-beating appears to have been accepted as a fact of life in many working-class communities throughout the nineteenth century.[55] When forty-six-year-old Betty Rowland was arrested in Manchester for poisoning her third husband, William, a weaver, she exclaimed 'Yes, I am guilty; I do not care how soon I die'. A senior police officer later told how she 'described a series of misconducts of her husband from the first night of their marriage to the time of his death'. It is not clear when exactly they married, but she claimed to have left him three days after the wedding, only to return within a week; they had lived together unhappily, over a period of some years, ever since. A neighbour confirmed that the couple often quarrelled. Although Rowland claimed that the poisoning had been accidental, the fact that she had not sent for a doctor told against her. Tried in April 1836, she was convicted and sentenced to death. Although her statements suggest that William Rowland was an abusive husband, she did not use this in her defence. And if, as a witness asserted, she had probably poisoned her two previous husbands as well, we must assume that there was some other, more calculating, dynamic at work.[56]

There is remarkably little direct evidence that abuse was ever the principal motive for husband poisoning, though it is entirely likely that, where it did exist, the fact was downplayed in court. A woman who killed was seen as an abnormal creature of unusual lusts, not simply the terrified victim of a violent man. Where living on 'bad terms' was taken as the motive for a wife poisoning, we may infer from the example of vindictive poisoning that disgruntled husbands wished to discipline – occasionally with fatal results – a wife who would not submit to their control or whom they had grown to hate. At least half of all spousal poisonings sprang not from fear and hatred, however, but from lust and love, powerful emotions that inspired men and women who wished to get out of one marriage and into another, or into a relationship that otherwise seemed impossible. Where matters of the heart were concerned, poisoning crimes were generally prompted by the desperation that a lack of options could foster. Sometimes, even murder seemed a reasonable alternative to a lifetime spent in unhappy union with the wrong person.

4

Suffer the Little Children

I know Sarah Bright, she had a bastard child. I have told David
Gray of it. I heard him say one day when we were at work together
that 'he should not mind killing it any more than he should a
sparrow, if it was not for the law'.

Emanuel Bright, 1847 [1]

Although women were at a disadvantage in Victorian society, children
were even more vulnerable. A remarkable set of statistics published in
1894 showed that, of the homicides registered in the period 1863 to 1887,
the victims were more likely to be children up to the age of five than
people of all other age groups combined. Worse, the younger the child,
the greater the risk of violent death. The same figures clearly indicate
a horrific toll of infant life: babies under the age of one constituted 61
per cent of all homicide victims, at a time when they made up only 2.5
to 3 per cent of the total population of England and Wales. (In the late
1970s only 6.1 per cent of all English murder victims were children
under the age of one;[2] the statistics have not changed much since then.)
Infant death rates from all causes were very high, standing at about 15
per cent from the late 1830s to 1900, down from a shocking 24 per cent
in the 1790s but a little higher than the 1910 level of 10.5 per cent.[3] By
comparison, the average death rate fell much more quickly. In 1841 it
was around twenty-four per thousand population, while the infant death
rate was thirty. Sixty years later, the gap had increased: the average
death rate was now only sixteen per thousand, but the infant rate was
nearer twenty-eight.[4] Such a high infant mortality tended to limit parents' emotional investment in young children, while widespread poverty
meant that many adults saw their offspring as a burden.[5]

The high infant mortality was of course due mainly to disease and deficiency, not to violence. A large number of arguably intentional deaths caused by neglect and passive cruelty were attributed, in official statistics, to symptom-based causes such as debility and atrophy; they were not classed as murder or manslaughter. This was also true of an undetermined number (probably thousands per year) of deaths caused by opiate overdosing. The result was that relatively few infant deaths were proven homicides; of these, most were due to suffocation in the first few weeks of life.[6]

The child victims of poisoning crimes, a tiny minority among the vast numbers of young lives lost, nevertheless help to illuminate important aspects of eighteenth- and, especially, nineteenth-century society. Of all poison cases, 162 (30 per cent) concerned the murder, attempted murder, or manslaughter of one or more children aged up to sixteen. Twenty-six of these involved a child or children plus one or more adult victims. In three cases the victims included an adult plus an adult child of the poisoner, and four cases stand alone in involving solely the adult child of a poisonous parent. One hundred and eight cases involved a single child (including those aged over sixteen), and thirty-five more than one child (usually between two and four in number) but no adult. Among lone victims, more than half were babies up to the age of about one year old. Of the rest, forty were aged between one and sixteen, and three were older than sixteen. Thirty-nine of these child victims were illegitimate; three other cases involved two illegitimate child victims of the same parent. In all, about half of child poisoning victims were infants under the age of one, and half of these were illegitimate.

Young victims were usually closely related to their killers. For lone victims, mothers and stepmothers formed the largest group of poisoners, at eighty-two cases. By contrast, fathers and stepfathers were less often given to poisoning their children and stepchildren, accounting for just twenty-eight cases. More women than men poisoned both their spouse and one or more of their children. This is unsurprising, given that mothers, whether married or not, bore most of the responsibility for childcare, especially at the youngest and most vulnerable stages of a child's life. In two cases both parents were charged with planning and carrying out poisoning crimes, but against different children in their family. Other deaths were, in equal measure, caused by medical practitioners (including local 'healers' and druggists), all unintentional;

servants or nursemaids (a mixture of accident and intent); and other family members (often grandparents). A small number of cases were attributed to neighbours, family friends, total strangers or an unknown relationship between poisoner and child victim.

Although it was most common for one person acting alone to poison a child or children, twenty-one cases involved two or even three accomplices. Usually these were the child's (married or unmarried) parents, occasionally the mother and her own mother or a female friend. One rare type of pairing resulted in a double execution. In 1873 Edwin Bailey, a thirty-two-year-old Bristol shoemaker, used his mistress, Anne Barrey, thirty-one, as a means of gaining access to his illegitimate baby daughter, Sarah Jenkins, for whom a court had ordered him to pay five shillings a week until her sixteenth birthday. He denied being the father, and hatched an elaborate plot to kill the child. Posing as a mother who had recently lost her own baby, Barrey began to visit the Jenkins home, where Sarah lived with her mother and grandmother, claiming that the girl reminded her of her own dead infant. She carried on this charade for six months, eventually suggesting that the family, which was very poor, should approach a charitable organisation for help in buying an expensive powder recommended to ease the effects of teething. When three packets of this powder, purporting to be from the charity, arrived by post, Sarah was given one, with almost immediately fatal results. The symptoms were those of strychnine poisoning, and the remaining powders were found to contain rat poison. It took a month for the police to trace Barrey and, through her, to discover Bailey's role in the death; handwriting analysis showed that he had sent the poisoned parcel. Although recommended to mercy by the jury, both were executed on 12 January 1874.[7]

The clearly unnatural death suffered by little Sarah Jenkins made an inquest unavoidable, but infants were generally the least likely members of society to be the subjects of inquest. Despite this fact, by the 1870s coroners had begun to recognise a trend: nearly a third of inquest subjects aged under one year were illegitimate. Unofficial estimates placed the proportion of illegitimate births at no more than 8 per cent, so the inference was clear: illegitimate babies faced a markedly greater risk of violent or unexplained death than legitimate babies did. Older children fared better: in 1869, for instance, only about 10 per cent of inquest subjects aged between one and seven were illegitimate. This contrast existed throughout the nineteenth century.[8]

The story of infanticide is primarily an account of the fate of illegitimate babies, those members of society who were a burden on both the state and their parents.[9] It was an almost impossible situation for all concerned, and the root of the problem lay in the conditions set out by the Poor Law, which regulated what we today call welfare benefits. In 1531 the first in a series of laws designed to provide support for the poor was established. In 1601 the Poor Law Act made justices of the peace (local magistrates) responsible for the welfare of the poor citizens of each of the fifteen thousand parishes in England and Wales. These provisions were funded by local taxation, the only such system in Europe – not even Scotland had such a thorough, tax-based scheme in place. But national expenditure on poor relief rose inexorably: from an average annual cost per citizen of 1s. 6d. at the end of the seventeenth century, it had risen to 9s. 6d. by the earliest years of the nineteenth century. The nation was then spending over £4,000,000 per year, about 1.9 per cent of the national income. For the more than a million people who were claiming poor relief, its provisions were set at generous levels: lone parent families could expect to receive about 78 per cent of the average income of a two-parent family.[10]

The children of single mothers were well provided for within this system. Under laws of 1733 and 1809, if an unmarried girl became pregnant she had only to name the putative father – with no other evidence required – and the parish poor law authority would bring him before the magistrates. There, he would be forced to agree to pay a weekly sum towards the upkeep of the child – usually two to three shillings – or face a prison sentence.[11] To many men this solution seemed unreasonably harsh, and they fled to avoid their responsibilities. Others revealed a vicious streak: instead of paying, fleeing or going to prison, they chose to remove the source of their trouble, murdering either their illegitimate child or its mother. It was in such circumstances that the infant daughter of Martin Slack, an eighteen-year-old Sheffield brace bit maker, died in November 1828.

Three weeks before Elizabeth Hague gave birth to her daughter, also called Elizabeth, she went to the Sheffield magistrates to name Slack as the father, a process known as 'filiation', or 'fathering'. On the following day, Slack was sent to the Wakefield House of Correction – then as now a large prison for serious offenders – because he could not make bail. He spent five weeks there before his father got him out, standing as guarantor of any maintenance order that might be made. Hague had not yet had time to go back to the court to get such an order, a necessity since Slack refused to marry her, claiming that his parents forbade it. But the child was now five weeks old, and Hague would certainly have obtained a court order sooner rather than later.

Slack knew this, and early on the morning of 23 November he visited Hague at her parents' house. She left him with the baby while she went upstairs to dress, but almost immediately heard a cry. Rushing down, she found little Elizabeth in Slack's arms; something yellowish was coming from her mouth, something that burnt when it touched her own skin. He claimed that he'd given her nothing, but the baby died within an hour. An inquest was held the next day, when several of Hague's relatives confirmed her version of events. Her brother-in-law noted that Slack had told him that he did not like children and would not have anything to do with his daughter. A work colleague told how he had suggested that Slack would have to return to prison if he did not pay for the child, to which Slack had replied that he thought he would not go. Shortly after this, Slack had commented on the ease with which poisons could be purchased. A surgeon confirmed that the baby had died from the searing effects of nitric acid, and stains and burns were found on Slack's clothing and hands. He claimed that these were the result of the child's sudden illness, but no one believed him. At his trial in March 1829, he was convicted and sentenced to death.[12]

The main difference between the Slack and Bailey cases pertained not to the men themselves (their motives were identical), but to the conditions that governed the maintenance payments they had to make. During the intervening years, the law had been changed quite drastically, much to the detriment of unmarried mothers, before yet another revision restored some balance. By the early 1830s the expense of the Poor Law had begun to weigh so heavily upon the nation that a House of Lords Select Committee was formed to study it, and a Royal Commission was charged with its reform. This resulted in the Poor Law Amendment Act of 1834, which transferred the direction of the poor law from local parishes to 643 specially created unions, each with a workhouse.

Workhouses were first established in the late seventeenth century, as shelters for the poor where the able-bodied were made to work; in the late eighteenth century a revision to the law allowed the able-bodied poor to be provided with work outside the workhouse. The new Act abolished this 'outdoor relief' for all but the sick and aged poor; all other paupers were forced to enter a workhouse. In this, conditions were controlled so as to make any form of employment seem preferable. The workhouse symbolised loss of self-respect to the working classes, and the stigma was such that many people would have done almost anything to avoid it.

This radical overhaul of the benefits system included those of unmarried mothers, who had begun to gain a name as profligates who took advantage of the laws on bastardy. The commissioners accepted the dubious argument that if responsibility for bastard children was placed solely on mothers, the illegitimacy rate would fall and, with it, the costs to the system. Women, they thought – erroneously, as it happened – would never kill their children from poverty alone. The new Act of 1834 imposed means testing on single mothers (to which widows had always been subject), and made the process by which maintenance proceedings could be set in motion both complicated and expensive. The local unions had to bring the actions on behalf of single mothers, a process that could be done only four times each year at the quarter sessions. Moreover, claimants were now required to provide corroboration of a man's paternity, leaving much to the justices' discretion. By the end of the decade the unfairness and impracticality of this system had resulted in some loosening of its restrictions, but in 1844 the law was changed to place the burden of beginning proceedings on unmarried mothers, a difficult task for the poor and ignorant. Even those who managed to scrape together the necessary funds balked at facing a humiliating ordeal in open court, where, before a largely male audience, they had to admit to their shame. The illegitimacy rate remained as high as ever, over 50,000 births per year during the middle part of the century, and a rise in infanticide was publicly linked to the poor laws.[13]

The invidious combination of ignorance, restrictive laws, poverty and high infant mortality could often lead to inadequate emotional bonds between parents and young children. From caring little about the life of a child, to hoping for its death, to helping it into the next world – this, for some, was a relatively easy progression. Nothing makes this resound more clearly to the modern reader than the comment made in 1847 by David Gray, a farm labourer in the Essex village of Little Dunmow. When discussing his illegitimate baby son with a work mate, he claimed that he would have few qualms about killing the child were it not for his fear of being caught. After the baby died, it was this remark that led authorities to charge both Gray and his ex-lover, Sarah Bright, with murder. In fact, the death of their baby seems to have been an accident: his mother had given him some medicine to ease wind, but had mistakenly used a laudanum preparation that was intended for external use only. Gray, however, had clearly wanted the child dead: his new lover testified that he had asked her if she would go away with him if the boy died, and that he had been fretting about being named before magistrates as the father. But there was no evidence that he had had anything to do with the poisoning, and both he and Bright, who were in their early twenties, were acquitted.[14]

It was not until 1872 that some of the restrictions and difficulties placed in the paths of single mothers were removed. A new law increased the maximum weekly support payable by fathers from 2s. 6d. to 5s. (the sum Edwin Bailey was ordered to pay), and enabled the boards of guardians appointed by each poor law union to assist mothers in recovering maintenance costs.[15] The money was payable even if a woman married someone else, but the corroborative evidence rule as to the father's identity remained. Only about a sixth of all new single mothers applied for maintenance, but a significant motive for mothers to kill their infants had finally been eliminated. And, as living standards and employment opportunities rose, the illegitimacy rate fell, to about 4.5 per cent of all births in 1914. Yet the statistics on poisoning cases speak for themselves: three-quarters of all child victims were actually legitimate. There were clearly other factors at work.

Poverty, frequently the cause of the careless attitude to infant life of the kind displayed by David Gray, was no respecter of marital status. During the first half of the nineteenth century, in particular, extreme privation led some women to abandon their traditional role as carers for one as killers, all for the sake of a few pounds. The growth of the insurance industry gave parents added incentives to murder. In this respect, legitimate children were worth more than illegitimate ones: the higher death rates suffered by the latter made them a greater risk. Since policy values were often ranked according to age, there was more to be gained by killing an older child than a baby. Insurance money provided the motivation for most of the cases that involved the deaths of older and even adult children, and for almost all examples of serial poisoning. Only a little less common were the cases of children poisoned by parents suffering from mental instability, poverty or other seemingly unbearable circumstances. To avoid unnecessary repetition, depression-motivated poisonings will be treated later, as will the small number of children who fell victim to revenge poisonings. Finally, cases of outright cruelty to children, though sadly frequent in society at large, were rare in relation to poisonings – there are only two clear-cut examples among the stories on which this book is based.

One of these was a crime of abuse perpetrated by a child on a baby, an almost certain indication that the killer's own childhood had been severely damaged by some trauma. In February 1894 Emily Newber, a fifteen-year-old servant, was tried at the Old Bailey for the murder of the ten-month-old daughter of her employer, Frederick Humphreys, a solicitor. Newber joined his household on 2 December; on the 8th baby Maud was found to have bruises on her face, and on the 10th she was discovered suffering from the effects of acetic acid, from which she died two days later. At Newber's trial, a doctor who had examined her stated that she was not suffering from hysteria, but had a homicidal mania – a diagnosis that today seems utterly inadequate. That she suffered from some kind of personality disorder is clear: it was revealed after the trial that Newber had been discharged from two previous situations for alleged cruelty to children. In light of this fact, the court's leniency is noteworthy, especially in relation to the present-day frenzy that inevitably surrounds any case of child abuse: Newber was convicted of manslaughter and sentenced to one week in prison and five years in a reformatory.[16]

The Newber case is reminiscent of modern times, when child abuse is known to be complicated and multi-causal. As such, it is a far cry from the sort of child murder that had been common half a century earlier, when the young were rarely shielded from abuse. Before the late nineteenth century, child abuse and child murder usually stemmed not from personal deficiencies in the perpetrators but from the effects of environmental problems, especially poverty and overcrowding, which led to widespread alcoholism, desertion, prostitution and social disaffection.[17]

Several notorious cases of the 1840s brought home to the British public the desperate measures that extreme poverty could engender. The date was significant: not only had tests for arsenic, the most common poison, become reasonably accurate and widespread, but the decade was one that gained its own sobriquet – the Hungry Forties. The economic distress suffered during the 1830s and 1840s, when about 7 per cent of the English and Welsh population were classed as paupers, occurred at the end of a lengthy cycle of boom and bust. Following the battle of Waterloo (1815), about a quarter of a million ex-servicemen flooded onto a contracting labour market, as the economy adjusted from war to peace. The inevitable result was unemployment, the effects of which were exacerbated by a rapid increase in the birth rate: there were more mouths to feed, but fewer jobs available. Industrialisation offered greater employment opportunities in the factory towns of the midlands and the north, but in the predominantly agricultural counties of the south, the job market shrank as cottage industries, particularly weaving and spinning, declined and mechanisation replaced human labour. The rural poor found themselves with few options but to work for daily or weekly wages as farm labourers, an occupation that led to seasonal unemployment, and generally to chronic underemployment.[18] In all parts of the country, men with skilled jobs were constantly under threat from competition from unskilled (frequently female or juvenile) labour, and by technological innovation.[19] In industrial areas, this was offset by increased family wages in factory jobs, but urban living standards could be horrendous. Filth and overcrowding combined with higher city prices and rents made life for many northern urban dwellers as bleak as it was for their underemployed southern country brothers.

After an initial post-war fall in prices, depression due to low grain prices was severe and widespread in two periods, 1821–23 and 1833–36, when excellent weather conditions led to large harvests; surpluses meant low returns for farmers, who paid their workers proportionally less. Low wages and insufficient employment, together with limited mobility (farm workers rarely travelled more than a few miles from their homes) and the increase in the rural population explained the prevalence of poverty in the southern agricultural counties, especially Gloucestershire,

Wiltshire and Suffolk. In the northern industrial counties, alternative
sources of employment led to generally higher wages in all occupations,
but when an industrial depression hit the country, in 1839–42, the stage
was set for a national crisis of unprecedented proportion.[20]

British trade operated under a protectionist system, whereby all imports of produce and manufactured goods were subject to stiff tariffs.
This worked well when the balance of trade was in Britain's favour,
when the net value of exports exceeded that of imports. But at the end
of the 1830s a series of events combined to plunge the country into a
depression that was blamed on protectionism. Bad harvests led to high
food prices and increased food imports, which had to be paid for from
the national budget. Expensive food reduced the average citizen's purchasing power for British manufactured goods. At the same time,
Britain's leading exporter, the textiles industry, entered a period of
stagnation: raw materials were expensive to import, and markets shrank
as foreign buyers balked at paying for goods that could be got more
cheaply elsewhere.[21] The worst period of distress occurred in the late
1830s and early 1840s, with 1842 suffering possibly the worst unemployment in the entire century.[22] People in the north west, where the textiles
industry was strongest, were at risk of starvation; the whole town of
Stockport was said to be 'to let'.[23] The number of workhouse inmates
rose to nearly 200,000, increasing 150 per cent between 1838 and 1843.
The fact that workhouses were tenanted at all gives the most eloquent
testimony to the depths of poverty suffered at the time.[24]

In 1842 disillusioned voters elected a new Tory government, which
tackled the ongoing economic problem by reintroducing income tax and
using the proceeds to reduce import duties.[25] Four years later free trade
was instituted when the Corn Laws were repealed. This was followed by
another agricultural depression in the late 1840s, but by 1851 British
agriculture and industry were flourishing as never before, heralding a
period of booming prosperity that lasted twenty years. Britain was now
the wealthiest nation in the world; its middle classes swelled as 'white
collar' employment expanded. As for the working classes, there is no
doubt that their standard of living did rise overall, but poverty and
unemployment remained constant fears for as much as 30 per cent of the
population. For some, 'life was permanently hungry and brutish' and
for others, 'according to the ebb and flow of prosperity, intermittently

anxious and deprived'.[26] In August 1849, the depths to which that anxiety and deprivation led some parents became painfully obvious.

In 1848 the Geering family lived in a three-room cottage in the Sussex village of Guestling. Richard, a fifty-six-year-old farm labourer, and his wife Mary Anne, forty-nine, had seven children ranging in age between early teens and late twenties; three other children had left home. Formerly all very healthy, the male Geerings began to die one by one. In September Richard fell ill after eating a meal prepared for him by his wife, suffering vomiting and burning pains in his stomach. Dr Pocock, employed by the poor law union to provide free medical care to the local poor, was called in; deciding that Geering was suffering from a fever, he prescribed 'blue pill', a medicine composed largely of mercury. Richard died on 13 September, and Pocock wrote out a death certificate giving the cause of death as heart disease. The widow collected £5 3s. 4d. from the Guestling Benefit Society, to which her husband and sons belonged; each member paid 1s. toward the cost of burying one of their number.[27]

In November George Geering, twenty-one, took to his bed. His mother nursed him, and Pocock treated him with copious quantities of blue pills, but he died on 27 December. Mary Anne collected about £5 from the Benefit Society. Next, the eldest son, James, twenty-six, fell ill in February 1849. Under the ministrations of Pocock and his mother, he suffered improvements and relapses for five weeks, before dying on 6 March. Once again the Benefit Society paid. One month later Benjamin Geering, nineteen, was seized with stomach pains, burning in his throat, vomiting and purging following a meal eaten at home. Dr Pocock, by now a regular visitor, treated him for two weeks before finally beginning to sense that something unnatural was going on. He decided to call in another medical man, Dr Ticehurst, who asked the family to move out of their cottage. Eating only what the doctors gave him, Benjamin began to recover, leading Ticehurst to send a specimen of his vomit to Alfred Swaine Taylor, who found it to contain arsenic. The three other men were exhumed, and arsenic was found in Richard and James. Although his symptoms suggested arsenic poisoning, none was found in George, who may in fact have been killed by the mercurial pills given him by his doctor.[28]

Suspicion fell upon Mary Anne Geering, who was found to have purchased arsenic on no fewer than seven occasions, and who had had constant access to all the victims and their food. It was she who had collected the benefit money, and who had seemingly emptied her husband's small savings account of the £20 it had contained before his death. Indicted for three murders and one attempted murder, she was tried in August 1849 and convicted of the murder of her husband. Described in the *Times* as a woman of 'masculine and forbidding appearance', she was removed from court 'apparently very little affected by her awful position'.[29] It is difficult to imagine the extreme poverty and despair that could drive a woman to murder three healthy wage-earning men for what today seem small one-off payments; perhaps only the desperately poor can ever attempt to understand such an impulse.

Two days after Geering's execution on 21 August, Rebecca Smith was hanged in Wiltshire for the arsenic murder of her month-old son, Richard. Aged forty-three, 'undernourished and in poor health, living in great poverty and almost illiterate', she had borne eleven children during eighteen years of marriage, but only one, the first-born, was still alive. After her conviction, the local authorities deemed it advisable to exhume the bodies of some of the other nine children; the first two selected had died in 1841 and 1844. Analyst William Herapath found arsenic in both, the first time that the poison had been detected so many years after death. Smith then confessed to a prison chaplain that she had poisoned eight of her babies, fearing that they 'might come to want'. Her husband was an alcoholic who never earned much money and frittered away the £100 that her father left to her; although a seemingly pious woman, Smith felt that murder was a kinder fate than slow starvation. Although the jury had not wanted to see her hang, a confession to eight murders made a reprieve impossible and Smith became the last woman executed in England for the murder of her own baby.[30] Seen by her neighbours as inoffensive and industrious, she claimed that her only fear was that her surviving daughter would be neglected after her death.[31]

The Smith case shows that desperate poverty could lead to child murder solely because of grim economic realities: if there were one less mouth to feed, there would be more for the rest of the family. That such events were not uncommon during the Hungry Forties is shown by the fact that four years earlier, in Suffolk, Mary Sheming poisoned her infant grandson for an identical reason, and paid the same heavy price.[32] But most of the child poisoners of the 1840s did it for money, often very small sums. Bolton housewife Betty Eccles, thirty-eight, was hanged in May 1843 for the murder of her teenage stepson William, at whose death she had received 50s., the amount paid by mill owners for the burial of young mill workers. The bookkeeper, suspicious because less than three weeks earlier she had tried to claim a payment for the death of a daughter, alerted the coroner and an inquest and autopsy were held; arsenic was found in the body. Then two more of her dead children were exhumed and arsenic was again detected. In fact, she had poisoned all three of the daughters born to her first marriage. The two younger girls died shortly before Betty's marriage to widower Henry Eccles in 1841, possibly killed so that their mother would appear to be a better (that is cheaper) catch. By September 1842, when the eldest girl and William died, Betty believed that she would be entitled to burial money for each child and stepchild; but, in fact, only mill workers and their children were included in the company scheme. Henry Eccles's other two children were clearly at risk, and Betty confessed to her husband that she would have poisoned the entire family had she not been caught. There was an additional victim, too, a baby boy she had been paid to nurse and whose father she defrauded out of a miserable 7s.[33]

Although Betty Eccles was a determined and prolific serial killer, she was less organised than other poisoners active in the region at that time. There was certainly money to be made from the deaths of children, but would-be poisoners had first to invest in the cost of burial insurance. This largely unregulated business was popular among the working classes, who, it was felt in some circles, tended to spend too much money on funerals. In order to pay costs that might amount to £5 per burial (more than a great many labouring men earned in a month),[34] some form of insurance had to be obtained. For a small weekly payment, as little as a penny or half a penny, a lump sum sufficient to pay for a funeral would be paid upon the death of a subscriber or a member of his or her family. Burial societies, or clubs, were especially prevalent in the industrial north west,[35] where the economic crisis had hit hard, and it is thus unsurprising that the first insurance-related child murders to come before the courts occurred at Stockport, a town known for the scale of the deprivations its inhabitants suffered. Hatter Robert Standring was suspected of poisoning his teenaged daughter with arsenic for club money worth just under £8, but at his trial in April 1839 the evidence against him was too weak to secure a conviction.[36] A similar lack of strong evidence almost derailed the next such case that the Stockport magistrates sent for trial.

Two Irish immigrant brothers, Robert and George Sandys, lived in adjoining cellar rooms in Stockport, where both worked as mat makers. Each could earn a maximum of 15s. per week if their wives, Ann and Honor, helped in the work, but it cost nine to twelve shillings per week to feed each family, and the rent was extra. Robert and Ann, both aged twenty-five, had five children: twins Robert and Edward, aged six; Mary Ann, four; Jane, two; and Elizabeth, six months. Four of the children were insured in the Philanthropic Burial Society, which had seven thousand members. For a weekly payment of one penny, the relatives of full members who died (those who had been in the club for a minimum of seventeen weeks) were entitled to 2s. for liquor and a net amount of £3 8s. 6d. to pay the funeral costs. George, twenty-eight, and Honor, twenty-seven, had also insured their children. The cost of a child's burial was perhaps 20s., so for a minimum investment of seventeen pence, each couple could expect a return of about three weeks' wages, a cost benefit analysis that the Sandys clan began to contemplate as the economic crisis deepened. Robert's older children and their mother had been entered in the club in April 1837 and Jane shortly after birth, but the first death did not occur until 1840.

Predictably, given the fate of so many Victorian infants, Elizabeth was the first to die, on 9 September 1840. Ann brought her to a doctor – a ploy later commonly used by parents to deflect suspicion – who thought she was suffering from diarrhoea; but when she died no death certificate was obtained. Nor did the burial society ask for one: Elizabeth had been a full member for a week, and so the whole amount was paid with no questions asked. Later it was recalled that Robert had twice asked how long he had to keep paying for her before she became a full member. On 12 October both Mary Ann and Jane developed severe stomach pains after eating a meal at home; the family dog also became ill after it ate their vomit. Ann and Honor took them to see two doctors in succession: one diagnosed arsenic poisoning and both prescribed emetics that the women failed to give the children. By the next day, Mary Ann was dead and Ann and Honor were under arrest. That did not stop Robert and George from collecting the burial money on 14 October, the day on which an inquest was opened.[37]

The insurance money, the dog's illness, Ann's apparent lack of concern at the death of her child, and the fact that everything in the house was washed within an hour of the girl's death, led authorities to widen the investigation, and the coroner ordered a series of exhumations. Elizabeth, a girl named Mary O'Neal, and George and Honor's daughter Catherine were all disinterred and their internal organs subjected to chemical analysis. O'Neal was a red herring: in order to draw attention away from herself, Ann told the police that Bridget Riley, Mary Ann's godmother, had poisoned both girls. But the analyst found arsenic only in the Sandys children, including Catherine, who had been insured in May 1838 and died in July 1840, aged just over two years.

In August 1841 both couples went on trial for the murder of Mary Ann, but all were acquitted. Robert and Ann were then tried for Elizabeth's murder. Robert was convicted but Ann was acquitted, since the jury mistakenly believed that a wife was acting under her husband's direction and thus could not be guilty. As there was less evidence relating to the death of Catherine, no one was tried for her murder. Robert was sentenced to death but reprieved to transportation to Australia for life.[38]

Similar poisoning cases, sometimes on an equally extensive scale, continued for almost fifty years, as mostly ineffective laws were passed in an attempt to break the connection between child life insurance and murder. Their weakness lay in the fact that they did not apply to burial clubs that failed to register themselves under the national system instituted in 1828, and it was not until the mid 1870s that such clubs were brought within the legal purview. There were some limits set: a child up to the age of five could be insured for a maximum of £5, rising to £10 for a child between five and ten; above that age there was no limit. Claimants had to obtain a certificate from the local registrar of births and deaths before any money was paid; the certificate was to be issued only after a doctor's, coroner's or other satisfactory evidence was produced.[39]

That certificates did not always prevent murder was shown by the 1878 case of Ellen Heesom, a thirty-two-year-old housekeeper at Lower Walton, Cheshire, who poisoned her mother and two daughters aged one and nine for the insurance money. A doctor certified the death of both girls as natural, and it was only because their grandmother died so soon after that any suspicion was aroused.[40] Although deaths from neglect, or murders made to look like accidents, may have continued for decades longer, the last of the known insurance-related child poisonings occurred during the 1880s. In Manchester, Mary Ann Britland, thirty-nine, was hanged in August 1886 for the strychnine murder of her lover's wife, Mary Dixon, a crime she committed only after she had first poisoned her husband and teenage daughter. Although her main motive was passion, money was important too: Elizabeth Britland was insured for about £10, while Thomas Britland and Mrs Dixon were worth nearer £20. That Thomas Dixon escaped indictment was a tribute to Britland's feelings for him: if she had told all she knew of his involvement, he would almost certainly have been convicted as an accessory.[41] At Liverpool, less than a year later, thirty-one-year-old workhouse nurse Elizabeth Berry was hanged for the murder of her daughter, who, in retrospect, seems to have been the fourth and last family member to fall prey to a determined poisoner. Berry's husband, mother and son had all died suddenly and were all insured (the adults for £100 each but the children for only £10); the fact that the deaths took place several years apart served to conceal the crimes. Berry was only exposed because of her own carelessness: she poisoned eleven-year-old Edith Annie with a mixture of creosote (a chemical similar to carbolic acid) and sulphuric acid, leaving telltale burns and stains on her victim's face. Given that the child died in the workhouse infirmary and that her mother used the common ploy of asking a doctor to attend the patient (intending later to ask him for a death certificate), it would have been extraordinary had he failed to notice that something unusual had occurred.[42]

Lest we assume that child insurance poisonings were solely the province of mothers, it is worth noting that the last known cases of the 1880s were the work of fathers. In July 1888 William Dawson Holgate was tried for poisoning his eleven-year-old daughter Lily with carbolic acid. The little girl, who suffered from general debility, had been insured for £20 for nearly three years. Although her mother paid the premiums, her father was well aware of the policy. He was almost certainly sparked into action by the arrival of bailiffs, who came to their house in Bradford a few days before Lily's death on 26 March and then returned to remove some furniture a few days after. As a coal dealer who earned £1 per week, Holgate, who was forty-one, evidently saw his weakly daughter as a means of paying off his debts; his wife and eldest son strongly believed in his guilt. But he was acquitted when it became clear that Lily might have taken the poison by mistake – even though Mrs Holgate claimed that there was none in the house at the time.[43]

A year later a collier, George Horton, thirty-seven, was tried at Derby for the strychnine murder of his daughter Kate, aged eight. She too was insured, and by the same company, the Refuge Assurance, which for a weekly premium of one penny would pay £7 if she died after one year. In this case the motive seems to have been less the money than Horton's general desire to be rid of all his children. A father of seven, his wife had died in October 1888 and he moved his brood into a house shared with another large family. His eldest daughter left in March 1889 because he mistreated her and had 'threatened to poison me out of the road'.[44] A colleague related how Horton had later told him that 'I've got shut of two of my children and I'll soon be shut of the lot'.[45] In May 1889 he took steps to do just that, as Kate was able to tell in the twenty minutes before she died: 'My dad gave me some blue stuff out of a bottle in a cup'. The 'blue stuff' was, of course, a vermin killer, although analyst Alfred Henry Allen was unable to determine exactly which brand. Despite a neighbour's testimony that all the children seemed happy and well cared for, and the surprise and shock that Horton evinced when told of Kate's death, he was quickly arrested and charged with murder. Apart from Kate's dying statement, evidence against him included the fact that he had paid the arrears due on her insurance policy on 18 May, two days before her sudden demise. He was convicted and sentenced to death, though later reprieved to life imprisonment.

We saw earlier how men who poisoned their own babies often did so to avoid the financial responsibilities of fatherhood. The Horton and Holgate cases are typical of a second important motive that drove men to poison their children: a sudden social, emotional or financial disruption. This could arise after the death of a wife, when fathers found themselves unable to cope with raising their children. Many men would have had a family network to turn to for help; others could simply have abandoned their children to the workhouse. The element of profit was sometimes the deciding factor in favour of murder, but the sad truth is that there have always been individuals who have chosen to kill in order to rid themselves of family commitments. To those who thought about it in advance, poison seemed to offer a means of doing so quietly.

By the 1890s, however, the number of known child poisoning cases related to insurance money had declined almost to zero, and the issue of murder motivated by child life insurance had begun to lose its urgency. This was largely due to a sustained campaign run by the National Society for the Prevention of Cruelty to Children, founded in 1888, which brought the issue of child cruelty and child insurance to the political and public imagination.[46] In 1889 the society secured the passage of the Prevention of Cruelty to Children Act, which, for the first time in England, placed legal limitations on parental power over children. By the end of the century, working-class people had begun to accept NSPCC inspectors as a means of rooting out child abuse and identifying children at risk.[47] Its rapidly expanding operations, together with stricter laws governing insurance and death certification, acted to defer the sort of child poisonings that had previously been all too common. By the time the insurance poisoners of the 1870s and 1880s embarked upon their crimes, the social situation had changed enough to make them the last of their kind. In the end, it was environmental and social improvements that removed the factors that tended to lead to child poisonings. Although poverty was by no means a thing of the past, there were now more social institutions in place to alleviate its effects and, equally importantly, to act as a deterrent to crime.

Yet suspicion died hard. In November 1904 (once again in the north west of England), Ellen Burndred, forty-nine, was acquitted of the arsenic murder of her fourteen-year-old foster daughter, Sarah Ann Jones, whom she had insured with two companies for about £30. As the girl's funeral cost just over £8, the profit margin was significant enough for the police to take notice and they began to investigate her background. They discovered that during the 1890s Burndred had had five children, all of whom had died insured. The doctor who had attended some of them, Patrick O'Keefe, now claimed that she must have poisoned them all with arsenic, and that she had seemed happy at their deaths. The last child to die was exhumed, but nothing was found. At her trial in Liverpool, Burndred's defence – that Sarah's death was a tragic accident and that she had in any case no need of the insurance money – convinced the jury of her innocence. If Ellen Burndred was a serial poisoner, it was impossible to prove.[48]

In the same year an unusual crime occurred in London, in essence a throw-back to earlier cases in which hungry extra mouths were removed for the benefit of older family members. Once again the motive was poverty, though certainly not on the scale suffered by the likes of Rebecca Smith. Chemist's assistant Arthur Devereux, thirty-four, lived in West Kilburn with his wife, Beatrice, and their three children: Stanley, six, and twins Lawrence and Evelyn, two. Devereux's mother-in-law later testified that 'he seemed to be very fond of Stanley, but he never took any notice of the twins',[49] and, indeed, it was this strong attachment to his eldest son that was to lead to murder. Earning a weekly salary of £2, Devereux had begun to resent the cost of keeping his younger children, estimating that he spent half a sovereign each week for milk alone. They had rickets and could not walk or feed themselves, and Beatrice devoted all her time to them; she disliked the fact that her husband did not show them the same amount of affection as he did Stanley. She confided to her mother that Devereux had told her that 'If I had not got all this bastard lot to keep I could get on better by myself'.[50]

This was clearly neither a happy nor a prosperous family and, by Christmas 1904, Devereux had decided to murder his wife and baby sons so as to be able to provide better for Stanley. He rented a flat in Harlesden and moved in with his family on 31 December; on 2 January he was given notice to quit his job, since sales at the chemist's shop were poor. The last time that Beatrice was seen alive was 28 January 1905, and at the beginning of February Devereux began to sell off household items and some women's clothing. On 7 February he and Stanley moved out of their flat, and a large tin trunk was sent to be stored at a warehouse in Kensal Rise.

Ellen Gregory, Beatrice's mother, began to worry when she was unable to find her daughter at the flat in Harlesden; questioning the neighbours, she learned of the trunk that had been removed. By the middle of March she had become so fearful that she contacted the police; but no action was taken until 13 April, when the trunk was traced and opened. Devereux had told the warehousemen that it contained books and chemicals, but beneath a shallow partition three decomposing bodies were found. The Home Office Analyst, Sir Thomas Stevenson, found that death was due to morphine poisoning. Devereux, who had been traced to Coventry, claimed that his wife had first murdered the children and then committed suicide. At his trial at the Old Bailey in July 1905 he unsuccessfully feigned insanity, and on 15 August he was executed in Pentonville Prison.[51]

Of the relatively few poisoners who targeted both their spouse and offspring, Devereux was unique in being motivated by an excessive love for one of his children; most cases involved insurance, or resulted from some form of quite obvious mental instability. There were, however, early poisoning cases in which the motive was a desire to be rid of all family commitments – not for the sake of profit, but to save money and gain personal freedom. In 1817 Lancashire weaver Henry Scholfield poisoned his wife and two children, whom he had often wished dead, following an argument over money. He was apparently inspired by an evil mixture of anger and jealousy sparked by the return of his wife's first husband, who had been assumed dead in the Peninsular War, and by the poverty that struck the country at the war's end.[52] It was a selfish desire to have more for herself that led middle-aged Susannah Holroyd to poison her husband and son in Ashton-under-Lyne, Lancashire, in 1816. She was heard to observe that it was no trouble to bury them on the same day, as they had done her no good these past two years.[53] These hard-hearted creatures, both of whom were hanged, believed they would be better off unencumbered by family responsibilities.

We have seen how easy it was for some parents to kill their own children, led by poverty, ignorance and indifference to end the lives of individuals who were little valued by society. Throughout history, many children were more neglected or ignored than loved or hated by their parents. It was not until the late nineteenth century, when contraception, humanitarian legislation, slowly improving economic conditions, welfare services and schools began to improve the lives of the children of the poor that they were able to secure their position within the modern, child-orientated family that we today take for granted.[54] The subsequent decrease in child poisoning crimes and its previous high incidence are thus readily understood to be part of the history of how parents treated children, itself the by-product of changing social factors that we might define, for want of a better word, as progress.

5

The Root of All Evil

Certainly he was ignorant that his life was valued at so little, his death at so much ...

Lancet, 1884 [1]

'To hell with the clubs – you won't get any money for me.' [2] With these belligerent words, coal deliverer Thomas Higgins made it clear to insurance agent Richard Jones that he wanted nothing to do with the product he was selling. Not for nothing had Higgins gained the nickname 'Crack of the Whip', but he had underestimated his wife and sister-in-law, who had managed – without his knowledge – to insure him in five different companies for a total of £108 10s. od. He died six months later, on 2 October 1883, the ninth and final victim of a pair of poisoners who had exploited the growth of an industry that had previously been closed to all but the wealthy: life insurance. A local newspaper claimed that Catherine Flanagan and her sister Margaret Higgins had 'poisoned for pence ... with no greater desire or hope of profit and advantage',[3] but this wasn't true. They had in fact been able to make a considerable profit, one that increased with each victim, as they became more familiar with the way the insurance companies operated. These middle-aged Scotswomen, both of whom had married Irishmen, lived in Liverpool in the early 1880s, in one of the city's notorious cellar dwellings. It was the nation's least healthy city, and had a well-deserved reputation as a haven for crime, alcoholism and social disaffection.[4] It is not difficult to see how two of its denizens, both poor, unskilled and illiterate women, came to see murder for insurance as a sound financial investment, when with one death they could earn more money than they could ever hope to do legitimately.[5] In the end, it was only by chance that Thomas Higgins was proved right: no one got any money for him, but it was not for a lack of trying.

Flanagan and Higgins were not the first of their kind: they were preceded by several cases of serial murder committed for a profit that usually took the form of 'burial money' – a branch of the insurance industry. Their execution in March 1884 did, however, mark the beginning of the end for serial poisoners of their class and type. The poor, uneducated and largely female serial poisoners of the period between 1840 and 1890 disappeared, to be replaced by perpetrators as middle class as the institution of insurance was originally intended to be. Nowadays, the stereotypical insurance murderer is a middle-class, educated male who, in a carefully planned operation, kills for a large sum of money.[6] The serial killers of today are a different breed: while they may occasionally stand to gain financially from their crimes, they are motivated primarily by the pleasure they obtain from the act of choosing, dominating and killing their victims. Serial poisoning, which is no longer common, is now, for reasons to do with controls on drugs, primarily the province of health care professionals. Recent English examples include the infamous and prolific Cheshire GP, Harold Shipman, convicted of fifteen morphine murders in 2000, and the nurse Beverly Allitt, convicted in 1993 of four child murders and a variety of serious assaults in which drugs – insulin and potassium – featured. Shipman is known to have profited from some of his crimes, continuing an infrequent but chilling pattern established in the first half of the twentieth century, when a handful of English cases revolved around medical personnel accused of poisoning for advantage.[7]

Insurance murders are themselves a subset of a broader motive to murder: the expectation that a killing will remove a barrier to financial gain, usually in the form of an inheritance. It was in this context that arsenic gained the sobriquet, 'inheritance powder', for its ability to hasten – seemingly naturally – a wealthy man into his grave. Although greed played a large part in most such poisoning crimes, the Victorian satirist Samuel Butler rightly noted that 'It has been said that the love of money is the root of all evil. The want of money is so quite as truly.'[8]

Of our 540 poisoning cases, 121 were clearly carried out for financial motives, of which there were four distinct types. The most common was the one that prompted Flanagan and Higgins in their crimes, insurance money, which accounted for forty-one cases, about a third of the whole. Next in frequency were poisonings committed in order to inherit the victim's money or property, thirty-seven cases (30 per cent). One fifth (twenty-four cases) of the crimes perpetrated for financial motives revolved around cases of fraud, most of which were related to attempts by the poisoner to hide a previous theft from the victim. One of the more interesting aspects of this motive concerned the sporting world: three cases involved racehorses that were poisoned ('nobbled') to affect the outcome of their races. Finally, nineteen cases (16 per cent) appear to have been carried out so that the poisoner could save money, as, for example, the cases of Cecilia Collier, Martin Slack, Susannah Holroyd and Arthur Devereux, all of which have been described in earlier chapters. In some of these, underlying feelings of anger or disgust seem to have sparked the crimes, and it is not always possible to determine which motive was uppermost in the poisoner's mind. Several were certainly instances of killing two birds with one stone.

Equally, there are cases in which the motive is simply not apparent. If a wife and her male servant conspired to poison her husband, how much was that due to a desire for sexual freedom and how much to a desire to inherit the husband's property? When a father poisoned two of his young sons, was it because he, like Robert Sandys, expected to make a small profit on the burial money, or was it for some other reason, one that is not made obvious in the documents which survive? [9]

Of the 121 cases, two involved perpetrators who acted together but were tried separately, under slightly different indictments, [10] and two involved the same people tried twice on different indictments. [11] This distinction has been maintained because it offers a useful way to examine jury behaviour and sentencing policy; it makes no significant difference to the proportion of poisonings carried out for the four financial motives identified above. It is, however, a detail that has to be taken into account in a gender analysis of the people who were thus accused. Hence, the total is taken to be 117 cases, of which forty-eight were carried out by men and fifty-two by women who acted alone. [12] It would thus be unwise to conclude that women were any more likely to kill for money than men. They were, perhaps, more likely to kill for money if doing so might lead to the consolidation of a sexual relationship. Only three cases

were attributed to two men operating together, and five to two women
– most notoriously, Flanagan and Higgins. Finally, nine of the cases led
to the trial of a man and a woman. Six of these couples were married,
another were lovers, one pair had a business arrangement and one pair
may have shared a little of both business and pleasure.

Of the 117 lone or collaborative poisoners, twenty-eight were suspected
of murdering, or attempting to murder, more than one victim, but that
does not mean that these were twenty-eight financially motivated serial
murderers. In fact, seven of these were cases of what might more
appropriately be termed multiple murder, meaning that in a single
incident more than one person became a victim – sometimes unintentionally. This could easily occur if poison was placed – accidentally or
not – in a source of food or drink that several people had access to.
The accused was suspected of murder if he or she stood to gain financially from the death of one of the victims, as happened to Jonathan
Barcroft, a washer in a Cheshire print works. His ten-month-old
daughter Sarah Ann and a two-year-old neighbour, Ellen Mills, died in
April 1851 after sharing a bowl of porridge that had somehow become
impregnated with arsenic. Sarah Ann was a member of a burial society,
her life valued at £2 10s., and her father had easy access to arsenic at
his place of work; the Mills child had simply been in the wrong
place at the wrong time. But was this an open and shut case? The jury
thought not, and acquitted Barcroft; the evidence against him was purely
circumstantial, and the deaths could easily have been accidental.[13]

Twenty-one of the twenty-eight cases that involved more than one
victim were indeed serial murders, in which one victim at a time was
killed, usually over a period of years but sometimes within a matter of
months. There was one exception to this general pattern. In May 1827
Jane Scott, aged twenty-one, poisoned her parents by mixing arsenic
into their porridge, and they died within hours of each other. Residents
of Preston, Lancashire, John Scott and his wife owned a cheese shop,
and Jane confessed that she had killed them in order to inherit their
property. A broadside of the period suggested that she had been robbing
her parents before she killed them; she explained that she wished to
make herself a more attractive marriage prospect to George Richardson,
a man who appears to have had little serious interest in her. Scott was
tried first for the murder of her father, but was acquitted when a key

witness failed to appear. Undaunted, the judge committed her for trial at the following assizes, on the charge of murdering her mother. She was convicted and executed in March 1828.[14]

What made Scott different from other poisoners who hoped to reap financial rewards was the fact that she was mentally unbalanced – several neighbours testified that she had suffered from violent fits for two or three years. Furthermore, she confessed to having poisoned her own illegitimate four-year-old son – the motive is unclear but probably related to her desire for Richardson – and also her young niece, following an argument with her sister in 1826. It is for these reasons that it is difficult to classify Scott, who did not kill for any one purpose: she poisoned on a whim (her niece), suggestive of insanity, and to a plan (her parents and, possibly, son). In the absence of detailed medical information about her physical and mental health it is impossible to reach a firm conclusion, but it seems possible that she would not have become a serial poisoner had she not suffered from some form of mental illness.

Later cases of multiple and serial poisoning were occasionally inspired by complex motives of which money formed only one part. These poisoners did not act on a whim, but planned their actions carefully. Mary Ann Britland, who wanted another woman's husband but who also stood to gain financially from the three deaths in which she was involved, is an obvious example. A year after Britland's execution in August 1886, the Surrey gardener Henry Bowles murdered his wife and stepson – both of whom were insured – with strychnine. He needed the money to buy an older son out of the army, but he also wanted to be free to pursue a relationship with another woman.[15] Mary Anne and Faith Sealey, sisters aged twenty-two and eighteen, were accused of poisoning their great aunt and their father at their home in the Somerset hamlet of Pickney in 1843. Their father was insured in a burial club for £8, but a possibly stronger motive was the girls' desire to be free of his strict moral dominance over their lives. A younger sister testified that she heard Faith say to Mary that they would be better off without him, as she (Faith) could stay at home dressmaking (rather than go into service), while Mary, following her father's death, took to entertaining a man named James Bond in her bed. Although they clearly had motive and opportunity, both sisters – after three separate trials – were acquitted of all charges.[16] William Palmer, the first Englishman convicted of a strychnine murder (1856), killed a gambling companion to steal his winnings, but had earlier poisoned relatives so as to inherit, or collect insurance money, creditors to whom he owed money and children that might have cost him money. A man addicted to women, drink and gambling, his addictions led him to a life of crime.

Palmer's trial for the murder of John Parsons Cook marked a watershed in legal history: a new law had to be created to allow him to be tried in London, rather than Staffordshire, because of local prejudice against him, and he was convicted even though no poison was detected in his victim's body. Shortly before his execution he hinted that he might have been guilty of poisoning Cook with brucine, rather than strychnine, and also of the murders of his wife and brother, but he refused to confess, claiming that he went to the scaffold a murdered man. In truth, Palmer had begun his career as a poisoner years before he met Cook, and his execution in June 1856 was long overdue. From his earliest days as a medical student, he had used his access to poison as a means of lining his own pockets.

The man who became known as the Rugeley Poisoner was born in that town in August 1824, the son of a wealthy man who died when William Palmer was thirteen. William turned to crime as a teenager: at seventeen he was sacked from his first job after being caught stealing. He then spent five years as a doctor's apprentice, during which time he fathered fourteen illegitimate children and practised as an abortionist. He worked briefly at the Stafford Infirmary, where he poisoned a man with strychnine to see how it worked, before completing his medical education in London. In autumn 1846 he returned to Rugeley and opened a medical practice. He was already in debt: at the age of twenty-one he had inherited £9000, but his passion for gambling meant that he was always short of money.

In October 1847 Palmer married Anne Thornton, the illegitimate daughter of an army officer who had committed suicide. She was conscious of her lowly social status, being a bastard, and found it surprising that any man should want her. But she was a wealthy woman by the standards of the day, and their marriage benefited Palmer financially. They had five children, of whom only the first survived, the other four dying in convulsions as infants. There is no proof that their father poisoned them, but he was heard to say that large families were ruinously expensive, and members of his household suspected he had had a hand in their deaths. He was also responsible for the death of his mother-in-law, in January 1849, whom he poisoned in the expectation that her daughter would inherit another large sum of money. He was disappointed to find how little cash there was, but got away with murder: another local medical man, elderly Dr Bamford, attributed the death to apoplexy.

In May 1850 Palmer poisoned one of his creditors, Leonard Bladon, who had won considerable sums at the Chester races. During a brief visit to Rugeley, Bladon died in Palmer's house and his winnings disappeared. Relatives urged his widow to inform the coroner, but she refused because she did not want Anne Palmer to suffer any unpleasantness. Bamford helped tend the dying man, again unaware that anything unusual was happening. The next victim was another creditor, to whom Palmer owed £800. Then one of his uncles died within three days of holding a drinking contest with the dangerous doctor. The uncle's widow, invited to stay with the Palmers, refused to take some pills that William offered her; she threw them out the window, and several chickens were found dead the next day.

If, as it has long been supposed, Palmer poisoned all of these people, it is not known what poison he used; strychnine seems most likely. He broke with habit for his next two murders, however. Early in 1854 he lost £10,000 when he backed the wrong horse at a major race meeting. He then insured his wife's life for £13,000; when she died in September that year, Dr Bamford certified her death as due to English cholera. A later analysis showed that she died of antimony poisoning, probably from doses of tartar emetic administered over a period of days. In 1855 he invited his brother Walter to stay with him, hoping that he would die naturally, of alcoholism. The motive was, of course, money: Palmer had insured him for £82,000. But Walter was an alcoholic with a strong constitution, so in August Palmer poisoned him with prussic acid. It was never possible to determine the cause of death, as the corpse was too putrefied when it was exhumed.

The bodies of Anne and Walter Palmer were exhumed in December 1855 as a result of William Palmer's final murder. When the insurance companies refused to pay after Walter's death, Palmer turned his attentions to John Cook, another heavy gambler. Cook had one asset, a racehorse named Polestar whom he backed with the last of his cash. On 13 November the horse won a major race and Cook's winnings amounted to thousands of pounds. Over the next few days, Cook experienced pain and odd symptoms when he drank anything in Palmer's presence. He took pills that Palmer gave him, and on 19 November he died in agonising convulsions. Unlike on previous occasions, his family were not prepared to accept Palmer's explanations: Cook's stepfather demanded that an inquest be held. Despite various blunders on the part of the medical men involved, and analyst Alfred Swaine Taylor's inability to find strychnine in Cook's body, Palmer was committed for trial on a charge of murder and his wife and brother were exhumed. Convicted largely on circumstantial evidence at his trial in May 1856, the short, chubby Palmer, who scarcely looked like a hardened criminal, was hanged before a large crowd at Rugeley a month later.[17]

In all, there were only seventeen cases of serial poisoning that were clearly carried out solely for money. The first of these was the Sandys case in 1840, the last that of Amelia Winters and Elizabeth Frost in 1889. A question mark hangs over the 1911 case of Edith Bingham: although she clearly stood to inherit something after the deaths of her father, brother and sister, it was never proved that she was motivated by money, or indeed that she was guilty of their murders. Regardless, there is no doubt that the heyday of financially motivated serial poisoning was between 1840 and 1890. The earlier date is significant, for it was in the years immediately before 1840 that burial clubs began to expand at an astonishing rate. Before then, serial poisoning was rare: there were a handful of known seventeenth-century cases committed for the sake of inherited money or by persons of dubious sanity;[18] logic dictates that there must have been others, throughout the seventeenth and eighteenth centuries, that remained undiscovered. But most poisoners tended to kill one individual for a one-time reward, or, like Henry Scholfield, two or three people at one time so as to remove the financial burden they represented. It was only under the unwitting influence of the fledgling life insurance industry that serial murder became a regular feature of English society.

A life insurance policy is a contract requiring the insuring office – now a company but in earlier centuries often groups of individual underwriters

– to pay a sum of money to the insurer at the expiration of an agreed period or at the death of the insured person.[19] The earliest life insurance policy recorded in England was registered at the Chamber of Assurance in London. Dated 18 June 1583, it insured the life of William Gibbons for £382 6s. 8d. for twelve months, for which he paid a premium of 8 per cent of the total insured. This short-term policy was probably effected to provide security for a fixed-term loan, so that if Gibbons died during that period the debt would be repaid.[20] The idea originated in the practice of marine insurance, which had been customary among sea traders since late medieval times. Italian merchants in the Mediterranean instituted the first life insurance policies around 1400, as an incidental condition when marine policies (which normally covered ships and their cargoes) happened to include passengers, crews or slaves on overseas voyages.[21] Contracts ran for the duration of a sea voyage, and indemnified the policyholder against the death, capture or ransom of the insured.[22]

Until the last decade of the seventeenth century, life insurance in England was limited to short-term policies on business partners and merchants' representatives, but the rise of a large professional class in London and the county towns led to a boom in life insurance promotions during the following quarter century. Lawyers, doctors and clergymen formed an increasingly visible and affluent segment of society but, unlike the aristocracy, their income ceased at death. Their families were thus at risk of being left with an elevated social standing but no money. Life insurance offered a way to avoid this fate.[23] Most schemes were distributive: members would pay an entrance fee and a regular subscription, thereby entitling their nominees to receive a lump sum at their death.

After a very slow start, the market for life insurance grew rapidly after 1800, as actuarial techniques improved and a law of 1774 removed its unacceptably close association with gambling. It remained, however, a strictly middle-class and often London-based habit until the middle of the nineteenth century. In 1845 the chairman of one company estimated that fewer than 100,000 people, in a national population of over twenty million, were insured with life offices; policies were issued mainly to members of the landed, commercial and professional sections of society.[24] Since the minimum policy value was then around £100, it is little wonder that working-class and lower middle-class people had to seek alternatives.[25]

Early forms of life insurance functioned in the same way as friendly societies (also called box clubs, from the communal money box in which members deposited their contributions); the main difference lay in the social class of the contributors. The first friendly society was established in London in 1687, its members including mainly skilled artisans who sought to insure themselves against illness and funeral expenses. This type of society began to increase rapidly in numbers after about 1760, to serve the needs of the growing numbers of industrial workers; by 1815 there were over 900,000 members of friendly societies in England and Wales. The societies were most common in highly industrialised areas of the country, where working people were able to afford what amounted to a self-funded system of incapacity benefits. For a weekly contribution of four to six pence, members could expect to receive around 10s. per week when ill and £10 at death. There was a third essential feature of friendly society membership: they brought members into closer social contact with each other, at events that included annual feasts and free drink at monthly meetings.[26]

For those who could not afford to insure themselves against illness and death in a normal friendly society, there was another option. Burial societies existed solely to ward off the spectre of the pauper funeral, a fate that working-class people dreaded. No one wanted their corpse to be handed over to the anatomists for dissection, a risk faced by anyone buried at parish expense under the provisions of the Anatomy Act of 1832.[27] Local in scope, such societies would, for a small weekly payment (perhaps a penny), pay at the death of an insured person a sum between £2 and £10, to be used towards the cost of his or her funeral. This was in effect a form of life insurance, one that was wide open to abuse because of the informality of the system. The Sandys and Geering cases show how easy it was for an individual to collect the money when not just one but a whole series of insured people died.

The friendly society movement was strengthened in 1834 when the Poor Law Amendment Act came into force; indeed, this eventuality was one facet of the policy that guided the administration of the law. The threat of the workhouse was a good way to drive poor men into friendly and burial societies, thus saving costs that would otherwise have been borne by ratepayers.[28] By the early 1870s, membership in many thousands of such societies had rocketed to an estimated four million. But there was now an alternative for the weekly wage earner, as life insurance companies had from mid century begun to expand into the market known as industrial life insurance. Led by the Prudential, which soon came to dominate its competitors, policies gave life cover for a small weekly outlay, with immediate payment of death claims (about £10, enough to pay for a funeral with a little left over) upon presentation of a receipt to the insuring office. An aggressive system of marketing focused on the activities of local agents, who canvassed for business and collected premiums door to door. The rivalry between insurance agents and the representatives of local friendly and burial societies was fierce, and continued throughout the nineteenth century.[29] At the trial of Flanagan and Higgins in 1884, the judge directed stinging criticism at the five insurance agents who had made their task so easy. These agents had not only made false entries on the proposal forms in order to increase their commissions, they had allowed policies to be taken out on people who did not know they were insured. When Ellen Burndred was arrested twenty years later and charged with poisoning her foster daughter, she had a quick response to an obvious question: 'As to the insurance, the agents pester your lives out to give them business.'[30]

The cases of accused poisoners like Burndred offer a way to trace changes in life insurance practices, since eyewitness testimony gives clear evidence of how the system operated. That it was open to abuse was a fact recognised early on: in 1737 a Southwark apothecary insured his wife's life with the London Assurance Corporation and then poisoned her.[31] Similar cases may well have occurred both before and after this one, but they have not come down to us in any detail. The first insurance-related poisoning for which we do have a full account was that of William Reed, who was fed arsenic in broth and then bludgeoned when it failed to act as quickly as expected. The crime took place in the village of Berkeley, Gloucestershire, in April 1794, where Reed was staying with his wife Mary and her brother James Watkins. Originally from Dorset, the trio had lived together with a lodger, Robert Edgar, a wealthy young man who became Mary's lover and who promised to marry her if her husband died. Since Reed possessed a fortune of several thousand pounds, Mary stood to gain a great deal at his death; the more so after he was persuaded to insure his life for £2000, payable if he died within seven years. He was examined by a surgeon hired by the insurance agent, and pronounced healthy. This was then common practice, as companies strove to root out frauds perpetrated by substituting healthy impostors for unhealthy applicants at the time a policy was drawn up. Reed had no defence against arsenic, however; though attended by surgeon Henry Jenner, brother of the pioneer of vaccination, Edward Jenner, he died eight hours after eating poisoned soup. Although both doctors believed the death was due to poison, Mary and Watkins were released; in early May, the latter was found shot dead at his father's house in Herefordshire. There the matter would have rested, with everyone assuming that Watkins had committed murder and suicide, had his sister not tried to claim the insurance money. The Royal Assurance Company refused to pay because the policy had only been in effect for two weeks, so she decided to prosecute. Evidence given by a witness (probably Edgar) at the trial led to Mary's arrest on suspicion of involvement in her husband's death. Tried for murder in March 1796, she was acquitted, the jurors apparently convinced that Watkins had planned the crime alone.[32]

The deaths of William Reed, Anne Palmer and Walter Palmer were relatively rare examples of poisonings committed for the sake of a life insurance policy (as opposed to the funds paid out by friendly and burial societies) before the 1870s, when industrial life insurance aimed at the working classes had become commonplace. There was, however, a poisoner who was never charged with murder, although he is thought to have killed four people for the sake of money. Thomas Griffiths Wainewright (1794–1852) was an intelligent and well-connected man who became a respected member of a literary circle that included the poet Wordsworth, but he turned to forgery and murder when faced with financial difficulties. In 1829 he poisoned his grandfather with strychnine, and inherited a large fortune and a house. But much of the money went to his creditors, and in August 1830 he poisoned his mother-in-law to save himself the cost of keeping her. Then he turned his attention to his sister-in-law, whom he insured for £18,000 with several companies before poisoning her in December 1830. The companies were suspicious and refused to pay, so Wainewright, like Mary Reed, decided to sue. After five years, judgement was given against him. He meanwhile had disappeared to France, where he poisoned a man he had first insured. Returning secretly to England in 1837, he was recognised as 'Wainewright the Poisoner' but tried only for forgery. Convicted, he was sentenced to transportation for life, and died unrepentant in Tasmania.[33]

Wainewright and Mary Reed had in common both their high social status and the fact that each was bent on maintaining that status at all cost, but poisoners of their class were extremely rare when it came to insurance murders. Why this should be so, given that wealthier people had long been poisoning each other for the sake of family inheritances, is puzzling. The answer is probably related mainly to a lack of detection. Wealthy people were a minority: any murders of the rich may have been so few and far between that most were never detected, a fact perhaps exacerbated by reluctance among doctors, relatives and neighbours to voice suspicions about influential persons. Certainly there were many more murders related to burial insurance than those identified and prosecuted as such.

The first known burial insurance poisoners, Robert Standring and the Sandys family, poisoned their own children for a few pounds during a time of great hardship, in the years around 1840. The subsequent frequency of similar crimes resulted from the difficult economic climate and the rapid increase in the number of friendly and burial societies after 1834; better tests for arsenic also meant that more poisonings were detected. During the next four decades, many such cases (even those that involved the deaths of adults – such as Mary Anne Geering) could be laid at the door of poverty. Those who had the luxury of full bellies and warm houses were horrified by what they considered despicable acts, but could not be surprised so long as such an incentive to murder was so readily available. By the early 1860s such cases were old news, each making local headlines only. When Alice Hewitt was condemned to death at Chester, it was only the rarity of a daughter killing her mother that prompted the clerk of assize to note that Hewitt had been 'executed 28 December 1863 for poisoning her mother with arsenic to obtain the burial money'.[34]

By the 1870s, life insurance among the working classes had begun a spurt of growth that was to continue unabated until the present day. Changes to the legislation that governed friendly societies (1875) encouraged them to adopt sound life insurance practices, so that many became indistinguishable from insurance companies. This led to the practice of insuring lives in more than one company, since policies were easy to obtain and relatively cheap: a minimum investment of a few pence a week could lead to payments of up to £10 from each insurer. This explains why, after a relatively quiet period during the 1860s, the number of insurance poisonings began to rise again in the late 1870s: poverty and want still existed and, to the criminally minded, the insurance system offered clear opportunities. There were seven cases of insurance-related serial or multiple poisoning in the 1840s, four in the 1870s and five in the 1880s, but only two from 1850 to 1870. By contrast, there were eight cases involving a single victim in those two decades, but only seven during the following thirty years. Although companies were now more careful to insist upon medical checks when policies were issued and claims were made, the fierce competition between agents meant that due care was not always taken. This was how Catherine Flanagan and Margaret Higgins (1883), and Amelia Winters and Elizabeth Frost (1889) were able to commit so many murders before they were caught – on both occasions via the intervention of worried relatives of their final victim.

It was in the late 1870s that poisoners of the type that we now associate with the typical insurance murderer first appeared in numbers: ambitious in excess of his or her abilities, greedy, selfish and acquisitive. Thomas Griffiths Wainewright was one such poisoner, but he stood alone in this regard for forty years, by which time the field had been opened to all comers. William Palmer was of a similar disposition, though he appears to have been something of a born criminal: a heavy drinker, gambler and womaniser, he killed to maintain his position and stay out of debt. But Ellen Heesom and Elizabeth Berry, for example, both wanted more from life than their education and status would allow, so they killed for the money that would enable them to attain a better place in society. In that respect, there was little difference between them and the poisoners who killed for inherited wealth or to hide an earlier financial misdeed, both of which were crimes that occurred long before the first insurance murder and continued long after murder for burial money had finally been eradicated.

The feature of the insurance and burial society system that made it so open to abuse by murderers was the fact that, to collect the money, a policyholder had only to produce a certificate of burial, issued by local registrars upon presentation of a death certificate. Problems arose when registrars accepted the flimsiest of evidence as to the medical cause of death, and failed to inform coroners of sudden deaths or cases where cause of death was unknown. Many murderers had only to register the fact of a death, being under little or no pressure to explain how they had occurred. Others called in a doctor at the final stage of a poison-related illness, failed to describe certain telltale symptoms, and were given a death certificate naming some natural disease. Sometimes insurance agents approved claims after they had viewed a dead body themselves. On occasion, coroners who were informed of sudden deaths declined, for financial reasons, to hold an inquest. Standards varied widely around the country, being worst in rural areas, and it was not until 1926 that it finally became law that no death could be registered without a death certificate stating natural causes or a coroner's order for burial.[35] Although friendly societies and, especially, insurance companies attempted to ensure that claimants were not able to collect cash without proper medical evidence of cause of death, their good intentions were sometimes hampered by their own agents and doctors. These men could falsify claims or ignore suspicious circumstances, and evidence from poisoning cases of the late Victorian period indicates that many were willing to do so for the sake of larger commissions or payments that bore a marked resemblance to bribery. An agreement between insuring offices to halt the practice of direct competition between agents (1901) was important in stamping out some of the worst of the competitive practices that had led to abuses. In the end, it became more and more difficult for poisoners to escape detection, as dead bodies became subject to the ever-closer scrutiny of doctors, coroners, registrars and insurers. But there long remained one exception: nothing prevented doctors from certifying the deaths of their own relatives.

While insurance poisonings were mainly clustered in the period 1840 to 1890, other cases related to money were much more widely distributed through time. The earliest example of poisoning for the sake of inherited money was in 1765 and the last in 1910; during the intervening years there were thirty-five others, scattered evenly throughout. As one would expect, many involved families that had property, capital, or both, and there was therefore a sizeable proportion of middle-class perpetrators in this group, including shopkeepers, doctors and large farmers. Some of the victims were wealthy, and one victim and his killer were members of the minor aristocracy. But poorer people too were suspected of murder for profit, albeit over fairly trivial sums (diligently saved by the hard-working victim) or very small cottages. By 1914 living standards had improved for millions of Britons, who were now able to save money and buy property, a fact we can see reflected in the criminal record. In the eighteenth century and the early part of the nineteenth, victims clearly had more wealth than the average citizen. By the century's end, however, the average citizen, finding himself in a better financial position than would have been possible decades earlier, offered a tempting target to friends and family members who hoped to profit from an untimely death. Since children, even those who came from wealthy families, did not have control over their money and did not make wills, they are almost entirely absent from the records of inheritance-related poisonings. There is only one exception: in 1842 twenty-two-year-old Ann Edge was tried at Chester for the arsenic murders of her much younger brother and sister. The only evidence against her was circumstantial, including her own admission that she had dreamed that her family was dead and she had inherited everything. This was enough to convince a coroner's jury to commit her for trial, but, since her family was poor and there was nothing to inherit while her mother remained alive and healthy, Edge was acquitted.[36]

The decision to murder was usually made for one of three reasons: impatient greed; a desire to escape a mounting debt that had resulted from a mixture of avarice and poor judgement; or the jealous belief that another's money or property ought rightfully to belong to the perpetrator. It was this third reason that led William Knightson, a Yorkshire farm worker, to attempt to murder his brother-in-law, Joseph Dodsworth, in 1818. The trouble started when Dodsworth married in January. He brought his new wife to live with him in his father Thomas's house in the village of Arkendale, at which point Knightson and his wife had to move out. Thomas Dodsworth, a wheelwright, owned the house and some land, which at his death was to go to his son Joseph; or, if Joseph had no sons, to his daughter, Mary Knightson. Once Joseph had married, the only way to ensure that he had no sons was to murder him, which

Knightson tried several times to do between mid February and mid April, each time using arsenic mixed with food. Although several family members became ill, no one died, but attempted murder was then a capital crime and Knightson, aged twenty-seven, was convicted and hanged.[37]

One of the most famous cases on record is that of Captain John Donellan, who was hanged in 1781 for poisoning his brother-in-law, Sir Theodosius Boughton, with prussic acid distilled from the leaves of the cherry laurel. Boughton died a few days after his twentieth birthday, but had he lived a year longer he would have inherited a fortune of £2000 per year. Instead, the money and family home, Lawford Hall in Warwickshire, reverted to his elder sister, Donellan's wife. This seemed motive enough and Donellan was convicted, despite the fact that there was no scientific proof of the presence of the poison, apart from the symptoms, and his claim that legal restrictions imposed at the time of his marriage prevented him from controlling his wife's money. Modern commentators agree that Donellan was guilty, his motive probably the fear that he might have to leave Lawford Hall, of which he felt he was master, when Boughton reached his majority.[38]

Where greed was concerned, the case of John Bodle offers a classic example. A dissolute youth of twenty who made his mark on history as the man who stimulated James Marsh to develop his famous test for arsenic, Bodle murdered his grandfather in 1833 because he wanted his share of the old man's estate, worth a total of about £20,000. It is likely that, had the crime gone undiscovered, his next victim would have been his father: a servant reported overhearing Bodle say to his mother that he wished his father and grandfather were dead, so he would have more money.[39]

The best known examples of poisoning crimes sparked by the killer's need to escape debt are those of Thomas Griffiths Wainewright, Dr William Palmer and Dr George Lamson, all of whom sought to maintain a lifestyle that demanded means well beyond their financial circumstances. Their social status meant that these men became notorious in their own day, and their crimes have as a result been well documented.[40] But lesser-known characters committed crimes from similar motives. In Suffolk in 1815, Elizabeth Woolterton, a forty-nine-year-old farmer's widow, tried to kill her aged uncle, to whom she owed £200 and at whose death she stood to inherit property worth £500. Having failed, she tried again, but by a series of mishaps a neighbour's child ate the arsenic-riddled cake intended for the old man and died, a crime for which Woolterton was hanged.[41] Among the very last of the poisoners to be executed was John White, a Coventry tool grinder who killed his elderly mother with cyanide in 1910 because he knew she had made her will in his favour. He had been living on her largesse for years, receiving what amounted to a weekly allowance. Eventually, he found himself in debt (thirty-two pawn tickets were found in his rented lodgings), and decided that, where his inheritance was concerned, he did not wish to wait for nature to take its course. What makes this case particularly interesting is the financial status of the victim and her son. Both were working-class (he was employed in the local Daimler factory), but she was a widow who lived much as modern pensioners do, in her own home on her own savings.[42] Where once a woman of her age (seventy-five) would have been dependent on a man or forced to work to earn enough to eat, by the Edwardian era many old people were able to retire from the work force and still live independently. White's crime, though callous in the extreme, is a good example of how much the social and economic condition of the working classes had improved by the turn of the twentieth century.

Some of the most unusual and complex poisoning cases ever to come before the English courts revolved around cases of fraud, hocussing and theft, which, like crimes carried out for the sake of inherited wealth, appeared regularly. The first, in 1778, saw William Turner tried and acquitted of an attempt to nobble a racehorse at Boroughbridge in Yorkshire; the last, in 1911, ended in the hanging of Frederick Seddon, a man who is still remembered for his unyielding greed. Between these two appeared a variety of con artists, tricksters and thieves of both sexes, half of whom ended their days on the gallows. It was these fraudsters, who appeared to have the clearest intentions of murder, who most often paid the ultimate penalty.

Turner's crime, though rare, opens a window on a feature of English society that is still of concern: the deliberate poisoning or doping of racehorses to affect their performance. Horse racing, an ancient sport, did not become common in England until the reign of Henry II

1. The house of Dr William Palmer, the Rugeley poisoner.

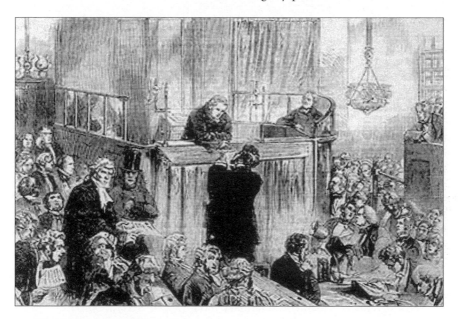

2. The trial of Dr William Palmer.

Borough of Leeds in the County of York〕 The ~~voluntary~~ Examination of Mary Bateman the Wife of John Bateman of Leeds in the said Borough Wheelwright ~~of~~ taken at Leeds aforesaid this 8th Day of January 1809 before me one of His Majesty's Justices of the Peace for the said Borough.

Who saith that all the Letters were written by Hannah ~~Nott except the last five or six~~ – That it is better than three Years since she was at Leeds – she has been from Manchester to Bedale, at Richmond and Masham – That she was not at Leeds when Perigo was to bring down the Wheat – that she gave him half of the Money to buy the Cheese with – he did not bring half a peck of wheat – that there was not a Letter that afternoon she never had any Honey or Powders – William Perigo's Wife never brought any Honey ~~a London~~ Pot to her this Examinants House – that she never talked to William Perigo or his Wife about any Honey – that her Husband or any one Else never fetched any Powder That William Perigo gave her a Bottle the night before she was taken when she met him and ~~that she gave the Bottle to~~ William Duffield the next Morning – That her Husband never did take any of it, but she ~~did~~ and she was very ill after it and many seed her pick up – that the Bottle was delivered to her by him – That William Perigo bought the Oat price and said it would make her Husband a Jacket – There is not half of the Money true some of it is and what they bought in Kirkgate is true – That she has sent Letters at different times She has paid 11s a shilling and fifteen pence for Postage. but it is utterly false that I ever did send for any provision ~~of~~ by any Person – Mary Bateman

it is utterly false

~~I never sent for~~

Taken before me.
Edw Markland

FATAL FACILITY; OR, POISONS FOR THE ASKING.

CHILD.—"PLEASE, MISTER, WILL YOU BE SO GOOD AS TO FILL THIS BOTTLE AGAIN WITH LODNUM, AND LET MOTHER
HAVE ANOTHER POUND AND A HALF OF ARSENIC FOR THE RATS (!)"
DULY QUALIFIED CHEMIST.—"CERTAINLY, MA'AM. IS THERE ANY OTHER ARTICLE?"

₊ The ease with which poisons could be purchased from druggists, afforded a menace to human life. Some fatal cases had recently
come to light.

4. A *Punch* cartoon on the ease with which poisons could be bought, 8 September
1849.

5. Mary Ann Cotton.

6. The trial of Florence Maybrick.

7. Charles Bravo, the victim of antimony poisoning in 1876.

8. Dr Hawley Harvey Crippen, waxwork model.

No 4 & 5. Newtown Assizes. Thursday 8th July 1886.

William Evans. } Feloniously making a false entry in
Mary Anne Home Jones } a marriage register.

The trial of Jones postponed to   Plea guilty
the next assizes – for on the   Sentence 12 months hard labour
ground of illness.
Witnesses bound by recognizance.

See Chester. Autumn assizes   Witnesses   2   5
October 1886. No 22   Mag Cts   1 . 15
                                              £ 4 . 0 . 0

G. D. Harrison }
for the Treasury }

No 6   William Samuel.   Murder   Poison. Strychnine.
                                     Same on Coroners Inq:

Jury.   Plea not guilty
3 . Evan Bumford   Verdict. guilty.
4 . Alfred Butler   Sentence of Death.   Executed
7 . Jonathan Davies   July 26th
10 . William Gwalchmay James   Witnesses   53 . 7 . 0
11 . Abraham Jones
12 . Cornelius Pryce Jones
15 . John Lewis   1 . 7 . 8 . 2 ag Cts   4 . 14 . 6
18 . Edward Morgan
22 . Thomas Phillips   38 . 1 . 8
23 . James Powell   1 . 7 . 8
26 . John Poyce   36 . 14 . 6
29 . Samuel Pugh   Grains
                         Analyst   8 . 8 . 0
                         2 days & ...
                         Bryl at 33   6 . 8 . 6
                         ...   15 . 6
                                     16 . 0 . 0

G. D. Harrison }   The Counsel from half past 1 to 5.30 on Thursday
for Treasury. }   & till 6 on Friday. Higgins Q.C. & Marshall for pros.
                            Douglas for prisoner.

9. Record of the sentence of death on and execution of William Samuel, July 1886. (*Public Record Office*)

(1154–89), and it was not until the early years of the seventeenth century that public races began. The Newmarket races were instituted around 1640, and the town eventually became the headquarters of British racing. The Jockey Club was founded there in 1751, and the sport grew rapidly in popularity through the rest of the century, appealing as it did to members of all classes. Gambling on the outcome of races was commonplace, and owners, trainers and jockeys could as easily bet against as on their own horses. If one wished to bet on a horse, some means had to be found to stimulate it, port and whisky being favourite choices. If betting against, the horse had to be slowed, and it was here that poison made its appearance. Historians of flat racing have stated that opiate balls were used for this purpose as early as 1838,[43] but that actual drugging of horses was very much a product of the American invasion of British racing that took place in the 1890s.[44] The Turner case, however, shows that horses had long been the potential victims of poisonous substances.

Turner, whose age and occupation are unknown, was accused of feeding putty and lead shot to a horse called Miss Nightingale, who died in convulsions two days later. She was worth £100, and had been brought to Boroughbridge in October 1778 to contest a race worth £50. Turner was arrested on circumstantial evidence: he had recently come to the town, had bought shot, putty and a chisel (with which he could have broken in to the locked stable), and had been seen loitering nearby. He was found hiding in a thick hedge after the horse's death, a fact that aroused further suspicion, and it seems likely that he was guilty as charged. But he was acquitted, as there was no direct evidence to prove that he had committed the crime.[45] Over thirty years later, the most famous horse poisoner of them all was less fortunate.

Histories of crime and of racing invariably refer to the case of Daniel Dawson (1765–1812), who was hanged in Cambridge for poisoning racehorses at Newmarket. The case was one that received widespread public attention, both because of Dawson himself – an educated man who had been reduced to earning a living as a tout – and because the victims' owners were members of the aristocracy. The story began in July 1809, when two horses died after drinking from a watering trough into which arsenic had been infused. The animals were each worth £20, and their owners appear to have done little to solve the mystery. This was not the case two years later, however, when four more horses died in similar circumstances. The intention was to nobble Pirouette (the favourite to win the Claret Stakes) by poisoning her drinking water and then to bet against her, a plot of which her trainer, Richard Prince, had been warned. For several weeks he watered his horses at another trough, but on one particularly hot day, having seen no evidence of poisoning, he allowed them to drink from the usual trough. Four of them died in agony, including Pirouette and Eagle, a colt worth £1000. It was sheer luck that none of the stable boys was killed, as they frequently drank from the same trough, and Prince set out to find the culprits.

Suspicion quickly fell upon Dawson, who had been paid by bookmakers who had bet heavily against some of the horses trained by Prince. A chemist named Cecil Bishop admitted that he had placed arsenic in the trough at Dawson's instruction, and became a prosecution witness in order to save his own neck. Tried in March 1812 for poisoning Eagle, Dawson was acquitted on a technicality.[46] He was then tried in July on several charges, and convicted of having poisoned one of the horses that had died in 1809.[47] The case was unique: although there had been many instances of poisoning horses for gambling purposes at major race centres like Doncaster and Newmarket, no one had been capitally convicted. Dawson himself had never intended to kill the horses: unaware that they were not using the poisoned trough, he had increased the amount of arsenic dissolved in it, supposing that he had underestimated the dose. But there was then no distinction in law between an attempt and an actual killing, of either people or animals. He may also have been made an example to others: the first acquittal annoyed local people, whose business had been hurt by the affair. That Dawson was not held in universal contempt was shown by the efforts of Lord Foley, Pirouette's owner, to secure a reprieve, and before his execution Dawson spoke bitterly of the hypocrisy of the Jockey Club, few of the members of which were above cheating.[48]

Although much about the Dawson case resonates with the modern reader, the early nineteenth century was a time in which ignorance and superstition flourished, as popular beliefs remained little changed from earlier centuries. Witch-hunting had all but disappeared in Britain following the repeal in 1736 of the laws against witchcraft, but belief in witches had not. It was the continuing conviction that some individuals were able to harness the power of the supernatural that led to the trial

of Mary Bateman (1768–1809), charged with the murder of an elderly
woman named Rebecca Perrigo, who had died from the painful effects
of corrosive sublimate. Theirs was a tale in which mutual greed figured
strongly, and one that could not have occurred had not a tacit agreement
existed between victim and poisoner. As a result of her actions, Bateman,
who was known as the Yorkshire Witch, became far more notorious
than any horse poisoner.

Married with several children, Bateman lived in Leeds, where she had
long earned a living as a fortune-teller, swindling gullible clients out of
cash, food and saleable possessions. She had no need to commune with
the supernatural, for 'her stock-in-trade was the ignorance, credulity
and superstition of her chosen victims'.[49] She invented a spirit medium,
from whom all the information she gave to her clients supposedly came,
and was so successful that by the turn of the nineteenth century she
had to invent another, a Miss Blythe from Buxton. In the spring of
1806, William and Rebecca Perrigo, who were in the clothing business,
sought her professional advice after the latter began to suffer chest
palpitations, and Bateman saw an opportunity to bilk the couple of
nearly all they had. Acting as intermediary for Miss Blythe, Bateman
promised that not only would Rebecca be cured within eighteen months,
but that four guineas sewn into their mattress would miraculously grow
to £30 or £40 in that time; but only if certain instructions were followed
to the letter. In obeying the many ensuing demands issued by Miss
Blythe, the Perrigos were within a year bilked of about £70 and a long
list of commodities.

In April 1807, knowing that no money would be found inside the
mattress and wishing to avoid exposure as a fraud, Bateman decided to
dispose of her victims. Accordingly, 'Miss Blythe' wrote them a letter
in which she stated that 'I am sorry to tell you you will take an illness
in the month of May next, either one or both of you, but I think both;
but the work of God must have its course'.[50] To avoid the worst effects
of this illness, the Perrigos were to mix six powders into their food for
six days, not to consult a doctor if they became ill but to take some
honey that Bateman would provide as an antidote. The powders were
corrosive sublimate, the honey contained arsenic, and, after slavishly
doing as they had been told, the Perrigos found themselves very seriously
ill. William almost lost the use of his limbs, but it was Rebecca that

suffered the most. Her lips and tongue turned black and swelled so much that her teeth wouldn't meet, and still she continued to eat the poisoned powders, dying on the eighth day, 24 May. The poison had caused such internal damage that her body was covered with black spots of gangrene; the smell was so bad that everyone near it was forced to smoke tobacco.

After her death Perrigo visited a surgeon, Thomas Chorley, who asked to see some of the food that had made them ill. A neighbour who had noticed tiny white specks in the fatal dish gave some to a cat, which promptly died.[51] But these first glimmerings of suspicion came to nothing and, in June, Perrigo renewed his contact with Bateman, whose feigned grief and anger convinced him to retain his faith in her. Miss Blythe now promised that his dead wife would rise again and destroy his sight unless he continued to pay. It was not until October 1808, nearly three years after he took up with the Yorkshire Witch, that he ventured to open the moneybags sewn into his mattress. Imagine his horror when he discovered that they contained nothing but lead and scraps of old paper!

What the loss of his wife could not effect the disappearance of his promised windfall did, and Perrigo contacted a police constable, who arrested Bateman when she arrived at a prearranged meeting with her victim. All his property was found in her house, and a search of her person yielded a pot of honey and a bottle of liquid that, later analysed by Chorley, proved respectively to be full of corrosive sublimate and arsenic. She was tried for murder at York in March 1809, where, lacking counsel, she made no real attempt at a defence. She was found guilty but, upon being asked if there was any reason why she should not be sentenced to death, shrieked that she was pregnant. The judge ordered that a panel of married women should examine her, but so fearful were they of the witch that the women present rushed for the doors. After order had been restored, twelve brave souls announced that Bateman showed no signs of pregnancy. So strong was the belief in magic that, at her execution on 20 March, the crowd saw her 'not as a murderess who had killed for gain, but as a martyr and mystic'.[52]

The strange tale of the Yorkshire Witch and the awe in which she was held by her neighbours and clients was one that – murder aside – was probably repeated over and over; today, we see a modern equivalent in the successes enjoyed by astrologers, tarot readers and mediums. People believe what they want to believe, and are prepared to pay for the privilege. What made Bateman different from the many other individuals who perpetrated similar frauds was her resort to poisoning her victims to conceal the fact that her prophecies were false. In turning to murder to hide earlier deceit, she allied herself with many less interesting but equally dangerous poisoners who sought to hide evidence of theft and fraud by committing an even more serious crime.

Sometimes, theft and fraud could only be accomplished with the aid of poison. In a phenomenon known as hocussing, which was confined to large cities, the intent was not to kill but to render a victim unconscious and easy to steal from, a purpose for which opiates were clearly suitable. Most perpetrators were tried for theft in the lower courts and have thus not been easily identified as poisoners; but if a death ensued, the case became one of murder. This is what happened to Charles Parton, who, at the time of his trial for murder at Liverpool, in March 1889, was an eighteen-year-old labourer who had already served short prison sentences for theft and non-payment of a railway fare.[53]

On 26 February 1889 John Fletcher, a fifty-year-old paper manufacturer who had recently been elected to Lancashire County Council, was discovered comatose in a Manchester hansom cab. He was rushed to the Royal Infirmary but died a few minutes before the driver could get there, at around 8 p. m. The surgeon on duty could smell alcohol, but tests for prussic acid, morphine and strychnine were all negative. Death was clearly due to heart failure, but the cause wasn't evident. An autopsy was made the following day, when the source was discovered: although Fletcher's body showed signs of liver damage, he was otherwise healthy. Death was due to the combined effects of alcohol and chloral hydrate.

Chloral hydrate, a powerful soporific, was introduced into British medicine in the 1870s. A crystalline substance that dissolved easily in water, as little as ten grains could be fatal to an adult; though considered a poison, it did not have to be signed for in a poison book. Most deaths from chloral were accidents and suicides, and Fletcher himself might have survived had he not been drinking so heavily. But his death was no accident: the cabbie reported that a young man had got into the cab with Fletcher, and then jumped out, and police enquiries soon uncovered the full story. On the day of his death, Fletcher had spent at least two hours drinking with a young man later identified as Parton. A witness who saw them noticed Parton pour fluid into a glass of beer, but, as it seemed to be his own glass, the witness did nothing. By 7.30 p. m. Parton was alone, flashing money about and showing off a valuable watch and chain which were, of course, Fletcher's. He was arrested on 2 March and placed in a police line up, where four witnesses picked him out; he was then charged with murder, robbery and administering a stupefying drug.

Once the newspapers had got hold of the story, other victims came forward. Charles Bromley, a Liverpool chemist, reported that Parton had stolen a large bottle of chloral from him on 19 February. Samuel Oldfield, a grocer from Ashton-under-Lyne, realised that he too had been drugged and robbed by Parton: on 8 January he had had four drinks with him, and awoke the next morning at a police station, his watch gone and his pockets empty. To add insult to injury, he had been fined for public drunkenness: a doctor who examined him had suspected opium, but, finding none, had concluded that he was simply drunk. Finally, John Parkey, a railway porter from Ashton, came forward to say that he had met Parton on 28 December and had spent time with him and a mutual friend in a pub. The last thing he remembered was being perfectly sober before Parton sat down next to him; he came to on the floor of his friend's lodgings the next morning, his watch and cash missing. Subjected to stiff cross-examination by Parton's solicitor, Parkey denied that he had been on a drunken spree and claimed that his health still suffered from the after-effects of the experience. (He died a few days after the trial.)

This evidence was more than enough to convince local magistrates that Parton had a case to answer and, as the assize court was then in session, he was tried just ten days later. Found guilty of murder and sentenced to death, he was reprieved and given a life sentence because he had not intended to kill Fletcher. A cocky youth, he later wrote his memoirs, bemoaning the mere eleven years that he actually spent in prison.[54] The question remains of how Parton managed to win the trust of total strangers so easily. Hocussing was the only poisoning crime in which victim and perpetrator could previously be completely unknown to one another and yet manage to develop a relationship, however fleeting. The fact that Oldfield and Fletcher were in Manchester alone and were both much older than Parton is suggestive. It is now impossible to know for certain, but they may have taken a fatherly interest in him, or perhaps there was a homosexual element in the ease with which the young man attracted his victims.[55]

Of all the poisoners led to their downfall by greed and avarice, the name of Frederick Seddon (1870–1912) stands alone as one whose mean and grasping nature so told against him that he was convicted entirely on circumstantial evidence. If he himself had not testified at his trial for the arsenic murder of his lodger, Eliza Barrow, it seems almost certain that the prosecution would have failed to prove a case sufficient to secure a guilty verdict.[56] The case was groundbreaking in many respects. Accused persons had only been allowed to testify on their own behalf since 1898, and lawyers had yet to learn that this could be a dangerous privilege. Moreover, Seddon was tried with his wife, Margaret, and the same evidence was offered against both; but the jury acquitted her and convicted him, despite a total lack of proof that he had ever handled arsenic. The scientific evidence too was unique. Toxicologist William Henry Willcox used an electrolytic version of the Marsh test, obtaining only slight deposits that, in earlier times, would have been considered too small to use for quantitative purposes. In order to calculate the amount of arsenic that must have been present in the body, a multiplying factor of up to 2000 was used, leaving a large margin of possible error. In this way, Willcox calculated that about five grains – a fatal dose – had been given to Barrow a short time before she died.[57]

In the Seddon case, motive and appearance were all. The story began in July 1910, when Barrow, a forty-nine-year-old spinster, moved into the Seddons' home in London. There she discovered that she and her landlord shared a mutual love of gold. Both were financially secure: Barrow owned stock and property; Seddon, ironically, was a successful district superintendent for an insurance company. During the next year, Barrow signed over all her assets to him, in exchange for a generous annuity of over £150 per year. On 1 September 1911 she was taken ill with what was assumed to be epidemic diarrhoea, and died two weeks later; the doctor who attended her gave Seddon a death certificate without viewing the body. Seddon had her buried two days later, and there the matter would have rested had not some cousins happened to hear of her death and subsequently to enquire about her money and property. Seddon's explanations did not satisfy them, and her body was exhumed in November. The police alleged that the arsenic that had caused her death had been obtained from fly-papers that Seddon's daughter had bought in August, but no one ever produced a credible theory of how or when the poison was taken or administered.

This was clearly not enough evidence upon which to convict either Seddon or his wife, but when he entered the witness-box at their Old Bailey trial in March 1912, all the possible prejudices against him were given full sway. He was unshaken and unperturbed, and had a plausible explanation for all sorts of seemingly inexplicable events. He saw nothing odd in the fact that he had bargained with an undertaker for a cheap funeral for Miss Barrow, or that he had accepted a small commission on it. His obsession with money and apparent lack of feeling became obvious in his detailed accounts of how he had come to acquire all of her assets, and it was these personal defects that convicted him. The jury may have had some difficulty in following the complex financial, scientific and legal details of the case, but they knew that Seddon had the air of a man quite capable of committing any crime for the sake of money. He continued to protest his innocence until his execution in Pentonville Prison on 18 April 1912. For Frederick Seddon, guilty or not, money was truly the root of all evil.

6

Fear and Loathing

The prisoner came to my house frequently in the evening. I have often heard him speaking about the disagreement he and his father had. I remember him on one occasion saying he wished his father's corpse had gone from the place – he would not shed a tear.

Edward Brown, 1846 [1]

When Ralph Joicey, aged twenty-six, went on trial for the murder of his father, the correspondent who covered the case for the *Times* noted that he had 'the appearance and manner of a person rather above the station of a farm servant'.[2] Moreover, he seemed to be a gentle, though sombre, man. Witnesses testified that he was faithful, honest and kind. This raised an obvious question in the minds of readers: why and how had he become a parricide? The prosecution's task was made easier by the fact that Joicey had confessed; his guilt was scarcely at issue, but his defence attorney tried valiantly to cast a reasonable doubt on the assumption that it was his client who had sent the victim a parcel of arsenic labelled as medicine. Unlike the strategy that modern lawyers adopt, relatively little was made of the complex emotions and events that underlay the crime, factors that today would almost certainly be seen as strongly mitigating circumstances. These were never spelled out in full, but it is possible to read between the reticence of the lines penned by the court reporter.

In the autumn of 1845 Joicey was living with his sixty-seven-year-old father, Robert, his mother, Isabella, and sister, Margaret, in a one-room cottage on the estate of the Duke of Portland, at Cockle Park in Northumberland. The men worked as day labourers; it is not clear whether the women had any paid employment. Margaret had only returned to live with her parents on 12 August, having left a position in domestic service. Although the problems that afflicted the family were almost certainly of a longstanding nature, it appears to have been her homecoming that triggered the tragedy.

All the evidence points to Robert Joicey as a man who victimised his own family and in turn became their victim. Everyone who knew the Joiceys agreed that there was a great deal of arguing and disagreement among them, but none of the trial witnesses seemed to know, or was prepared to state, the cause of it. At the inquest, a former servant girl told how, not long after Margaret's return, she had been heard to warn her father that she would poison him; later she told the witness that if her mother were better, she would soon make her father a corpse, and would poison him.[3] What did Margaret's reference to her mother mean? The testimony of the family doctor, Arthur Hedley, provides a clue. He stated that he had been sent for on 11 October to attend Isabella Joicey, who had suffered a series of fits following a family quarrel. He seems to have suspected that she had attempted suicide, for he asked her if she had 'taken anything'. Both her children then claimed that their father was the cause. Although the old man denied it, Isabella said he was not telling the truth. Hedley also noted that he had often told Ralph Joicey not to quarrel with his father.[4] It is uncertain whether the elder Joicey had beaten his wife, forced her to take something, hectored her into some sort of minor stroke or driven her to attempt suicide. Regardless of the exact nature of this incident, it is likely that father and son clashed repeatedly because Ralph could not tolerate his father's behaviour toward his mother.

But this wasn't the only reason. Robert Joicey abused his son as well as his wife, so that Ralph described him as an 'out-of-the-way' man.[5] By this he meant that his father's actions, when behind closed doors, were worse than those that were exposed to view, and he told their neighbours, Edward and Hannah Brown, that he wished his father's corpse had gone from the place. The old man was rarely seen to behave badly but, one day in the harvest fields, the farm steward had heard him use 'very improper expressions to his son'; Joicey had then denied Ralph's accusation that he had threatened to kill him.[6] The quarrelling – apparently about the same thing that had led to the argument on 11 October – continued throughout the month, until on one occasion Robert nearly pushed his son into the fire. This drove Ralph to breaking point, and he bought poison the next time he went to Morpeth, on 25 October; a chemist there recalled selling an ounce to a young man whom he could not positively identify. He hid the parcel in a hedge and did nothing with it until the end of November, when, heavily disguised, he brought it to a local pub and said it was medicine to be delivered to Robert Joicey. The timing was deliberate: Robert had recently consulted Dr Hedley about a medical problem, and was expecting him to send something. Unaware that the two coloured powders contained arsenic, he took one before he went to bed on 1 December. An hour and a half later, he began to vomit. His symptoms thereafter followed the classic pattern of arsenic poisoning, marked especially by the extreme pains that he suffered until his death on 8 December 1845.

The evident agony that his father experienced aroused such feelings of guilt in Ralph Joicey that he was led to confess to the farm steward at Cockle Park, a week after the death. Walter Weallens testified that Margaret sent for him; when he got to their house he found all three of them waiting. Ralph then told him that he had poisoned his father, insisting that no one else was involved. But the local constable, William Dickinson, was already suspicious of Isabella and Margaret. As bailiff of the duke's estates, he had visited the family during Robert's illness, and had been struck by their apparent apathy and the speed with which the women removed the vomit and faeces from the house. After the cause of death had been confirmed, Dickinson decided to arrest all of them; the coroner's depositions show that there were three prisoners in custody during the latter stages of the inquest. Ralph's state of mind is apparent from the declaration he made to the arresting officer, who had tracked him to his brother's house in Newcastle: 'He said he had dreamt three times he was to make it known ... and he would be forgiven. He said he had no peace, as he thought he saw his father everywhere.'[7]

Tried at Newcastle in February 1846, Ralph was convicted and sentenced to death. Margaret was tried separately, as an accessory after the murder, but was acquitted. It seems unlikely that a woman who had threatened to poison her father was unaware that her brother had actually done so, but it takes little imagination to see that they might have agreed on a story that cast the blame squarely on Ralph's shoulders. Why should they both suffer if the law could be persuaded that only one was guilty? At his execution on 17 March, which took place before

thousands of unusually silent and contemplative spectators, Ralph behaved with a great deal of composure. He had prepared a statement in
which he again asserted that no one else had known of his crime – until
he had confessed first to his mother and sister, and then to Weallens.
He thought his trial had been fair, commended the kindness shown to
him by the prison governor, officers and chaplain, and bade farewell to
his family. He exhorted them to follow God's commandments, 'and
there need no fear overtake them'.[8] It is easy to believe that Joicey
recognised the sad irony of this expression, knowing that he had become
a victim of his own fear and hatred.

When poverty, jealousy and financial gain are removed from the diverse
equations that lead to murder, two other motives emerge as important
precipitating factors. Of these, a strong desire for retribution formed
one of the last links in the chain of events that tended to give rise to
poisonings; the other was mental illness. Such crimes were frequently
unplanned; those that were given a degree of prior consideration were
often carried out in a fog of rage or depression over which perpetrators
seem to have had little control. Of all poisoners, it was those stirred by
some form of fear or loathing who were most likely to suffer extremes
of guilt and regret, often prompting them to confess even when they
knew the consequence might be their own death. In contrast to the
selfish and remorseless killers motivated by greed or lust, here we
examine the personal experiences of poisoners motivated by deep feelings of despair and vengeance, opening a window into distressing
examples of anxiety, dread and self-doubt. Men, women and children
endured such crises. Many of them were members of the second largest
occupational group in nineteenth-century Britain, domestic servants.

About a tenth of poisoning crimes (fifty-eight cases) can be clearly
attributed to a desire for revenge, including most of those committed
by servants and children, and those against animals. Of the individuals
who confessed, most seem to have been resigned to their fate, sometimes
teetering on the brink of mental imbalance, or were so young that they
were unable to lie convincingly to their adult interrogators.

Poisoning crimes provoked by fear (of the real or the imagined, the
present or the future) and loathing (of oneself or another) raise issues
whose boundaries are fluid. Mental illness features in a few of the

revenge cases, but it is impossible to know whether the perpetrators would have committed a crime had they been of sound mind. Servants made up one third of those who sought vengeance, but two thirds of them were children; how clearly can we distinguish between the individual as servant and the individual as frightened child? And both adults and children could become the victims of desperation so extreme that murder seemed an obvious solution.

Ralph Joicey did not poison his father on a whim, or for any benefit save the general wellbeing of his beloved mother and sister. It took months, if not years of abuse to drive him to the deed, but once his mind was made up he did not shy away from the consequences. There were few other poisoners motivated by vengeance who exhibited the same strength of purpose or, indeed, who suffered the same provocation; in only one other case were the precipitating stresses of an equal or greater intensity. In 1862 William Robert Taylor, with the cooperation of his wife Martha Ann, poisoned his three young children before stabbing dead his landlord, shooting a bystander in the arm, and then calmly waiting for the police to arrive. Taylor and the victim, Evan Meller, an estate agent, had been in dispute for five months, ever since a gas boiler in the house rented by the family had blown up and killed their eldest child, a girl. Taylor demanded repairs and financial compensation; when the latter was refused, he stopped paying the rent. Meller then entered the house and removed some of the family's possessions, to try to recoup the money owed him. A stalemate ensued, during which Taylor became more and more embittered. On 16 May, armed with a knife and a gun, he went to Meller's office in Manchester; knowing that their next stop would be a prison cell, his wife brought a basket of toiletries. Cornering Meller on a staircase, Taylor stabbed him to death, telling one witness that the man had ruined him and his family. He apologised to the man whom he had shot accidentally, and sat with him to await the police and a doctor. When Sergeant Henry Bateman arrived, Taylor gave him his address and keys, and told him to search the house. There the bodies of three children were found, dressed and arranged, each with a note pinned to their clothes:

> We are six, but one at Harptry lies and thither our bodies take. Meller and Son are our cruel murderers, but God and our loving parents will avenge us. Love rules here and we are all going to our sister, to part no more.

Chemical tests failed to determine what had killed them; at a guess, it was chloroform. There was insufficient evidence to try the couple for the murders of their children, but the Meller case was watertight and, as we might have expected of the Victorian justice system, William Taylor was convicted while his wife was exonerated. Hers was perhaps the worse fate: although he was hanged, she was left alone with nothing but the memory of her husband and four dead children.[9]

Typically, parents killed their own children not from a desire for revenge but from misguided love. Children became the targets of vengeance killings only when their deaths served to hurt someone else, someone who had inflicted emotional pain on the poisoner. The victims themselves were rarely directly related to the killer. It was in such circumstances that Ann Dickson, twenty, attempted to kill six-year-old Rose Catherall by feeding her a mercury compound, before taking a dose of oxalic acid herself. Both survived. Tried at the Old Bailey in September 1873 on charges of administering poison and attempted suicide, Dickson explained that she wanted revenge against the child's father, a married man who had seduced and abandoned her. As she told the magistrate at her committal hearing: 'I wish to say that I had cause to do it'. The judge seems to have accepted this and gave her a light sentence: two terms of one year in prison with hard labour, to run concurrently.[10]

Children were always easy targets for killers, but cases like that of Ann Dickson were rare, amounting to just a handful of the total number of poisoning crimes in which children featured. Jane Scott, hanged at Lancaster in 1828 for murdering her parents with arsenic, had poisoned her niece following a quarrel with her sister in 1826.[11] In 1789 Hannah Whitley, a married woman, was convicted of poisoning her neighbour's child in very odd circumstances. The depositions show that she was guilty of placing arsenic in the victim's food, but why did she do it? A tiny, ragged, misspelled note preserved by the court suggests witchcraft or, at the very least, a deep-seated hatred. Covered all over with tiny inked crosses, it is just possible to make out the words: 'God damn you all for I can come again and I will send the devil to [?] you in [?] by god.' It is now impossible to unravel the web of unhappy relationships that must have surrounded Whitley, and perhaps others, in the Yorkshire village of Hampsthwaite at that time. She may indeed have written the mysterious note, which alarmed her neighbour Thomas

Rhodes considerably; it was she who pointed it out as it lay on the ground (though no attempt was made to identify the handwriting). Immediately after that she went into Rhodes's house and offered to help make a pie, food that made the whole family ill and killed five-year-old Joseph Rhodes. Arsenic was found in the crust, which she had rolled out. In her defence, Whitley claimed that a local linen weaver, William Horseman, had given her a powder to put into Thomas Rhodes's food, threatening to kill her if she refused. Rhodes seems to have believed this, so the source of the trouble may well have been a dispute between himself and Horseman; his children were not the intended victims. But the law demanded a life for a life and, though Horseman never faced any formal legal proceedings, Whitley was executed.[12]

Where disputes between neighbours erupted into violence, a poisoner's target was more usually an animal than a person. Eight out of fourteen examples of animal poisoning are attributable to revenge; all the perpetrators were male, though one man involved his wife. In March 1839 Thomas and Rebecca Mallett were tried at Ipswich for poisoning four bullocks and two pigs, the property of Mallett's former employer, the farmer Charles Stanford. He claimed that Mallett had been plotting revenge since January 1838, when he had been dismissed from his job as head horseman after being found in the granary at three in the morning with an unauthorised duplicate key. After the animals died in October, Rebecca told Stanford that it was a visitation from God, and that he would not prosper if he treated her husband badly. Although chemical tests proved that arsenic was the cause of death, no local druggists recalled selling any to Mallett; the newspaper report does not state whether they were asked to identify his wife. Though Stanford certainly had good reason to suspect them, there was no direct evidence: the couple was acquitted.[13]

If disgruntled ex-employees were obvious suspects when farm animals sickened or died in suspicious circumstances, their indoor equivalent, when people fell ill or died, were domestic servants, a ubiquitous presence in Georgian and Victorian England. In 1806 there were just over 900,000 servants in England and Wales, of whom 800,000 were female.[14] By 1891, according to the official census, the numbers had swollen to a total of 1,400,000 indoor domestics, a mere 58,000 of whom were male.[15] Always principally a female career – male servants were more expensive to employ and men generally had far more job opportunities – domestic service was the second largest occupation after agricultural work. In the early 1880s, approximately one third of all working women were in service; and, even after child labour had been abolished in mines and factories, it continued to flourish indoors. In 1891 there were over 100,000 girls and about 7000 boys between the ages of ten and fifteen in service.[16] The work was physically very demanding, involving long hours of scrubbing and carrying, and most women saw it as a job to keep them only until marriage.

The proportion of servants was highest in towns and cities, and lowest in the mining and manufacturing areas, where alternative occupations for girls and women existed. Although child servants were paid about as well as beginners in other fields, older women could earn more in shops, factories and offices. The average wage rose with age: in the 1890s it was about £7 per year for under sixteens and around £25 for those over forty.[17] In contrast to the stereotypes portrayed on film and television, only a small section of the servant community was employed in the houses of the very rich; most worked for members of the growing middle class. Ninety per cent of all domestics worked as general servants ('maids-of-all-work'), cooks, housemaids and nursemaids in small households. The insufficient supply of domestics became a persistent problem from the 1880s, as the suburban middle classes, conscious of their new status, sought to employ at least one servant. By the early twentieth century, the minimum annual income needed to keep a resident general servant in London had risen from about £150 in 1860 to £300, but this remained lower elsewhere.[18]

Servants were, for the most part, regarded as inferior beings, one of the reasons why first men and then women came increasingly to see domestic service as a choice of last resort. Employers held the whip hand when it came to giving a character reference: no servant could get a new position without one, but no employer could be forced to give one. Dismissal without notice or compensation was legal for a variety of offences including wilful disobedience, unlawful absence, drunkenness, immoral conduct, theft, abusiveness and entertaining at the master's expense without his permission.[19] Servants were often the first to be blamed when items went missing from the home, and surviving legal records indicate that petty larceny was a constant problem for employers, who in most cases preferred immediate dismissal rather than the publicity of legal action.[20] Yet employers who had nothing good to say about a former servant did not always exercise their right to tell the truth, for fear of unpleasantness.[21] This would explain how a girl like Emily Newber was able to obtain more than one position as a nursemaid, even though she was suspected of child abuse.[22] Although such cases were not commonplace, they did occur with distressing regularity, the victims being most often young children whose deaths were not always recognised for what they were. In 1862, in a precursor of the Newber case, thirteen-year-old Elizabeth Vamplew was convicted at Lincoln of the strychnine manslaughter of a baby. Two years later, a renowned toxicologist claimed that she had probably killed three babies during her short career as a nursemaid.[23] The reason was one given repeatedly by servants suspected of harming youngsters: children hindered them in their duties, and generally made more work for them. Violent crimes perpetrated against adults by servants were rarer, usually provoked by greed or anger at an employer's treatment.

Among the 540 poisoning cases in the period for which records have been analysed are fifty-six in which the accused poisoner (ten male and forty-six female) was employed by the victim as a servant, nursemaid or housekeeper, or was a fellow servant within a household. Of these, twenty committed poisoning crimes in pursuit of revenge. This excludes the eleven servants who had a financial motive for poisoning their employer, or who sought to hide an earlier misdeed. It also excludes nine cases that were obviously due to accidents, and those in which the motive is unclear or had nothing to do with vengeance. Guilty verdicts were secured in twenty-six of the fifty-six cases, two thirds occurring after 1850, when servant numbers began to rise rapidly. That so many faced charges which did not stand up in court can be interpreted as a sign of employers' prejudice: when something went wrong, blame was cast immediately on the servants, regardless of the evidence. It was just such an attitude that brought about one of the most infamous miscarriages of justice in early nineteenth-century England.

On 7 April 1815 Elizabeth Fenning, a twenty-one-year-old servant, was tried at the Old Bailey on what was then a capital charge: attempting to poison her employer, lawyer Orlibar Turner, his son and his daughter-in-law. She had been employed as a cook about seven weeks before the incident, which occurred on 21 March. On that day, the family ate some yeast dumplings which Fenning had made, despite the fact that the dough had failed to rise properly. Charlotte Turner described them as 'black and heavy, instead of white and light'.[24] All three complainants became ill, with burning pains, vomiting and swelling which began to abate after about six hours. Fenning and an apprentice who had eaten the same dumplings were also ill with similar symptoms. Orlibar Turner claimed that he suspected arsenic, presumably because he knew there was some kept in the house to kill mice; on checking the next day, he found it gone from an unlocked drawer. He then tested the pan in which the dumpling dough had been mixed (it had not been cleaned), by adding a little water to it, and found that a white powder settled out of the mixture. Finally, he noticed that the knives used by the diners to cut the dumplings had turned black. At the trial, a surgeon, John Marshall, confirmed that the symptoms were those of arsenic poisoning; that the sediment given to him by Turner was arsenic; and that the poison could have turned the dinner knives black. (Arsenic will in fact not turn metal black; and there was no real evidence that what made the family ill was arsenic, only that it was something which prevented the dumplings from rising.)

Orlibar Turner suspected that Fenning was to blame because she had gone into his office to light the fire and might have opened his desk drawer; she could read, and the packet of arsenic had been labelled as poison. She might have wanted to harm the family because she had been reprimanded for going into the room of the male servants partly undressed. For her part, Fenning vigorously denied any part in the mischief, and claimed that, if they had been poisoned, the poison had been in the milk, not the dumplings. But Turner's position within the legal community meant that he could rely on support for his prosecution. Although Fenning's parents sold their possessions to pay for legal counsel, her lawyers seem not to have considered that someone else might have put poison in the food, or that the poison was not arsenic. As the defence could not sum up the case or cross-examine witnesses, the jury simply failed to notice the weakness of the prosecution's case and brought in a guilty verdict. Elizabeth Fenning was sentenced to death.

What happened next rested largely on the shoulders of the judge, Sir John Silvester; it was he who had to recommend a reprieve to the king. The popular outcry against the verdict aroused the concern of so many influential citizens that the execution was stayed for three months. Finally convinced that arsenic could not turn knives black, Orlibar Turner was almost persuaded to ask for mercy for Fenning, but Silvester told him that, if he did, it would cast suspicion on a member of his own family. Even at the time, his son Robert was rumoured to be mentally unstable: a modern theory holds that he framed Fenning in revenge after she rejected his sexual advances. She was executed on 26 July 1815 because the established order could not conceive that a servant's word should be taken above that of her master.[25]

Fenning protested her innocence in a series of moving letters to the *Examiner* newspaper, to her parents and to a fellow convict, a rapist who died with her. At her funeral, five days later, a crowd of thousands accompanied her coffin to the grave; and mourners set upon a man who spoke against her at the cemetery.

Her fate was still the subject of heated debate in the London press when, only seven weeks later, another servant girl was accused of poisoning. On 13 September 1815 two-year-old Elizabeth Anne Newman, the daughter of a butcher, died in the London suburb of Kennington; one of the servants, Elizabeth Mary Miller, nineteen, was accused of murder. The way the child died was not in dispute: she had eaten gruel made with oatmeal that contained arsenic. Miller admitted to having made the gruel, which she had refused to eat after the child fell ill. The question was how the arsenic had got into the oatmeal.

Miller was tried at the Kingston assizes in April 1816, prosecuted by Isaac Espinasse, the barrister who had prosecuted Elizabeth Fenning a year earlier. This was no twist of fate: in his opening statement to the jury he noted how both Orlibar Turner and Richard Newman had been 'hooted from society for doing their duty in bringing the case before a legal tribunal'. But where Fenning had the most perfunctory of legal representation, Miller was more fortunate: a respectable solicitor gave his services for free, and her barrister's fees were raised by public subscription. Between them, these two quickly ascertained the root cause of the child's death. Newman admitted that his property was infested with rats and mice; three different ratcatchers told how they had left poisoned oatmeal in the shop; and a former servant recalled that he had placed one such parcel on the kitchen windowsill. Another former servant noted that he had seen the poisoned oatmeal and thought it looked perfectly harmless. At this stage, the jury decided there was no need to call on Miller, who was nearly senseless throughout the trial, for her defence. The judge ascribed death to an accident and she was acquitted.[26]

There is no doubt that Miller benefited from the increased vigilance shown by members of the public and the legal profession in the wake of the Fenning case, which served as something of a *cause célèbre*. Although servants were subsequently accused of poisoning crimes that were later proved (or at least found) to be accidents, there is no evidence to show that an error on such a massive scale was ever made again.[27] In trials where a servant's motive was known or believed to be revenge, over two thirds nevertheless ended in a guilty verdict. What was it that inspired servants to bite the hand that fed them? We have already noted that some servants poisoned their employers' children so as to cut down on their workload; there was no antipathy involved, simply a badly thought out plan to make life easier for themselves. In a similar show of muddled thinking, Jane Riley attempted to poison her employers and their four children in 1859 simply because she wanted new mourning clothes. Despite confessing that she was aware that green copperas (iron sulphate) could kill the children, Riley, who was described as a girl, was acquitted, perhaps because the Nottingham jury could not quite believe the stated motive.[28] Other servants, finding themselves in a position in which they had access to young children, may have taken advantage of a situation that they would otherwise have sought elsewhere, having already developed an urge to harm others. Or, if never placed in such a household, perhaps such urges might never have arisen within them. Emily Newber and Elizabeth Vamplew took their first positions as nursemaids when they were themselves still children, and were allowed to continue caring for infants even after coming under suspicion of cruelty and abuse. We are left to wonder at what point their proclivities developed, and whether there were any early warning signs.

Regardless of the variety of intentions, one unifying theme stands out: the accused were all young and female, almost certainly lacking more than a rudimentary education, and perhaps sometimes simple or mentally defective. Finding domestic service to be a limiting and frustrating experience, they lashed out in a way that has left a written record. Others must have found less drastic outlets for their discontent.

When a servant of any age made an attempt on the life of their employer, the motive was usually personal. Many, particularly youngsters, were unable to live happily in their new homes and wanted to leave. Some, instead of just running away, reasoned that, if their employer were dead, they would be free to leave. This rationale underlay eleven-year-old Lily Cartwright's attempt to poison Ellen Reynolds with a liniment containing aconitine (which she found on the top shelf of a cupboard): wanting to go home to her mother, she dosed Reynolds's tea with enough of the liniment to kill her. Tried at Stafford in December 1891, the child was found guilty but released into the care of her father.[29] Fifteen years before, a thirteen-year-old Devon farm servant, William Dodd, had attempted to poison his master with a sheep-dipping powder that contained arsenic. He admitted what he had done; with a child's logic, he explained that he was tired of the man. He was under the age of intent (fourteen), but the jury were satisfied that he was aware of the consequences of his actions and that he had intended to kill the victim. Without counsel to plead for him, the court was disinclined to show Dodd much lenience, though allowance was made for his age: the judge sentenced him to six weeks' imprisonment with hard labour, to be followed by three years in a reformatory.[30]

Had William Dodd's victim actually died, he might have suffered a far worse fate, probably many years in prison; his age, though, was an insulation against the worst that the law could do. Thirty years earlier, a boy only a little older than Dodd, but over the crucial age of awareness, was sentenced to death for the murder of his employer. Samuel Kirkby, fifteen, was apprenticed to a Lincoln butcher, John Bruce, but often quarrelled with him; a consequence of this was that Kirkby was frequently beaten, and said more than once that he wished Bruce dead. One Sunday in April 1838 matters came to a head: Bruce forbade Kirkby to leave the house, presumably for his monthly day off, claiming that a lamb had died because the apprentice had neglected it. On the following Saturday, Bruce died suddenly after breakfast and other members of the family became seriously ill. They called in a surgeon who had seen two other cases of arsenic poisoning and had the sense to secure the breakfast dishes for examination. Arsenic was found in the kettle. An autopsy confirmed that the appearance of the stomach was exactly similar to that found in arsenic poisonings, although the newspaper account does not state whether any chemical tests were done. When it emerged that Kirkby had bought arsenic, ostensibly to poison rats, and that he had threatened to 'serve his master out', the case against him was complete. He was confined to the city gaol until his trial in August, when he was convicted and sentenced to death. As the government of the day had no wish to hang a fifteen year old, he was reprieved and sentenced to transportation for life.[31]

A large proportion of the servants accused of revenge poisonings were very young, teenagers for the most part, or in their twenties. This suggests that their actions were born as much of the thoughtlessness of youth as out of malice. This is not to deny that children like Samuel Kirkby were fully capable of planning and carrying out a murder; in many respects their place in the workforce meant that childhood had ended and adult life, with all its responsibilities, had begun. But it is important at least to consider that to anyone with experience of life such courses of action would have seemed senseless. Of twenty servants accused of revenge poisonings, only four, possibly six, were over the age of twenty-five; two of these were male, and their exact ages are unknown. The age structure of the servant population played a major role. Of the fifty-six servants involved, thirty-three were aged under twenty-five; only ten were definitely older, most only just older. The 1870 Education Act expanded the school system for the working classes, and children now had to attend school from the age of five to thirteen, with exemptions from the age of ten. This opened a door for many into the growing job market and led to a decrease in the number of child servants.[32] The larger number of older women in service at the end of the century tallies with the numbers of older female servants accused of poisoning crimes, three of the four cases occurring after 1875. This date also marked the last time a male servant (young William Dodd) was accused of poisoning. Thereafter, according to commentators of the day, the demand for servants was such that those who disliked their position could simply find another. Only those (like Lily Cartwright) too young to make their own way in the world, or those who had a serious grudge to satisfy, took to poisoning. The last known case occurred in

1899, when, angry at having been given notice, a sixty-year-old cook, Sarah Vyse, added arsenic to the last meal she served to her employer's family. Luckily, they all survived.[33]

After poverty, jealousy, money and retribution, mental instability caused by problems ranging from suicidal urges to postnatal psychosis provided another, less common, motive for murder. Less than a tenth of poisoning crimes can be clearly attributed to some form of emotional duress, but those for whom state of mind was at issue were in a somewhat better position than other killers, as they were unlikely to be held legally responsible for their actions. The crimes of forty-three poisoners were considered by the courts at the time to be the more or less direct consequence of some form of mental illness. This instability was variously termed 'insanity' or 'depression', and, for reasons that will become clear, more female than male poisoners were sufferers. Suicidal urges lay at the root of three-quarters of these cases, which are divisible into two types. One in five (eight cases) were failed suicide pacts between consenting adults. Nearly all the rest involved the murder or attempted murder of children by their parents (usually mothers), two thirds of whom attempted suicide at the same time. Nearly all confessed. Within the group as a whole, the only people (six in all) who did not make a confession of some kind were those who were so unbalanced mentally that they were unable to give any account of their conduct. The emotional problems of one boy who made an attempt on the life of a younger sibling were not vastly different from those of the adult poisoners in this category. One case of spousal homicide completes this group. Many men and women whom the courts deemed to be insane murdered their partners, usually in violent outbursts, but insanity was acknowledged as the sole precipitating motive in only one case of spousal poisoning. In 1908 Londoner Henry Morger poisoned his wife and then tried to cut his own throat, a fact that was taken as evidence that they had not made a suicide pact; rather, he had intended it to be a murder-suicide.[34]

These crimes stemmed from a sense of inner despair that gnawed incessantly at those involved, so that even those who did not attempt suicide felt compelled to try to expiate their crime by acknowledging their guilt. Fully 84 per cent of the poisoners in this group confessed; almost all the rest showed evidence of long-standing mental problems and – at best – a tenuous grasp on reality. It was mere chance that brought most of them to the bar: had they not failed in taking their own lives, their stories would have closed in the coroner's rather than the criminal court. To some extent, then, this is a microhistory of suicide and its causes.

The incidence and causes of suicide have been under debate by social scientists, historians and medical professionals for well over a century; earlier, the opinions of theologians and philosophers held sway. Early Christian doctrine condemned suicide as a violation of divine and natural law, and a series of secular and religious penalties were enforced. In England, suicides were denied normal funerary rites, and their corpses were often desecrated before burial; their property was also forfeited to the crown. In practice, however, coroners regularly found ways to excuse suicides and their families from these penalties, by attributing death to some other cause or by finding a verdict of lunacy. In the eighteenth century, legal penalties were relaxed as attitudes to suicide became more forgiving. Enlightenment ideals of humanitarianism, science and toler-ance introduced a philosophical justification for suicide, which was increasingly attributed to mental illness or individual pathology. If a suicide was insane, or had reacted rationally to an unendurable situation, it was illogical, even pointless, to punish him or her.[35]

The medical profession contributed little to debates about suicide until the nineteenth century, when psychiatry began to emerge as a distinct discipline. Physicians ascribed suicide to mental disease, and those who attempted it were given medical treatment, usually in asylums. But closer medical scrutiny of the problem led to the realisation that not all suicides were caused by mental illness: social factors such as poverty, alcoholism and family problems also played an influential role. At the same time, another emerging science, sociology, began to lay claim to the study of suicide, adopting a statistical approach that, in the nineteenth century, was most effectively propounded in France. This culminated in Emile Durkheim's seminal work, *Suicide*, published in 1897.[36]

One of the founders of modern sociology, Durkheim investigated the basis of social organisation and the effects of industrialisation on tradi-tional social and moral order, seeking to establish the subject as a respectable and scientific discipline capable of diagnosing social ills and recommending possible cures. He was not original in his use of suicide statistics to show social causes for an apparently individual act, but he did provide a focus for subsequent arguments about how the term 'social' should be defined. Durkheim rejected the medical notion that suicide was caused primarily by individual pathology, claiming instead that it was promoted or discouraged by the strength or weakness of the social norms in a society or group. He took as his starting point the realisation that suicide rates tend to be regular over time and show a clear correlation with factors such as religious belief, economic depression and war. Both he and his student Maurice Halbwachs believed that suicide rates had increased markedly during the nineteenth century, and sought to explain this as a feature of modern urban industrial society.[37] (It is actually impossible to determine precisely what the suicide rate was in earlier centuries.)

In his *The Causes of Suicide* (1930), Halbwachs claimed that, no matter the precipitating motive for suicide, its unique cause was an agonising feeling of solitude that was 'definitive and without remedy'. By identifying 'isolation from involvement in the nexus of community relationships' as the sole cause of suicide, Halbwachs was able to subsume all possible motives into one theory. This held that all problems stemmed from unexpected events (psychological, organic or social in nature) to which individuals were unable to adapt. The inability to adapt led to a feeling of social isolation, unbearable loneliness, and the decision to commit suicide. Such events are produced more frequently in a more complex society, where change is both common and rapid; hence, rates of suicide tend to rise as society becomes more modern.[38]

In reality, it is the state of society that determines suicide statistics, and in the second half of the twentieth century some sociologists began to recognise that official statistics can be so faulty as to be useless for analysis. In the nineteenth century it was notoriously difficult to identify all cases of suicide, since some methods (especially drowning) were easily mistaken for accidental death. Concealment was widespread, the procedures and criteria used for registering suicides were not applied systematically throughout the country, and varying levels of efficiency at all stages of the process led to random inaccuracies. For historians, this is not an insurmountable problem: if the limitations of the official figures are recognised and accepted, marked trends, and differences in scale or relationships in the relative incidence of suicide, can be legitimately identified.[39] In so doing one tends to find, as do modern clinicians, that a blending of pathological and quantifiable social factors is required to explain suicide.

The historical study of suicide needs a detailed look at manageable evidence. This task has been ably begun for Victorian and Edwardian England, and several reliable conclusions have been established: suicide was not promoted by urbanisation; and it was less common among women than men, and more common among old men than among young ones.[40] Methods of suicide varied in popularity according to region and time period, as well as social class and gender. Men usually hanged themselves or cut their own throats, while young women, particularly those in the south, chose drowning. The use of poison was more common among women than men (by about two to one); at mid century it was found more frequently in London than elsewhere. It was also more common in cities and industrialised areas than in the countryside. By the end of the Edwardian era the proportion of male suicides in England and Wales who used poison had risen from 7 per cent in 1861 to 14 per cent; the proportion who hanged themselves declined in the same period from 48 to 29 per cent. In most neighbourhoods, suicide among the upper and professional classes was always considerably underregistered. And, as is still the case today, male suicides outnumbered their female counterparts by about three to one.[41]

In 1860s London the actual triggers for suicidal behaviour were similar for both sexes. Drink and its accompanying financial and family troubles predominated, apparently affecting three-quarters of both the men and women involved; other important factors included illness and mental disorder. Economic and emotional triggers were far less significant. In contrast, in rural Sussex most suicides tended to be preceded by pain or sickness and the depression associated with them; alcohol was rarely involved. The methods used were those associated with the countryside: water, knives and guns. Poisoning was rare, perhaps because country work did not by then involve the constant use of poisons, so people lacked both the knowledge of how they worked and the access to them that city dwellers had (via shops).[42] By 1911, in both wealthy and poorer districts, alcohol and economic distress were rarely the cause of suicide;

the reasons lay rather in some real or imagined threat to comfort or self-esteem, prompted by dread of disease, insanity or professional inadequacy.

These findings echo features found in the cases of those emotionally unstable poisoners who were brought before the assize courts, particularly the large number (70 per cent) detected in urban centres like London and Manchester or towns like Bury, Bath, Leeds and Oldham. But it is impossible to make a direct comparison: there is a clear difference in intent between suicide and attempted murder-suicide, the latter being the crime of which most mentally unstable poisoners were guilty. To look at the additional factors operating in the poisoning cases, the obvious place to begin is with the gender differential: women were about three times less likely to commit suicide than men, but three quarters of the suicidal poisoners were female.

The answer to why this should be so rests largely in the identity of the victims: of the thirty-one female poisoners, all but two killed or tried to kill one or more of her own offspring. In one unusual case, the victims had actually reached adulthood, but all the rest were babies or young children. This is in keeping with the statistics of child murder, where most of the perpetrators were mothers rather than fathers. Only three fathers attempted suicide after first killing one of their children, for motives that mirrored those of the women: the worry and despair caused by financial difficulties. Female suicides were more likely than males to choose poison, but another reason for the disproportionate number of maternal killers was the fact that women were at an economic disadvantage in comparison to men; money troubles usually hit them much harder. It is no coincidence that half of the women involved were single mothers or had been abandoned by their husbands. But both the women and men who experienced emotional turmoil as a result of sudden or grinding poverty killed their children from one misguided belief: it was better for them to be dead than to face penury and slow starvation. Only the attempt at suicide separated them from people like Rebecca Smith. In a few examples where family units had broken down, women who faced being permanently parted from a child they loved killed the child and attempted suicide, allowing an element of vengeance to creep into a psyche already unbalanced by misery. Only one mother (none of the men) was a known alcoholic, but she too suffered the belief that the world was a bad place from which her children should be liberated.

In August 1844 Eliza Joyce became the last woman to be executed in England for a murder to which she had pleaded guilty. An alcoholic aged thirty-one, she had been married for about four years to William Joyce, a prosperous gardener in Boston, Lincolnshire, who had two children by his first marriage. His eighteen-month-old daughter died in October 1841, when Eliza was heavily pregnant with another girl, who was born in January 1842 and lived only three weeks. By the end of that year the third child was also dead, in clearly suspicious circumstances. Fifteen-year-old William, who had been ill for some time, went into a sudden decline in September 1842. His father realised the cause when, in a chance encounter, a local chemist told him that he had sold arsenic to Eliza. Joyce informed a doctor of his suspicion that the boy had been poisoned, and analysis of a sample of vomit showed the presence of arsenic. Young William recovered enough to state that he had become violently ill after taking some medicine given him by his stepmother, but died in December. Eliza Joyce was then charged with murder, but a clerical error led to the postponement of her trial. When she did eventually appear in the dock, in July 1843, the charge had been reduced to attempted murder; she was acquitted after claiming that she had accidentally allowed arsenic to get on to the spoon she had used to give William his medicine.

William Joyce refused to have anything to do with his wife, whom he believed guilty, and Eliza went to live in the local workhouse. Evidently tormented by guilt, in June 1844 she confessed to the work-house manager that she had poisoned all three of the children. She claimed to have killed the two girls with laudanum, though a doctor had certified their deaths as due to convulsions. Asked why she had done it, she replied that she did not know, except that it seemed 'a troublesome thing to bring a family of children into the troublesome world'. There was no evidence that what she said was true: she was convicted solely on the strength of her confession.[43]

No medical evidence as to her state of mind appears to have been sought, but the modern reader will surely recognise that Eliza Joyce was not a typical calculating child killer. She almost certainly suffered from some form of mental illness, perhaps depression exacerbated by alcoholism, but she ended her days on the gallows rather than in an asylum because she did not obviously appear insane. Two factors singled her out in the eyes of the legal authorities: she did not attempt suicide, and she was not living in a state of deprivation. This was in stark contrast to three other cases that occurred at about the same time. The perpetrators (James Brain, Ann Rothwell and Hannah Leath) had fallen on hard times and were obviously very poor; and all three confessed to murder. Brain and Rothwell were single parents who showed signs of insanity, not the least being the fact that they had attempted suicide after poisoning their children. Leath had the sympathy of both judge and jury at her trial at the Old Bailey: the judge noted with deep regret that he did not have the authority to commute her death sentence immediately.[44]

Only a few parents poisoned their children for reasons to do with dire poverty, not greed, and each case shows a correlation with a period of economic distress. The cause of the melancholy that struck at these individuals was clearly social. There was, however, another type of depression for which the origin was in little doubt. It was a form of mental illness that only women endured: postnatal depression. Known as puerperal insanity, it was one of the few clearly recognised entities in nineteenth-century psychiatry. The entry of this condition into obstetric textbooks was well defined: it was seldom mentioned in the eighteenth century, first appearing as a concern in childbirth in the 1820s and 1830s. By the middle of the century doctors believed it to be 'a common cause of a form of insanity which was usually manic, often severe and occasionally fatal'.[45] Patients who suffered from what was thought to be an emotional imbalance attempted acts of violence or suicide, and an average of about 7.5 per cent of all female admissions to lunatic asylums were due to puerperal causes, usually mania rather than melancholia. It seems that manic cases exceeded melancholic ones by a ratio of about four to one, even if allowance is made for cases that may have been due to delirium caused by infection, and for those that were the subject of erroneous diagnosis. The predominant form today is postnatal depression, with violent mania occurring only very rarely.[46] Recent estimates note that 'baby blues' set in after eight out of every ten births, but depression in only 10 per cent. The incidence of puerperal psychosis (including delusions and rejection of the baby) is one in 200, while the most extreme cases of infanticide, suicide or murder (of other children, husband or parent) happen once in every 125,000 births. Symptoms do not necessarily manifest themselves immediately after birth, but may set in after a few weeks or months.[47]

By the middle of the nineteenth century, doctors had become familiar with the possibility that suicidal and homicidal patients may have been suffering from some form of mental illness. Although all were deemed to be 'insane', an important factor in diagnosis was the existence of a prior or family history of mental disease, or recent confinement. Among the poisoners, the most common problem was depression, often of puerperal origin. Half the women involved were found to have murdered their infants, and/or toddlers (in one case, husband), while suffering from the effects of postnatal depression. The earliest example dates from 1853, with a steep rise in numbers after the 1860s, reflecting the increased interest and influence of the medical profession. A typical later case was that of Lancashire housewife Alice Lucas, who poisoned two of her children with carbolic acid. In early 1909 she had three children ill with measles and gave birth to a new baby, John, on 8 January. By the end of the month her daughter Ellen had pneumonia and John was ill; Alice had to nurse them around the clock, and began to suffer from insomnia. In mid February she told her husband that she was sure she was suffering from typhoid fever. On the following day her slim grasp on sanity snapped and she poisoned John and Ellen before taking carbolic acid herself. She was saved when her husband gave her salt and water to induce vomiting, but John died the next day and Ellen three weeks later. Alice Lucas's physician, Thomas Sharples, who had often told her to get some help with the children, was called in and found her repeatedly crying 'I have done wrong'. In his opinion, the lack of sleep, anxiety about the sick children and the fatigue of nursing had brought on an acute attack of melancholia, at which time she was insane and not responsible for her actions. The trial jury accepted his opinion and she was committed to an asylum.[48]

Among middle-class married women, child poisonings were almost always due to depression following childbirth, and juries usually found verdicts of not guilty by reason of insanity.[49] Sometimes it became evident that a woman was suffering from more than post-natal depression, as when Catherine Groocock, the wife of a Leeds shopkeeper, swallowed a packet of vermin killer and gave her seventeen-month-old daughter another. Insanity ran in her family. Her sister had died 'raving mad' the year before; her father and another sister suffered from depression; and she herself had long battled with suicidal depression compounded by religious mania. Groocock, who was thirty-two, was committed to an asylum after her trial in August 1872.[50] Insanity could strike at any age. Five years later, the Dorset shepherd's wife Lucy Tizzard was fifty when she attempted to poison her two adult daughters with arsenic, fearing that she was going blind and believing it would be 'better for them to be in heaven'. It was thought that her mind had been affected by chloroform administered during several unspecified operations, and magistrates ordered her to be taken directly to an asylum, as she was mentally unfit to stand trial.[51]

Of the cases under consideration here, only one occurred prior to 1840. There are a number of possible reasons for this. We know that it was not uncommon for the authorities to recognise that some murders were the result of insanity or some form of mental problem most easily labelled as insanity. Furthermore, urbanisation did not necessarily lead to increased levels of suicide. However, changes in the structure of society (including migration), the harsh 1840s, the introduction of the workhouse in the 1830s and the difficulties faced by single mothers may all have combined to place some people in a vulnerable position that might once have been easier to cope with. By far the most important factor, however, appears to have been the changing standards of the medical profession in diagnosing mental illness and suggesting methods for treating those who suffered from it. Juries had always been willing to give some defendants the benefit of the doubt; now they had a medical reason for doing so.

A final category in poisoning crimes is that of intended double suicides where one partner survived to face trial for murder. Of eight cases, two occurred in the 1860s, one in 1887 and the rest after 1900, a pattern that fits with the established fact that suicide by poison had become far more common at the end of the century. Despite the restrictions of the 1868 Pharmacy Act, which limited the sale of poisons to doctors, pharmacists and registered druggists, the sheer number of these people in business meant that a would-be suicide had only to visit two or three shops to procure a fatal dose of almost any poison. The testimony given by failed suicides confirms that they were able to purchase small amounts of poison from several different chemists without having to travel very far, leaving no time for a cooling-down period in which to decide against death. Those who did not already have poison at home (oxalic acid was used in cleaning, carbolic acid for disinfection) had to be plausible enough to allay the suspicions of the chemists they approached. It was common for vendors to refuse to sell poison, or even to call a policeman, if they suspected that suicide was intended. This probably explains why so few would-be suicides survived: they were among the minority who, by chance or accident, did not swallow enough poison to kill themselves outright, and were then found and taken to hospital. (Hospitals, of course, were more common in towns and cities than in the country.) That more people seem to have survived after the 1880s was partly due to the tighter controls placed on the sale of arsenic and strychnine; to avoid suspicion, suicides had to choose other, less reliable poisons. Favourites were laudanum and oxalic acid, both readily available and cheap, but they did not necessarily complete the job if the victim was found in time. They also required larger doses. Moreover, while the sentence for attempted suicide was reduced to two years' imprisonment in 1882, the abetting of suicide was made punishable by life in prison. Few cases were brought to court except suicide pacts.[52]

In the exploration of the motives that drove poisoners to their crimes, the poison actually chosen is of secondary importance. The cases that ended in partial failure provide a record of what led friends and partners to suicide. In the eight cases in which the decision to die was clearly a mutual one, fear of the future lay at the heart of the problem, and the decision to die together was prompted by the emotional and sexual ties between the two individuals. Among married couples (two cases, both middle-aged) the decision was a practical one: it did not seem sensible to remain alive in the face of poverty, illness and the separation these might entail. For younger couples (all, interestingly, unmarried), a seeming inability to attain personal goals incited suicide pacts. Unemployment and its associated financial problems, unexpected pregnancy, and lack of freedom to marry (because of an existing marriage or family disapproval) were all triggers for suicide attempts. In only one case were the two individuals of the same gender, but they too shared similar feelings of powerlessness and hopelessness. In 1887 the close friends John Allcock and John Jessop found themselves in distressing circumstances. Both had contracted venereal disease and were ashamed of the fact, both were out of work, and both had experienced family difficulties; Allcock had become homeless. The survivor explained their thinking:

> We both got ourselves into disgrace, and we did not know what to do with ourselves. Allcock proposed doing away with himself somehow. He said to me, shan't you die with me? I said I am not at all particular. Allcock pulled a bottle out of his pocket with laudanum, and said this would do it, if we could only get some more.[53]

Although it was Allcock who decided upon suicide, his friend Jessop, fearing his own inadequacies, could not find a reason to dissuade him, or indeed not to join him; he survived only because he drank less of the laudanum.

The sad personal stories of these suicidal individuals offer a counterpart to the traditional image of the poisoner: the use of poison did not always indicate malicious intent and careful planning. Sometimes it could become a weapon that, in the hands of vulnerable people – the disappointed, depressed or mentally ill – was turned to most devastating effect against themselves. The sufferings of those who died – children, husbands and lovers – were short in relation to the lifetime of regret that the survivors faced.

7

Inquests Duly Held

This deponent sayeth that her late husband Peter Davies was on the third day of this instant taken violently ill, of frequent and uncommon purgings and vomitings. That upon continuing so for some short time, he said that doubtless that rogue Luke Mapp had poisoned him.

Mary Davies, 1771 [1]

Deliberate poisoning has long had a justifiable reputation as the ultimate secret crime, since its true nature is easily overlooked or misinterpreted. Before the advent of dependable investigative procedures and controls on the disposal of dead bodies, the successful detection of such offences depended primarily upon the vigilance of those members of the community who knew or had contact with the victim. Family and friends, lodgers, servants and neighbours, as well as doctors and police officers, had a role to play. Unprompted confessions were relatively rare, so the first step in the process was the most crucial: someone who knew the deceased had to suspect that death might not have occurred entirely naturally, and so inform the appropriate local authorities. Only then could an investigation begin, usually with a coroner's inquest, often held concurrently with or prior to investigations carried out under the auspices of local magistrates; both could result in the committal of an individual for trial. For most, or perhaps all, of the period before modern times the initial phase was at best haphazard: in 1876 an anonymous correspondent to the *Times* noted that 'except in cases of murder and manslaughter and being accessory before the fact, the coroner is not bound to take any depositions at all, and, as a matter of fact, often does not take any ...' [2] There was evidently an element of chance in this crucially important first stage of investigation, as coroners had to adopt some system for identifying the potentially criminal cases from among the hundreds that they heard.

The same correspondent, who seems to have been a coroner, went on to explain that, in cases of death from accident or disease, he sometimes jotted down a few notes for his own guidance in addressing the jury. For cases that at first seemed suspicious, he started off taking very careful notes of witness depositions, but if it began to appear that no crime had been committed he stopped doing so. Moreover, when he held a serious inquiry, he was forced to hire a lawyer's clerk to write down the evidence, so that he was free to devote his full attention to the proceedings. This gives us a good deal of information about how coroners went about their task. First, it suggests that they opened inquests with some prior notion about whether there might have been criminal involvement in a death. Such ideas were most likely formed at the time the coroner was notified of the death, as many sought reasons for not holding an inquest at all. The full weight of conducting inquests, examining witnesses and writing down their evidence fell mainly upon the coroner alone.[3] Inquest jurors were free to ask questions but, like a judge, the coroner summed up the evidence before the jury retired (often going into a huddle in a corner of the room) to consider their verdict. Usually held in meeting halls or public houses, inquests could become raucous public affairs, unlike the more staid proceedings that magistrates conducted. For all its faults, however, the inquest stood as a bastion in the nation's system of medico-legal investigation.

The inquest's importance in detecting secret homicides was clear: if no doubts were raised at the time of death, or no action taken, a murderer could reasonably hope to escape justice. That so many serial poisoners operated with impunity for years before at last coming under suspicion suggests that many more managed to conceal their criminal activities completely. The continuing immediacy of this problem was brought home to the British public by the media furore surrounding the Cheshire GP and serial killer Harold Shipman, convicted in January 2000 of fifteen murders. If from the first a death is assumed to be natural, there will be no perceived need for an investigation until that supposition is abandoned. And even then, although the police can investigate complaints made long after the fact, and corpses can be exhumed and subjected to chemical tests, the evidential trail may have grown cold: it has proved impossible to say for certain how many people Shipman killed.[4] Added to this, earlier examples show that, after the passage of many years, it becomes difficult to make a case even against those who have actually confessed.[5] It has always been important to act while the evidence is fresh.

The hundreds of poisoning cases that were investigated offer a detailed picture of the ways in which such a secret crime could be revealed, showing that, regardless of how suspicion was first raised or by whom, the actions taken thereafter tended to be consistent in structure, if not proficiency. Crucially, few victims of poison (with the exception of suicides) died in isolation; even those who lived or worked alone with their murderer were likely to be surrounded by other people during their illness and at the time of death. Though often unaware of the later importance of their observations, these people were potential witnesses, well placed to note symptoms and observe the actions of a possible murderer. Ideally, of course, at least one was a qualified medical practitioner, but it did not always require a formal education to spot the external signs associated with unnatural death, or to recognise some typical symptoms of poisoning. After death, those who washed and laid out a body for burial had the opportunity to view the corpse and note anything unusual. If at this point death was still thought to be 'natural' – and people of the time were prepared to accept causes of death that the modern reader would find surprising – local gossip could quickly inflame suspicions: odd behaviour, strange coincidences and casual remarks did not go unnoticed. Neighbourhood suspicions (and, possibly, the opportunity to satisfy old grudges) account for many poisoning accusations later shown to be false. If, however, a crime had in fact been committed, it was vital that such doubts were raised, the earlier the better, even if in response to mere rumour: the exposure of poisoning crimes hinged upon questioning how and why a person had died. In a process that was continually refined, those at the forefront of an investigation were primarily local coroners and doctors, acting on information supplied by friends of the deceased and in conjunction with a chemical analyst.[6] On occasion, though, the investigative process was begun before a death had occurred, sometimes inspired by the victim himself.

Apart from the mineral acids (which could destroy the throat) and a large dose of prussic acid (which caused death within minutes), none of the poisons commonly used for homicidal purposes acted quickly enough to prevent a victim from speaking or thinking clearly in the first moments after poisoning. Even strychnine, which could kill an adult within half an hour, left the mind clear until the point of death. Despite the swift onset of excruciating spasms, the Welsh shopkeeper William Mabbott was able to explain exactly what had happened to him and who had been responsible; the killer, his business rival William Samuel, was quickly arrested. Even young children could describe the circumstances that had led to their suffering, as Kate Horton did after her father gave her a cupful of blue-coloured vermin killer.[7] Victims of arsenic poisoning, who lingered for hours or days before dying, were even better placed to point a finger of suspicion, though their minds became increasingly clouded as death approached. But many victims failed to recognise that an unnatural fate had befallen them, or, if they did, were unable or unwilling to assume a murderous intent. The Samuel and Horton cases were atypical in that the poisoners made no effort to conceal their actions from the victims. Most people who fell ill shortly after eating or drinking inferred a direct association, and some suspected that they had somehow been poisoned. But to link their symptoms with deliberate poisoning was by no means an obvious assumption. Given that most poisonings were domestic affairs, to do so meant presuming that someone with whom they shared a close relationship desired their death. In the absence of explicit proof to the contrary, to most it would have seemed more likely that they had contracted some natural ailment. But there were also victims who, perhaps made wary by experience or expectation, did not hesitate to make a direct accusation against an alleged poisoner, usually someone whom they already had cause to mistrust.

There would otherwise have been little reason for the Herefordshire farmer Peter Davies to suspect that his son-in-law, Luke Mapp, had poisoned his breakfast. That the food was contaminated was clear: 'it had an uncommon taste and was very gritty'; the trial indictment named the poison as white arsenic. In early December 1771 the entire family, with the possible exception of Mapp (the depositions are unclear on this point), fell ill after eating flour and milk mixed in hollowed out pieces of bread. Only Davies, who had eaten the most, died, claiming repeatedly before his death that Mapp was to blame. He swore to Zacheus Wyke, a surgeon, that he had no poison in the house, and Wyke assumed it was not a suicide because Davies had drunk oil in an effort to bring up the poisoned food. There was no evidence against Mapp apart from the fact that he had 'breaded the dishes', or hollowed the chunks of bread used as bowls; the victim's wife had mixed the flour and milk. Although Davies's death was believed to be a case of murder, Mapp was given bail, an indication that he was thought unlikely to flee (and was thus probably innocent). It is unsurprising that he was acquitted.[8]

Mapp may well have been guilty of murder, but the lack of any systematic investigation of Davies's death ensured that no one could be successfully prosecuted for it. Although an inquest was held four days after death and an autopsy performed, the coroner questioned only Wyke, Davies's widow and daughter, and another woman who was probably a neighbour. Magistrates examined the same four witnesses a few days later. The brief trial record made by the clerk of assize shows that a fifth witness, a woman, was called, but it is most likely that she was asked to relate what she knew of the family's circumstances, or that she too had heard the accusations made against Luke Mapp. It is possible that she knew something about the arsenic; but, unless she had bought or sold it herself, this seems doubtful. In fact, there is no evidence to show that any effort was made to discover where the arsenic had come from or in what part of the breakfast it had been placed. Wyke fed some of the suspect flour and milk to a dog, which was unaffected, but he had no way of knowing whether this sample was the same as what Davies had actually eaten. The bread was not tested: given that the family lived on a farm, it may have been made with flour accidentally con- taminated by arsenic. Nor did Wyke know what exactly Mapp had eaten, if anything. If Davies's daughter had not also become sick, Wyke would have supposed his illness was due to 'some cold or surfeit', despite the dying man's assertions to the contrary. Finally, nothing gritty was found in the stomach. The entire affair was clouded by lack of information, a situation typically found at the outset of suspected poisonings and one that could only be relieved by thorough investigation. In this case, the fact that a culprit was identified and put on trial seems to have been due solely to Davies's persistence and the willingness of local authorities to act posthumously on his suspicion; they had nothing else to go on.

Had it not been for his allegation, the inquest jury might well have reached a verdict of 'murder by person or persons unknown', or 'died by the visitation of God'. Neither was unusual in the days preceding the increasingly rigid investigative standards introduced during the course of the nineteenth century.

The investigative norms that pertained during the eighteenth century and much of the nineteenth were highly dependent upon local conditions, particularly the capabilities, zeal and financial wherewithal of coroners, magistrates and police. Any history of the investigation of sudden or suspicious deaths must, therefore, begin with the coroner's system, the earliest of these offices to be established in England.[9] The first county coroners were elected in 1194, and thereafter an ever-increasing number of boroughs (towns that governed themselves) and liberties (areas that possessed, usually by royal grant, a degree of freedom from royal officials and laws) obtained the right to elect coroners of their own.[10] Medieval coroners were usually large landowners, and had to own property within their jurisdiction. This ensured not only that the coroner would have time to attend to his duties, and would appear quickly when summoned, but also that his assets could be confiscated if he made off with money due to the crown. This was of central importance, since the medieval coroner's numerous functions and obligations were all of potential pecuniary interest to the monarch.[11]

The most important and frequent of these duties was to hold inquests upon all who died unexpectedly, from other than natural causes, in prison, or in circumstances which appeared or were reported to be suspicious.[12] When such a body was found, the coroner was supposed to be sent for by the first person to find it; if it had been buried before he arrived, it had to be exhumed. The local sheriff (the king's representative) or bailiff (sheriff's agent) assembled a jury of twelve to sixteen men (at times more) drawn from the township in which the body had been found, and from three adjoining communities. The jurors were expected to acquaint themselves with the situation before the inquest, at which they viewed the naked body with the coroner, examining it for any relevant external signs, such as bruises, cuts or wounds. It was their job to identify the deceased, and to determine the time, place, cause and manner of death. There were four options: natural death,

homicide, accident and suicide, of which only the first was not subject
to financial considerations. Until 1483 a suspected felon's possessions
were forfeit to the crown (forfeiture of the 'goods and chattels' of suicides
continued until 1870), and it was the coroner who ensured that, in cases
of homicide and suicide, these were correctly valued and the monies
paid. If death was accidental, a deodand (god-gift) had to be assessed
and collected. This stemmed from the ancient idea that an object that
had caused death had sinned, and that the sin could be expiated if the
object, or its equivalent value, was given to the church. From the end
of the twelfth century, however, most deodands went to the crown, a
practice that persisted until finally abolished in August 1846 as 'unrea-
sonable and inconvenient'.[13] Thus, for centuries following the creation
of his office, the coroner's concern for the monarch's fiscal rights was
at least as important as the exhaustive investigation of sudden or unnatural deaths. This circumstance was compounded by an even greater
hindrance.

The most serious defect in this early system was the fact that the office
bore no remuneration, a situation that led to widespread corruption:
many coroners became embezzlers, or would hold inquests only if paid
a bribe. Consequently, in 1487 an Act was passed permitting the coroner
to collect a fee of one mark (13s.) for each inquest into a homicide
(murder or manslaughter), plus 4d. from the goods of the guilty man.
In practice, the money came entirely from the assets of the accused, or
from the town if the suspect fled or lacked possessions. This provided
little incentive for enquiries into accidents (deliberate suicide was self-
murder), a fact recognised in 1509 when any coroner who failed to hold
an inquest or demanded a fee in cases of misadventure became liable
to a fine of 40s. This law included a clause that, centuries later, was to
have what one commentator has termed 'the most disastrous consequences': it gave local justices of the peace administrative (and hence
financial) power over coroners.[14] And despite this early attempt at
reform, the system remained ineffectual and corrupt: in 1723 an early
English textbook on medical jurisprudence claimed that the office of
coroner had sunk into disrepute, and too often into the hands of the
low and indigent; gentlemen avoided the job.[15]

It was not until 1751 that a serious effort was made to remedy the
worst of these problems: a new law allowed the coroner a fee of £1 for

each inquest held plus 9d. for each mile travelled in the course of his
duties. The old fee of 13s. 4d. was still to be paid in cases of homicide.
Where once there had been no mechanism to allow the removal of a
coroner from office (for most it was a lifetime quasi-sinecure), at last it
became possible to eject those found guilty of extortion, misdemeanour
or neglect of duty. These changes certainly offered greater encouragement to intelligent and honest men willing to take up the burden, but
coroners did not become salaried officials until 1860. Moreover, the only
prerequisite that candidates had to satisfy was ownership of property
within the district, a regulation that existed until the Coroner's Amendment Act of 1926. It was this law that finally introduced one of the
features of office now taken for granted, by stipulating that coroners
must have either a legal or a medical qualification. There had formerly
been no educational standard, with the result that the aptitude and
relevant training of coroners varied enormously between districts.

Studies of the historical development of forensic medicine make much
of the fact that the first medically qualified coroner, Thomas Wakley
(1795–1862) was not elected until 1839. Better known as the founder of
the *Lancet*, he used the journal as a platform from which to lobby for
reform, regularly publishing the details of cases in which coroners who
lacked medical training had failed to recognise the importance of certain
evidence. Based in west Middlesex, Wakley was a key figure in a many-
sided campaign to promote the role of scientific and medical expertise
in the modern state,[16] but he was not actually the first coroner to hold
a medical qualification. Although they may well have been unique, that
honour seems to belong to the county coroners of Wiltshire: each man
who held office during the second half of the eighteenth century is
described as a surgeon or surgeon-apothecary.[17] But in 1830 a survey
conducted by the *Lancet* revealed that not a single coroner had medical
training. The campaign for reform soon bore fruit, however, as by 1839
there were twenty-five coroners who did. At the end of the century the
number had risen to about fifty, 15 per cent of the 330 then serving in
England and Wales. Throughout the nineteenth century, however, most
coroners were solicitors, as they are today.[18]

There is little doubt that the slow reform of the coroner's office delayed
the development of medico-legal investigative procedures in Britain,
thus allowing an unknown number of murderers to escape detection.

Whether or not the coroner had any medical training was, however, probably the least of the flaws inherent in the system. Of far more importance was the frequent lack of medical testimony or a proper medical examination, something which threatened the functioning of the entire practice.[19] Although a basic lack of interest in or understanding of the advantages of medical evidence were real problems, the root of the trouble lay firmly in the financial structure that underlay the inquest process.

From 24 June 1752 provision was made for the payment to county coroners (borough coroners were excluded until 1836) of the expenses they incurred for all inquests 'duly held', as well as for reimbursement of their travel costs (one way only). Local justices of the peace retained the financial power over coroners first granted to them during the sixteenth century, as payment of the fees was dependent on their approval. This approval became notoriously difficult to gain as justices sought to reduce levels of expenditure: the fees were to be paid from the county rates, levied since 1738 and earmarked (much like today's council tax) for many different and competing needs. The 'disastrous consequences' to the development of forensic medicine as a learned science in England – it lagged behind advances made on the Continent until well into the twentieth century – was partially due to the misguided zeal for economy exhibited by the justices.[20] Of more central importance was the fact that English common law procedure offered little scope for the formal participation of dispassionate experts in criminal trials, unlike the continental system which derived from Roman and canon law.[21] In England, however, the inquest lay at the heart of the process of uncovering secret poisoning, and it is clear that, where this was suspected, coroners regularly sought the opinions of 'experts' from at least the late eighteenth century. The financial control that JPs held presented a potential impediment to that process.

Justices of the peace received their title in 1361 and, despite being unpaid and part-time, rapidly became the most important officers of the law in England. Drawn mainly from the landed gentry, there were about twenty active justices in each county at any one time, each capable of wielding considerable power. By the Elizabethan era a single JP acting on his own could arrest, examine and imprison suspected felons; two JPs together could fix the poor rate, supervise the repair of roads and bridges, set and receive bail payments, and decide on paternity in cases of bastardy. At quarter sessions, established in 1363 and so called because they were held four times a year, JPs sat as judges in criminal trials and fixed punishments for those found guilty.[22] Local justices acquired so many administrative duties that they have been nicknamed the 'Tudor Maids-of-All-Work', and they became even more powerful in local government after the Restoration of Charles II in 1660. Their numbers increased steadily, to well over five thousand by the 1830s, of whom perhaps half were active. They were finally deprived of most of their decision-making functions in 1889, when county councils were created, and thereafter settled into the purely legal role that they maintain to this day.

In keeping with the provisions of the Act that granted them payment for their work, it became the practice of county coroners to submit their accounts to the local JPs at quarter sessions; if the bills were not large they were submitted perhaps once or twice each year. The law clearly stated, however, that the justices had to reimburse coroners only for those inquests 'duly held': it was left to the JPs themselves to decide how to interpret this term. In practice, most chose to pay only for those cases in which death had obviously been violent. Not only did justices refuse to pay for inquests they did not deem necessary, frequently leaving coroners and witnesses out of pocket, but some attempted to prevent the notification of sudden deaths to the coroner – a quiet word to the local constables and parish officers was all that was needed. This made coroners understandably reluctant to incur costs that might not be repaid. Moreover, those who took the trouble to call in a medical man could not guarantee him proper payment, making doctors equally cautious.

The obstruction of coroners by JPs at quarter sessions was primarily a feature of the first half of the nineteenth century, though the first clear evidence of it dates from 1791. When a coroner in Norfolk applied to the High Court against the local justices' refusal to pay for inquests held on drowned persons, the judges' remarks upheld the justices' view that inquests should be held only when marks of violence were visible on a corpse. In 1809 an even stronger blow was struck against coroners when the Kent justices refused to pay for an inquest and were again upheld by the High Court. The Lord Chief Justice himself gave it as his opinion that the Act of 1751 granted JPs the absolute right to determine

which inquests had been 'duly held', and no court could interfere with
their decision. There then followed a series of humiliations for coroners
around the country, who were hindered at every turn. They were
dependent upon information passed to them by the community. Letters
from members of the public (often anonymous) and doctors were
important sources, but they also relied heavily on local officials whose
job it was to deal with the disposal of dead bodies – the police and
parish officers. But by 1851 most quarter sessions had decided that
coroners should be informed of sudden deaths in certain cases only,
and, despite inflation, refused to allow them an increase in travel rates.
This antipathy to coroners on the part of local justices may to some
extent be attributed to resentment. Despite the fact that coroners had
had the power to commit suspected felons for trial long before the office
of JP was founded, the justices still saw that role as interference with
their own courts. Regardless of motive, the dire consequences of such
policies did not go unremarked. The Registrar General's first annual
report, published in 1838, noted that the customary lack of medical
involvement in inquests made poisoning crimes difficult to detect.
Newspapers claimed that the incidence of secret poisoning was highest in those counties where the justices most obstructed coroners,
Devon, Norfolk and Staffordshire, and regular media reports of actual
or suspected poisonings led to rising public hysteria.[23]

Coroners continued to fight a losing battle against the justices throughout the 1850s, resulting in a considerable fall in the number of inquests
held in England and Wales (in some counties by as much as 50 per cent)
– despite an increase in the national death rate. The government was
finally forced into action by intense press coverage of the frequent and
often horrifying deaths of children who had been entered in burial
clubs, and of poisoning crimes. Following the case of William Palmer,
the Staffordshire surgeon hanged in 1856 for the last in a series of up to
eleven poisoning murders, public outrage achieved what the Coroners'
Society, founded in 1846, had been unable to do. In 1859 a royal commission looking into the costs of prosecutions condemned the
interference of JPs and recommended that coroners become salaried
officials. This suggestion became reality with the County Coroners Act
of 1860. Coroners were largely freed of the control previously wielded
by JPs,[24] and the number of inquests held rose immediately. Also in

1860, a parliamentary select committee on coroners stated that inquests should be held in every case of sudden or violent death, and where there was reasonable suspicion of criminal involvement in an apparently natural death. This proposal became an important foundation of the Coroner's Act of 1887, establishing much of the authority and autonomy that modern coroners possess. The office underwent its next metamorphosis in 1888, when the Local Government Act abolished the election of coroners, in favour of lifetime appointment by city or county councils.[25] Although not yet wholly free to act as they saw fit, it was from this date that coroners gained markedly wider powers to investigate cases of unnatural death.

It was one matter for coroners to hold – in theory if not always in practice – the power to launch a death investigation, but another entirely for them to act upon it: they were barred from initiating their own enquiries. The inquest process could begin only after a coroner had received information passed on by members of the community.[26] During the medieval period the person who found the body (the 'first finder') was required to attract the attention of anyone nearby ('raise the hue'). A message was then sent to the coroner, while the town was held legally responsible for guarding the corpse until his arrival. From the reign of Henry VIII, it became usual for deaths to be reported by the parish clerk or overseer. Under the Poor Law of 1536 overseers had the right to order the use of parish funds to pay for coffins for the dead, a financial concern that could lead to a local enquiry that might ultimately involve the coroner. By the late sixteenth century it was becoming common for parish officers to form a decision as to cause of death by relying on information gathered by the searchers they sent to view the body. These were normally impoverished old women paid a pittance by the parish carefully to 'search' a body, originally for signs of plague, later to report all causes of death. Since the searchers relied on what they could see and what they were told by people nearby, it is highly likely that they misreported causes of death as often as they got them right. Not only did the usual assumptions about visible signs of injury hold sway, so too did bribery and simple ignorance. By 1833 the searchers' role in reporting causes of death had largely become obsolete, but they were clearly still active in some, mainly rural, parts of the country.[27]

The activities of the searchers anticipated the similar duty of the registrars of births and deaths, who finally replaced them in the 1830s. This was a turning point in the history of death management and death investigation in England and Wales, since provision was made for the formal and universal registration of death. The Births and Deaths Registration Act of 1836 called for far more systematic record keeping than had the parish-centred registers of baptisms, marriages and burials maintained since 1538. It now became unlikely that a person's death would escape official registration, since disposal of a body, previously unregulated, was prohibited without a registrar's certificate or a coroner's burial order. But every new system has loopholes. The law was optional and not comprehensive, as it applied only to those who died as baptised members of the Church of England – infants who had not been baptised and persons of other faiths were excluded. It was administered by a network of district and local registrars, who were required to obtain a death certificate from a medical practitioner – but nothing stipulated that this must be a doctor or, if he was a doctor, that he had to have direct knowledge of the deceased's final illness. In practice registrars accepted death certificates, often no more than scrawled scraps of paper, from chemists, local healers and midwives, as well as from doctors called in only after death had occurred. Many were willing to register deaths without any certificate at all: in the late 1850s over 10 per cent of registered deaths were uncertified. Local registrars should have reported such deaths to the coroner, but many were unaware of this duty, which was in any case not enforceable as the law then stood. This allowed serial poisoners to provide for the disposal of their victims quite legally, a fact noted after the trials of, among others, Mary Ann Cotton and Ellen Heesom in the 1870s. In 1874 the law was changed slightly, restricting the issuing of death certificates to 'registered' medical practitioners – those who met the standards set by the General Medical Council, since 1858 the arbiter of medical practice in the United Kingdom. These practitioners were legally required to issue a death certificate for anyone whom they had attended shortly before death; a rider added in 1885 stated that registrars were to inform the coroner of any death not so certified. But local registrars continued to apply their own haphazard standards, so that by the turn of the twentieth century there were still ten thousand registered but uncertified deaths in England

and Wales. It was not until 1926, a year already noted as crucial in the evolution of the modern system of death management, that it became illegal for a death to be registered without a doctor's certification of death from natural causes or a coroner's order for burial. In a related development, the Coroner's Amendment Act of the same year gave coroners the power to order a post-mortem examination without holding an inquest, something they had never before been able to do.[28]

The legal changes wrought nearly a century before were similarly vital. The year 1836 was significant not only because it ushered in a formalised system of death registration, but because it marked the point at which medical witnesses in the inquest process were for the first time given official legal status. The reliance by coroners on medical evidence to establish cause and time of death is a relatively new development: for most of its eight hundred year history there was no tradition of medical testimony at inquests. It was the coroner's duty to examine a dead body for injuries, even though he had no special training, since most people believed that an external examination was all that was required to ascertain the cause of death.[29] Medieval coroners were assisted in the task by the members of the inquest jury, a practice that gave rise to the time-honoured 'view' of the naked body by coroner and jurors together, usually before any evidence was heard. By the sixteenth century viewing protocol had become enshrined in law, and the view remained mandatory for coroners until the Second World War. Jurors, however, became increasingly squeamish about it. After the 1926 Act gave them the right to refuse, no inquest jury ever chose to view a dead body. By then, of course, there was no need: medical experts did it for them. When the view was abolished the last vestiges of active civic participation in death management were removed, in favour of the model familiar today: expert-oriented investigations carried out by recognised professionals employed by state and local government.[30]

There appears to have been little or no call for medical testimony at English inquests before the seventeenth century, and those few cases in which it was given were limited to murders that had aroused wide public or political interest. The first recorded occasion on which medical evidence was given at both an inquest and the subsequent murder trial occurred only in 1678, when the Earl of Pembroke, who had kicked a man to death, was found guilty of manslaughter.[31] The only cases in which medical evidence was automatically required were those of still-born children, under the Bastardy Act of 1624. When this law was repealed in 1803, it removed the sole legal requirement for medical evidence at any inquest.[32] The unsavoury air that surrounded any court proceedings made reputation-conscious medical men reluctant to become involved, a problem compounded by the fact that they were not entitled to payment for their time or services. But it is clear that, irrespective of apathy, financial constraints and ignorance, there was a subtle but appreciable increase in the authority credited to medical witnesses in eighteenth-century law courts.[33] If they were called to testify at trials, it is safe to assume that medical men also testified at preliminary hearings before a coroner or magistrate. Studies of inquest records in various parts of the country show that they did, though more so in London than in regional centres.[34] This supposition is also supported by evidence from poisoning crimes of the second half of the century. Of thirty-eight cases that occurred nationally, there were twenty-nine of murder, in twenty of which an autopsy was performed; two horses suspected of having died from poison were also 'opened' and their innards inspected. Violent assault, and above all murder, dominated the circumstances in which medical testimony (usually from surgeons, but occasionally apothecaries or physicians) was sought. Poisonings, being particularly difficult to prove, were (where suspected) more likely than not to demand the careful attention of a medical man.

It has long been fashionable to describe such individuals as 'expert witnesses': the first explicit discussion in a legal text was published in 1795, noting that they were a growing class of witness whose personal opinions on medical and scientific matters were, exceptionally, of evi-dential value to the court.[35] But, generally speaking, many medical witnesses were anything but expert: they were asked for their opinion merely because they happened to have been located conveniently near to the scene of a crime, or what might have been a crime. The death of Peter Davies is a good case in point. He fell ill at about ten o'clock on the morning of 3 December 1771, and someone sent immediately for the local surgeon, Zacheus Wyke, who arrived within half an hour. Little suspecting that his patient was dying from arsenic poisoning, Wyke at first took no particular interest in the breakfast dishes. It is to his credit as a diagnostician that the similar illness of Davies's daughter 'raised [a] suspicion that some poison might have been taken', and Wyke then made some attempts to identify its source.[36] He performed a post-mortem, almost certainly at the order of the coroner (whom he may have informed of the death) but, as was long common, examined only the stomach and alimentary tract. Not all medical men were as perceptive: legal records show numerous examples of doctors who tended patients (sometimes more than one patient) for hours or days yet never considered that they might have been poisoned. Without that suspicion, there was a good chance that the coroner would not be informed, nor an autopsy performed, the death being instead attributed to disease. Even when an autopsy was done, there was no guarantee that the surgeon who performed it would know exactly what he was looking for, where to look for it, or how to isolate a poison and identify it chemically. There was also a great deal of sloppiness when it came to ruling out other possible causes of death. This, when combined with local rumour, could become a factor in the prosecution of innocent people.

One of the most notorious examples of such a case occurred in Sussex, when Hannah Russell and her lodger, Daniel Leney, were tried for the supposed arsenic murder of her husband, a farm labourer in his mid thirties. The trio lived in the village of Burwash where, on 7 May 1826, Benjamin Russell died suddenly while out with Leney. They had been committing a burglary, and the family's efforts to hide this fact led to gossip and suspicion surrounding Hannah's purchase of arsenic to kill mice. At the inquest, a local surgeon claimed that he had found nearly an eighth of an ounce of arsenic in the dead man's stomach, and Hannah and Leney were consequently sent for trial on a charge of murder. They were convicted on 26 July, largely on the strength of the surgeon's evidence. Leney was executed on 3 August, but Hannah languished in gaol while lawyers debated a legal point. Dr Gideon Mantell, famed for his discovery of the iguanodon, now became involved, convinced that Russell had died too quickly to be the victim of arsenic poisoning and dissatisfied by the surgeon's description of the tests he had performed. Several well-known medical and scientific men confirmed his view, and witnesses were found to testify to Russell's recent heart problems. The Home Secretary was persuaded that death was caused by heart disease, not arsenic, and Hannah Russell was pardoned in February 1827. Had it not been for Mantell's interest in her story, she would certainly have been executed.[37] Doubts continue to surround this case: later expert commentators disputed Mantell's claim that arsenic could not have killed so quickly, and believed that the autopsy findings suggested the action of a mineral poison. But the evidence of when and how the victim took poison, and the tests used to identify it in his body, was far from satisfactory.

Medical men who were prepared to give their opinion in court could find themselves hopelessly outclassed by a clever attorney intent on eliciting greater degrees of certainty from them.[38] This was a feature mainly of cases in which the accused could afford to hire legal counsel; many poor poisoners faced the prosecuting counsel alone. (Although Hannah Russell had a lawyer, he was given only two hours to prepare for the case.) It was more common for medical witnesses to appear for the prosecution only, but even this was too much for some, who, scenting the danger of a probable court appearance, refused to be drawn into a case. But there were others who conscientiously sought additional medical corroboration. As in so many aspects of death investigation, much depended upon local circumstances: it was not unusual for people to be indicted by coroner's juries on the strength of inaccurate medical evidence, only to be acquitted at trial.[39]

When a coroner wished to obtain a medical opinion, the usual method was to summon the practitioner who had attended the deceased before death. If he refused, he could (like any other witness) be subpoenaed. If no one had treated the deceased, then the nearest medical man was selected, regardless of his qualifications for the task at hand. In the eighteenth century this was usually the parish surgeon, who could be compelled to attend even though he might not be paid. This practice did not change significantly after the Act for the Attendance and Re-muneration of Medical Witnesses at Coroners' Inquests (1836) became law. This authorised coroners to ask a medical man to attend an inquest and, if necessary, to carry out an autopsy and toxicological analysis; the maximum fee to be paid for these services was two guineas. Anyone who refused a coroner's summons could be fined, and inquest juries were free to request the opinion of a second doctor (and a second autopsy). Further legislation allowed coroners an additional 6s. 8d. for each inquest, but required them to pay all witnesses themselves at the close of proceedings. Since the fees were to be met from the county rates, local JPs held the financial reins. Medical men, now guaranteed payment, were less likely to shirk their duty, but coroners had to continue to exercise financial caution when it came to seeking medical evidence.[40]

Although medicine now had a formal role in the inquest, no special allowance was made for its needs. Autopsies were held on a table in the house where the victim had died, while family members and friends milled about. Edward Heesom, who was tried for three murders along with his wife, was present at the autopsy on his mother-in-law, remarking that 'it's a curious thing there should be all this bother when we'd got a doctor's certificate'.[41] During the autopsy on his final victim, William Palmer stood close to the table, contriving to jostle the surgeons so that some of the stomach contents were spilled, and even attempting to tamper with the sealed jar in which the organs were placed.[42] Fewer autopsies were performed in private homes as more and more people were taken to hospital to die, but inexperienced doctors continued to be allowed to carry them out until very recent times. The London County Council set up a panel of experienced pathologists to carry out coroner's post-mortems in 1906, but their lead was followed slowly, and only in other urban centres.[43] The first purpose-built mortuary was opened in London in the early 1890s, but other cities and towns were again slow to follow the example. The situation that pertained in 1914 differed little from that which existed in 1836.

The weaknesses in the system are obvious, the more so if the records of routine inquests are examined. Despite the fact that medical testimony became more and more commonplace during the nineteenth century, its quality was often a hit and miss affair, very much dependent upon chance. Some medical practitioners had little idea of what to look for during an autopsy, while others were vigorous and competent. In an unbroken link with medieval standards, some were still prepared to state the cause of death without the benefit of an autopsy. An unknown number of deaths were wrongly or too hastily attributed to suicide and accident, and some murders (including many poisonings) were never detected. It is ironic, then, that those poisoning cases that were investigated were often the focus of some of the most expert medical testimony in the country. In common with invocations of the insanity defence, poisoning prosecutions were medically so complex that the law demanded certainty from witnesses; those who could offer that certainty were sought after, developing local and even national reputations as toxicologists. In England, the most famous of all was Alfred Swaine Taylor (1806–82), a lecturer on chemistry and medical jurisprudence at Guy's Hospital and the author of numerous texts on poisons and forensic medicine. He had rivals both in London and in the provinces, where regional experts tended to dominate all but the most notorious cases. Below is a list of the experts whom legal officials around the country consulted most frequently.[44]

Table 5

Experts Consulted in Nineteenth-Century Poisoning Cases

Name	Active	Cases	City	Institution
Alfred S. Taylor	1844–69	31	London	Guy's Hospital
Thomas Stevenson	1872–1905	24	London	Guy's Hospital
William Herapath	1834–67	22	Bristol	Medical School
Henry Letheby	1844–71	12	London	London Hospital
Frederick C. Calvert	1847–72	7	Manchester	Royal Institution
Thomas Scattergood	1856–97	6	Leeds	Medical School
J. Baker Edwards	1856–64	6	Liverpool	R. Infirmary M.S.
William E. Image	1846–64	5	Bury St E.	Infirmary
Richard H. Brett	1840s	5	Liverpool	Medical School
John Rayner	1838–53	4	Stockport	Infirmary
Francis Sutton	1870–77	4	Norwich	County analyst

Of this group, only Taylor and Stevenson – for reasons that will shortly become evident – were regularly called in to cases outside London, where they were based. Herapath, although widely known in his day (hence his participation in some London trials), was mainly associated with cases in the west of England. Letheby was similarly a London expert. The others, some of whom had business and academic interests that made them known around the country, were called upon to do forensic chemical analyses only in cases that occurred in or near their home towns. With only two exceptions, all were chemistry lecturers in teaching institutions, usually medical schools; many taught toxicology or forensic medicine. These academic positions – which bore an attendant social status and intellectual authority – automatically made the men who held them an obvious source of expertise to coroners and police whenever cases of suspected poisoning emerged. It is thus unsurprising that most were located in large urban centres, and notably in the first cities outside London where medical schools and chemical laboratories were established. Between 1824 and 1858 eleven provincial medical schools were set up, one result being that the professors of chemistry (most of whom had medical degrees) were liable to be called in locally as expert witnesses.[45] In London, where nine teaching hospitals had been established by 1850, professors from all were liable to be called upon, though Taylor and Letheby were the clear favourites among legal officials. Unlike many of their colleagues, they relished the opportunity to enter a witness box, where their calm manner, lucid explanations, sharp memories and critical minds made them superb scientific witnesses.

In contrast to the academics, Image and Rayner were hospital-based surgeons whose chemical skills were evidently so reliable that they became local experts. Their training allowed them to do both autopsy and analysis, and their performance under pressure impressed legal officials. The established practice prior to this era had been similar: a local surgeon (most usually functioned also as apothecaries in their home town) would perform both procedures. Although no pre-eminent expert appeared before the 1830s, individuals gained local reputations in such matters. For example, surgeon-apothecary Mark Edward Poskitt was twice called to perform a chemical analysis when, in 1816 and 1821, poisoning crimes occurred in the West Yorkshire town of Rothwell, where he had established his medical practice.[46] Although his role in the earlier case came about more by chance than design, he was doubtless well respected in his day; but Poskitt's name has come down to us solely because of his involvement in these poison cases, for which one woman was hanged. The surgeon Benjamin Sykes, a graduate of Guy's Hospital, had earlier built a name for himself in the small towns west of Wakefield, in Yorkshire. In 1794 Ann Scalbird was convicted and executed on a charge of poisoning her mother-in-law with arsenic. The Scalbirds lived in Batley, and the victim's son called in George Swinton, a surgeon based a mile away in Dewsbury, to treat his mother. After her death on 19 June, following six days of misery and pain during which she claimed repeatedly that her daughter-in-law had poisoned her, the usual procedure would have been for Swinton to inform the coroner and conduct the autopsy. However, it may be that Swinton did not at first take Mary Scalbird's accusation seriously: the inquest was not held until 28 June. Then, given the serious nature of the case, the coroner called in Sykes, who lived about three miles away in Gomersal, and the two surgeons performed the post-mortem together that morning. The records state that Sykes gave it as his opinion that the dead woman had been 'destroyed by the effects of arsenic', and Swinton concurred.[47] Seven years later Sykes became involved in another family tragedy, this time in Heckmondwike, a village four or five miles west of Batley. A cloth-maker named Alvera Newsome was arrested on suspicion of poisoning a four-year-old girl, the product of an incestuous relationship that he had with his own daughter, Elizabeth. As Newsome did not ask anyone to fetch a doctor, the child died in the presence of family members and neighbours; but the news soon reached the coroner. An inquest was held three days later, on 9 August 1801, when the coroner asked Sykes to conduct an autopsy. Although he did not name the poison, Sykes confirmed that death had been due to poisoning. At the next assizes, seven months later, Newsome's entire family acknowledged the incest, but, unlike Ann Scalbird (who had bought arsenic on the day her victim fell ill), there was no evidence to show that he had ever had access to poison and the grand jury refused to indict him.[48] Medical evidence was important in poisoning cases, but circumstantial evidence could often be more persuasive to the layman. This might prove fatal to some, such as Daniel Leney, or of benefit to others, including Alvera Newsome, depending upon how a jury chose to interpret events.

Many factors important to the rise of expert witnesses came together in the 1830s. The Marsh and Reinsch tests made it easier to detect arsenic deaths; but the complexity of the Marsh test made it difficult for amateurs to use; poverty led to an increased number of poisonings; medical schools and chemistry laboratories offered a supply of skilled doctors and analysts. The building of the railways facilitated cooperation between experts in different cities. Thus, although it had for decades been common for the same individual to perform autopsy and analysis, by the early 1840s this was becoming increasingly infrequent. More usually, at the coroner's (or JP's) order the post-mortem was performed by the first doctor on the scene. It was his responsibility to obtain samples and remove organs, and to give them (or to send via post or

police officer) to a trained chemist for analysis. It was not necessary for
the analysts to be present at the autopsy: unless they had medical
credentials, they were not qualified to state cause of death, merely the
quantity and nature of the poison found. Although most were prepared
to affirm that what they had detected was or was not a fatal dose, their
testimony had to be linked with that of a doctor. For their part, doctors
frequently stated that they could not be sure of the cause of death
without a chemical analysis. Many were forced to revise their opinions
in the wake of an analysis. The two types of expert evidence had to
work together. Those analysts who had both chemical and medical
experience were clearly best placed to make a strong presentation in
court – hence the success enjoyed by Taylor, Letheby and Stevenson.
Herapath, although he was largely self-taught in chemistry and had no
medical training, appears to have been unique in that by the 1840s his
fame was such that no court was likely to question his statements as to
cause of death.[49] As they grew in forensic experience, other chemists,
including Calvert, also tended to form opinions that strayed into medical
territory, but this was a feature mainly of the mid nineteenth century.
By the 1870s, which saw the widespread appointment of public analysts,
the division of labour in forensic toxicological matters had become
distinct.

Despite an occasional tendency to overlook the objective scientific
data and form opinions on the basis of intuition and personal conviction,
Taylor's international reputation as a toxicologist and medico-legal
expert was well deserved.[50] His great contribution lay in recognising,
and setting down in print, what was required by the courts: evidence
had to establish legal proof, an issue that will be explored in more detail
below. As his fame grew, Taylor began to accept samples for analysis
from all over the country, and it was his insistence on receiving a fee
that adequately reflected the expenses incurred that set a standard. The
law of 1836 had considered only the cost of analysing the contents of
the stomach and intestines, for a fee of one guinea, but in practice
several different organs and samples had to be analysed. This was not
a cheap process. In the 1840s Letheby estimated the cost of a single
arsenic analysis to be about £1 in materials and two days of his time,
for a case that required him to make six such analyses.[51] Around the
same time, Herapath charged the county of Monmouthshire fifteen

guineas for a series of analyses that took him three days to complete.[52] Taylor's fee was then about two guineas per sample, including materials and time; it was more if he had to consult with a client or travel to give evidence.[53] Given the financial constraints that coroners had to endure, many must have balked at the thought of the potential cost when faced with cases of poisoning. But those who seemed unwilling to hire the best analysts were sometimes persuaded to do so by the medical men involved in the case, or by public opinion. When Jane Wooler died in suspicious circumstances in 1855, the coroner claimed that the necessary analysis could be done in Newcastle as well but more cheaply than in London, but was at last persuaded to call in Taylor in support of the Newcastle analyst, Thomas Richardson.[54] Six years earlier, jurors at an inquest in Bath, dissatisfied by the coroner's failure to appreciate the gravity of the case, had pressed him to send for the surgeon and analyst of their choice. They were allowed one of the two, William Herapath, to bring another arsenic murder to light.[55] This was, however, a discretionary power that jurors rarely exercised.[56]

Despite his pre-eminent position in English forensic toxicology, Taylor never attained the formal status that his successor, Thomas Stevenson, later did – the result of changes initiated long before his retirement. The process began in the 1850s, stimulated by Thomas Wakley, the tireless medical reformer and activist, and editor of the influential journal the *Lancet*. Under the aegis of the journal, Wakley established an analytical sanitary commission to investigate food adulteration in London; its various reports were published in 1855. As a direct consequence, the government appointed a parliamentary committee, its report resulting in the passing of the Adulteration Act of 1860. This permitted the counties and the districts of London to appoint analysts to be responsible for ensuring food standards and the purity of medicines; but it was not compulsory. To remedy its defects and extend the law's provisions to all boroughs, it was revised in 1872. Two years later the Society of Public Analysts was founded, including among its first members the public analysts of Sheffield, Manchester, Bradford, Cheltenham and several districts of London.[57] It is remarkable how many of these men were soon to appear as expert witnesses at inquests and poison trials; records show that some had been doing so even before formal appointment. Many of the earliest members of the society were as interested in food, water and drug analysis as in toxicology – and vice-versa. Moreover, the Public Health Act of 1875 required the appointment of a medical officer of health to every district in England and Wales, codifying sanitary legislation that had been developing since the cholera epidemic of 1848. These men were often also public analysts, while many of the analysts had medical training; by 1874 there were seventy-seven public analysts holding 110 appointments.[58] Those who filled these new public positions quickly became sources of expertise to other branches of the state apparatus, including coroners and the police.

One public analyst above all made a lasting mark on the science of toxicology and the practice of forensic medicine. Thomas Stevenson (1838–1908) was a brilliant student who had won prizes in medicine, surgery, physiology, chemistry and forensic medicine by the time he graduated MD from the University of London in 1864, the year in which he took up a junior post in the chemistry department at Guy's Hospital. An obvious choice, he succeeded to Taylor's lectureships: chemistry in 1870, then medical jurisprudence in 1877. He was also medical officer of health to St Pancras, Middlesex, a post he held for ten years from 1868. He then became public analyst for St Pancras, as well as the counties of Surrey and Bedfordshire. On top of these duties, he added one other. In 1872 he took up a position that was to involve him in nearly all the most notorious poisoning cases of the next forty years: Stevenson was appointed Scientific Analyst to the Home Office, becoming Senior Scientific Analyst nine years later. A classic example of the indefatigable Victorian who maintained the most exceptional standards, his services to the nation were given official recognition when he was knighted in 1904.[59] He had the same clear yet sophisticated courtroom style as Taylor, but also suffered from the same tendency occasionally to allow personal opinion to cloud the scientific evidence. Both preferred to appear for the prosecution, the only difference between them being the formal relationship that Stevenson had with the state: the annual retaining fee that he received from the Home Office meant that his services were, in practice if not in theory, available only to the state. His position as a skilled and trusted servant of the nation led to his appearance in every case that seemed especially complex, sometimes as a second opinion but usually as the prosecution's principal scientific witness. Like most Home Office analysts after him, Stevenson was closely

associated with catching criminals. Those who sought to defend themselves against charges of poisoning had to look elsewhere for an expert
opinion.

Although in many respects a flawed system, the English inquest was
nonetheless an important factor in the detection of secret poisoning.
Nothing can be said about the crimes that no one ever suspected or
which were never formally investigated, except to note that time and
numerous enhancements have closed many loopholes but cannot make
the system foolproof. A clever murderer always finds a way to hide the
truth. The less clever, or the unlucky ones, are another matter. Until
the late 1860s the majority of suspected poison homicides were brought
to light by an inquest. There were sometimes simultaneous magisterial
investigations, and there were occasions when only the intervention of
magistrates ensured that an individual was sent for trial, but it was
primarily through the inquest that questions about a death were formally
raised and answers sought. When the victim survived (and in cases of
animal poisoning) the coroner had no jurisdiction; it was therefore
magistrates who took witness depositions and directed any formal investigation. But from about 1850 the role played by police courts,
presided over by stipendiary magistrates, began to increase markedly,
as new legislation regularised the legal system and established the modern police force and its central responsibilities in crime investigation.
Where the wider picture is concerned, it could be argued that the inquest
failed to make any real contribution to the discovery or detection of
crime.[60] In the rather specialised area of poisoning deaths, however, it
long served as an essential part of the process of revealing what was by
its very nature a hidden offence.[61]

8

The Rule of Law

One enormous case, however, occurred at York – that of Elizabeth
Ward, seventeen years of age, who was convicted of the horrid
crime of administering poison to her sister, and is to suffer death:
a sister and a younger brother were the chief witnesses!

The Times, 1816 [1]

Contrary to the reports that initially appeared in the press, the teenager
Elizabeth Ward was convicted of the attempted murder not of her sister
but of her sister-in-law, Charlotte Ward, a correction noted two weeks
later when a full transcript of the trial was printed in the *Times.* By
then the girl expected to live just nine days longer, as her execution
had been scheduled for 24 August. Despite her youth, the fact that she
had no legal representative and called no one to speak on her behalf,
and the obvious reluctance of the principal witnesses against her, the
judge refused to commute her sentence, claiming that to do so would
only encourage others to commit similar crimes.[2] He had a valid point.
Ward was clearly guilty: all the evidence pointed to an intentional act,
and she later confessed that she had wanted to remove Charlotte because
she was jealous of the control she had assumed in the family home
following the death of Elizabeth's mother eleven weeks earlier. For her
part, Charlotte plainly regretted her role in the drama, and it was with
the greatest difficulty that she could be persuaded to answer the questions put to her at the trial. George Ward, aged only nine, was ordered
to testify against his sister because he believed that if he lied he would
go to hell, a statement which furnished sufficient proof that the boy
understood the nature of an oath and was thus competent to give
evidence in an adult setting. They were followed into the witness-box
by two chemists, Mark Edward Poskitt (who was also an apothecary)

and John Sutcliffe. Realising that she had probably been poisoned and knowing that she needed a stronger emetic than was available at home, Charlotte had gone to Poskitt for treatment. He dosed her on the spot and collected her vomit. From it he isolated a few grains of arsenic (nearly half a gram). Poskitt dissolved these in water and gave the solution to Sutcliffe, who did several tests. Though unable to state how much arsenic the liquid contained, Sutcliffe was certain that arsenic was present.

What is perhaps most astonishing is that the whole case was played out within a matter of days. On Friday 26 July 1816 Elizabeth visited Leeds, a few miles from her home in Rothwell, West Yorkshire, where she bought two ounces of arsenic from a druggist who afterwards identified her. The next morning, when only three people were in the house, her younger brother saw her mixing a white powder in a jug before adding part of the contents to a posset (a thin mixture of milk and oatmeal), which she then gave to her sister-in-law. Since the food tasted odd and a chalky deposit had formed on the bottom of the bowl, Charlotte quickly realised that something was wrong; George immediately told her what he had seen. She had the presence of mind to lock up the jug before drinking oil to cause vomiting, but George saw Elizabeth throw the remainder of the posset into the swine tub. Charlotte took the jug with her when she went to see Poskitt, though it emerged at the trial that no tests were made on its contents, a failing for which no reason was sought. Nor does anyone seem to have enquired whether the pigs became ill. Two days later Charlotte had recovered enough to make a statement to a JP, who interviewed the other witnesses before committing Elizabeth for trial on a charge of attempted murder.[3] The assize court was then in session at York Castle, and she was tried within a week of purchasing the arsenic.

Two of the most interesting things about this trial were its swiftness and the concerns raised about the accused girl's sanity. We do not know precisely how long the proceedings lasted, but it cannot have been more than an hour or two. There were only five witnesses, all for the prosecution: Charlotte and George Ward, the druggist Henry Bingham, Poskitt and Sutcliffe. Each was asked to testify and was then subjected to questioning by the judge. In the absence of a defence lawyer, the judge, Mr Justice Bayley, was supposed to act on behalf of Elizabeth

Ward. All he did, however, was to give her the opportunity to ask questions of each witness, to which she invariably replied in a faint voice, 'No, I am innocent'. The first witness, Charlotte Ward, suggested that Elizabeth might have become insane as a result of a bout of scarlet fever the year before, but close questioning from Bayley forced her to admit that her sister-in-law seemed capable of distinguishing right from wrong. Furthermore, there was no way of knowing what her state of mind had been on the morning in question. Next came little George Ward. Given his age, the court had first to ascertain that he understood what was happening and the importance of his role as a witness. Satisfied that he did, his testimony was straightforward, as was Bingham's.

As one might expect in a poisoning case, the evidence of the two chemists was more complex. The judge was particularly interested to know how much arsenic could cause death, a question he asked both men. Poskitt replied that it was difficult to say, as the substance sold in shops was adulterated with whiting (calcium carbonate); his estimate that an ounce and half of this arsenic would kill was far too high even given the adulteration. Sutcliffe refused to answer the question, as it pertained to medical matters he was not qualified to discuss. He was certain, however, that the liquid he was asked to test contained arsenic 'in a very minute degree'. The important point for the court's purpose was that the scientific witnesses agreed that the victim had been poisoned by arsenic. It is also interesting to note that Sutcliffe lived in York, the seat of the assize court: the fact that Poskitt gave him the sample to test indicates that the apothecary was determined to obtain corroboration of his findings. Why he should have wanted to do so was revealed towards the end of the trial. In answer to the judge, he stated that he had never treated a victim of poison before, nor performed an autopsy on one; he had formed his opinion on the subject purely from books.[4]

At the conclusion of the case for the prosecution, Elizabeth Ward was called upon to offer her defence, but said only 'I am innocent of the crime'. One of the jurors then wished to question Poskitt about her state of mind, so he was recalled. Although he was her family doctor, he said that he had never heard that she was of unsound mind or treated her for insanity. The town's physician had attended her when she had scarlet fever, but was not called to testify. Had her family had time to consider the possible importance of his opinion, or to hire a lawyer for her, the insanity defence might have been engaged more strongly in court, perhaps even successfully.

In his summary to the jury, the judge began by explaining the charge against the prisoner. Under a law of 1803 (Lord Ellenborough's Act),[5] attempts to commit murder were deemed the equivalent of actual murder, and thus punishable by death. In poisoning cases, juries had to decide whether the defendant had administered a 'deadly poison' to another person with the intention of killing them; also, whether the quantity given was likely to kill. If the answer to either was 'yes', the defendant was guilty. (So, even if an amount insufficient to kill had been given with the intention to kill, guilt was established.) In Elizabeth Ward's case, the jury had also to consider her state of mind. In the judge's opinion, there was nothing to suggest that she had not been in her right mind at the time she had mixed arsenic into the posset because, although she had done so in front of her brother, she had then attempted to destroy the evidence. The rest was circumstantial: she had bought arsenic but not said anything about what she had done with it, and arsenic had been found in the victim's vomit. Bayley then reminded the jurors that 'if there remained a single conscientious doubt upon their minds' as to what she had done or her intentions, they had to give her the benefit of the doubt and acquit. If they had no doubts, they must convict. According to the press reports, the jury then left the courtroom for about ten minutes, before returning with a guilty verdict. It was only after she had been sentenced to death that Ward attempted to tell a tale different from that offered by the prosecution, but by then it was far too late.[6] The judge was adamant that she should hang, and there was no court of appeal; yet there remained a final hope of mercy.

Had he wished to commute her sentence, the judge had the power to do so: the judges who presided over the Lancaster assizes in September 1816 reprieved four out of five of the death sentences they handed down.[7] Judges could also recommend to the government that a free pardon be granted. Finally, petitions seeking commutation or pardon could be made directly to the government or the monarch. Given the mental incapacity of George III, his eldest son had been Regent since 1811, so all petitions for mercy had to be addressed either to the Prince Regent or the Home Secretary, Viscount Sidmouth. Luckily for her, Ward became the subject of a vigorous campaign for mercy. Her 'friends' included Lord Lascelles, a member of one of the most important families in Yorkshire, and it was probably his intervention that saved her. He first persuaded Bayley to postpone her execution, though this obviously rigid man merely rescheduled it for 21 September. But the additional time was crucial: Lascelles wrote to Sidmouth in Ward's favour, while many of York's most influential citizens, including the Lord Mayor, organised a petition asking that her life be spared on the grounds of her penitence and the distress her death would cause to others. The petition was sent to the Prince Regent, who immediately ordered a reprieve. Elizabeth Ward was freed, amid hopes that she would go on to lead an exemplary life.[8]

Elizabeth Ward's trial and narrow escape from execution offer a fascinating glimpse into the workings of the English legal system. Among the many points highlighted by her case, those at once familiar and alien to the modern reader include the statutes that related to poisoning crimes, the practice of criminal law, and the penalties applied by the state to those deemed guilty of felony. Much may seem familiar to audiences who digest a steady stream of dramas and documentaries devoted to crime and the criminal justice system, but the past two centuries have brought marked changes to the details. The law itself, trial procedure, lawyers' duties, defendants' rights, sentencing – these have all evolved in an ongoing process intended to deliver justice in a manner that the general public finds fair and appropriate. Of the many cogs in this legal mechanism, all but one featured in Ward's case: the police were conspicuous by their absence.

In early modern England, law enforcement operated on both macro- and micro-levels. The macro-level was centred on the justices of the peace of each county, men whose responsibilities included bringing people to justice, either summarily or by referring cases to higher courts. Most crimes came to light as a result of a complaint made by the victim, most easily done by approaching the nearest JP. Although a citizen could bring his or her case directly to a court, these met infrequently, and only in certain towns; but there was usually a JP resident in any large village. At the micro-level, in each of the roughly 15,000 parishes in England and Wales, the petty or parish constable held responsibility for

every aspect of enforcing the law. Most importantly for the purposes of
criminal justice, they had the power to arrest and detain suspected felons,
and to execute warrants sent by superior officers. Although not members
of the gentry, as JPs were, these men were among the leading citizens
of each parish and acted, in effect, as one-man police forces.[9]

Despite this network of law enforcement, however, there was a decline
in the number of prosecutions and convictions between the Civil War
and the late eighteenth century, due mainly to shortcomings in the
system's efficiency. At county level there were too few JPs: many of
them were virtually inactive, while the rest were seriously overworked.
At the local level, constables served for one year only, giving them little
time to get to grips with the job. Moreover, they had no assistants or
formal protection and, as elected officials, they had a responsibility to
the community that could conflict with their role as servants of the law.
It was often possible to avoid taking a case to court, as a range of
alternatives existed, chiefly arbitration or some form of communal
disciplining, effective both in crimes against the person and those against
property.[10] This was desirable because involving a court could be a costly
business, the expense being borne entirely or mainly by the prosecutor,
who was usually the victim. In addition, the legal process was stiffened,
making it more difficult to secure a conviction. In the early eighteenth
century defence witnesses in felony cases became subject to testimony
under oath, making hearsay evidence increasingly unacceptable and
verdicts consequently safer.[11]

Poisoning cases of the late eighteenth and early nineteenth centuries
show that the investigative process frequently bypassed the parish constable. If the victim died, the local coroner took up the matter,
questioning under oath all those who might have had knowledge of the
case. If the victim survived, he or she lodged a complaint with the nearest
JP, who then gave instructions to the constables. This could include
orders to search a house (also issued by coroners), or to arrest a suspect,
but did not usually involve formal questioning of anyone connected to
the alleged crime – that was done by the magistrate himself. However,
given the constables' status within the parish – as neighbours or even
friends of the accused – they could elicit, often in the most casual
manner, information later used in court. When Cecilia Collier was sent
for trial on a charge of poisoning her husband at Barton upon Irwell,

in Lancashire, the warrant of commitment to the county gaol was issued by a JP and executed by one of the town's constables, Samuel Mee. It was his duty to escort her to Lancaster, but, since he took her into custody late in the day, he decided that they should stay in a public house until the next morning. During the course of the night they sat in chairs, not speaking, until Cecilia suddenly confessed to him. In his deposition, Mee admitted that they had addressed each other by their first names, suggesting that they already knew each other. But although he stressed that he had made her no promises and the confession was wholly voluntary, it was not enough to convince the jury who, though she was probably guilty, acquitted her in March 1813.[12]

Even as Collier was confessing, such methods of policing were becoming inadequate: population growth, urban migration and civil unrest made it increasingly impossible for small numbers of part-time, occasional officers to keep the peace and pursue suspected criminals. Although the idea of a uniformed police force patrolling the streets had long been contemplated with horror by a British populace suspicious of continental-style central authority, changing times demanded changing practices. As a result of its size, London led the way: in 1792 seven magistrates' offices were created, each staffed by three stipendiary magistrates and six constables paid full-time salaries. These were, in effect, the first district police offices, and they were followed in 1798 by the founding of a force to police the Thames. By the time of Napoleon's defeat at Waterloo there were about three hundred officers of various sorts employed in the city, which then had a population of over a million. In the provinces, policing focused mainly on the protection of property, under the general assumption that each locality should pay for its own protection against criminals. Local business owners formed associations to seek out and prosecute thieves, while private acts of parliament allowed local rates to be used for the improvement of towns or districts – a task often accomplished by the appointment of nightwatchmen and day constables. Local magistrates continued to be responsible for these organised forces.[13]

Changes in this laissez-faire system were achieved slowly, led by the example of London. There the driving force was the Home Secretary, Sir Robert Peel, whose Metropolitan Police Act of 1829 established the ideal of a well-disciplined, preventative force of waged police officers under central control, uniformed, impartial and easily visible as they patrolled the streets. It is from Peel that the term 'bobby' for a British policeman comes; also the more antiquated term 'peeler'. The Metropolitan police were quickly accepted by the middle classes, though the working classes feared a curtailment of their civil liberties, and antipolice sentiment simmered for years. But the London model, which was by and large successful, was not directly transplanted to the provinces. Rather, provincial forces sought to employ former Met officers, who already had expertise and training, while continuing to make their own local policing arrangements. Community forces became subject to the oversight of watch committees under the Municipal Corporations Act of 1835, which required boroughs that did not already have police forces to create them. This should have resulted in the establishment of forces in each of the 178 boroughs in England and Wales, but many failed to comply or made only half-hearted attempts to do so. Rural policing was affected by a series of laws that maintained the local flavour of the endeavour, encouraging the establishment of police forces for whole counties or any part of a county. Magistrates were to make the appointments, which were paid for out of local rates, and this led to the appointment of more men at the parish level: by mid century numbers had grown, though their primary aim – the prevention of property crimes – remained unchanged. And, like the boroughs, many counties failed to act on the legislation. To counter this inertia, the 1856 County and Borough Police Act made the creation of uniformed police forces in all counties and boroughs mandatory, and established a national inspectorate to ensure efficiency. The timing was affected by two factors: the granting of parole to prisoners (1853) and the ending of the Crimean War (1856). In the face of concerns about large numbers of unemployed ex-servicemen and parolees roaming at will throughout the nation, policing in England and Wales was at last brought under a uniform code of standards, with a greater degree of involvement by central government.[14]

It is clear that the quality and amount of policing varied immensely in the first half of the nineteenth century, dependent as it was on local attitudes and activities, not to mention training and funding. Although there were increasingly more officers, their number varied widely, the police to population ratio in some areas being as low as one to several thousand. After 1856, when the parish was at last abolished as the principal unit of policing, crime prevention remained at the forefront of policing aims: the 'new police' contributed to the statistical decline of theft and violence in the second half of the nineteenth century.[15] The number of police officers rose steadily, from just over 20,000 in 1861 to more than 54,000 in 1911, London accounting for about 40 per cent of the total; but turnover remained high until the end of the century. Insubordination, drunkenness, incompetence, corruption and neglect of duty were regular grounds for dismissal at every rank, as were other failings associated with lack of moral character. The quality of applicants for the job improved, however, as the nation's labour force became better educated and more disciplined. Regular pay, perks, pensions, internal promotions and improved work conditions all contributed to the emergence of career policemen and their gradual acceptance as an integral and respectable part of English society.[16]

As the number and professionalism of police officers increased, so their role in the investigation of poisoning crimes became more visible and immediate, overtaking their earlier function as mere instruments of the local coroner or magistrate. Instead, they became a crucial link in the investigative chain, assuming what was eventually to become a principal role as intermediates between the victims of crime and those who delivered justice. This role most often took a form familiar to us today: a response to a complaint made by a member of the public. Cases like that of Elizabeth Ward, which did not include any police involvement, became increasingly infrequent from the 1820s onward, tying in with a trend already identified. The inquest was for centuries the primary means by which poisoning crimes were exposed, but by the late 1860s emphasis had shifted from the coroner to the police, who were involved in all stages of an enquiry. This police concern was at first more precautionary than investigative, as when Jane Scott murdered her parents at Preston in 1827. Despite their agony, the unfortunate couple remained clear-headed enough to accuse their daughter of the poisoning; fearing that she might disappear, a relative called a constable to arrest her. Once the victims had died, however, the coroner took over.[17] On other occasions police officers 'received information' or 'heard reports of poisoning' and went to investigate. This is how a constable named

William Alcock explained his decision to search the house of a silk weaver, William Davis, where a baby had just died. The records of this case indicate that a JP held an inquiry at Leek, Staffordshire, on 20 November 1825, two days before an inquest was opened. As the infant, which had been seen by a doctor, had died a week earlier, the timing suggests either that the doctor said something to Alcock or that neighbourhood rumours made the constable curious. When his search turned up an empty laudanum phial, he reported his suspicions – made all the stronger by the fact that the child's mother, Elizabeth Nixon, was unmarried – to a magistrate. Nixon and Davis's wife, who had bought the laudanum, were tried for murder but acquitted, probably because three surgeons were unable to state with certainty what the underlying cause of death had been.[18]

As more police forces were established, an even more informal mechanism for securing their intervention fell into place. Officers were alerted to crimes by local gossip, overheard on their daily beat or passed on by their neighbours, who were free to approach policemen in their homes.[19] Similarly, officers living near a house where a death had occurred might visit the family to see what was going on; once there, they could act purely as friends and neighbours or, if necessary, adopt a formal role and begin an investigation.[20] Even police wives could become involved, as when in June 1842 a Welsh officer asked his wife to search a female prisoner he had brought to their house in Holywell. The prisoner stayed overnight, sleeping in the same bed as the officer's wife.[21] The ideal of community policing remains to this day, but codes of conduct now forbid such a blurring of the personal and the professional.

Most early examples of police involvement in poisoning cases took place in cities and market towns, reflecting the larger numbers and easier accessibility of the urban policeman over his country cousin. In some cities – Manchester in the 1840s, for instance – a senior policeman took on the role of coroner's officer, visiting the scenes of sudden deaths to determine whether an inquest should be held.[22] From the late 1830s – the first example in a poisoning case came in Stockport in 1839 – the police became a customary presence at exhumations and autopsies, just as they are today, their aim being to preserve the chain of evidence and maintain control of the investigation. The weak link lay in the financial constraints imposed by county JPs: until their control over coroners

was dismantled between 1860 and 1888, routine coopera
the police and coroners was often poor, and many poss
homicide were disposed of without inquest. The evidence fi
ing cases, however, suggests that, as the local profile of
increased, they began to be seen as a first port of call for worried
individuals who might previously have gone directly to a coroner or
magistrate to report their suspicions. Until the advent of fingerprinting
and the forensic science service, which did not become established in
England until the twentieth century, the modus operandi of the 'new
police' was not much different from that of their predecessors. Yet, a
significant transformation had taken place. By the end of the nineteenth
century, murder investigations had become entirely police centred.

The 'new police' also played one other important, though now unfamiliar, role in the legal process: they often took on the burden of
bringing a prosecution against a suspect. Under the English legal system,
every private citizen has the right to initiate a suit and, until the twentieth
century, most criminal prosecutions were conducted by the victims of
crime, or by individuals acting on their behalf. Local magistrates were
empowered to try cases involving a wide range of petty crimes, but the
more serious offences were sent to a higher court, either quarter sessions
or the assizes. To ensure that the prosecutor and his witnesses would
appear when required, magistrates used a system akin to bail: individuals
entered into recognizances, becoming legally bound to pay large sums
of money if they later failed to appear in court. The amounts varied at
different times and in different regions, and in relation to the supposed
severity of the crime, but in cases of poisoning appear to have been set
at about £40 per person during the late eighteenth and early nineteenth
century. Witnesses were usually liable for smaller sums than prosecutors.[23] The system placed a heavy financial responsibility on private
prosecutors, who had to pay the fees and charges associated with taking
a case to court, typically between £10 and £20. Added to that were the
travel and subsistence costs for themselves and their witnesses: the higher
courts sat only in the main county towns, and the volume of work that
they dealt with meant that it could be several days before a given case
was heard. The cost and inconvenience were long significant deterrents
to prosecution – often more so than the prospect of sending someone to
the gallows.

Prosecution associations, first established in the seventeenth century, offered one way to finance the cost, but poor people who could not afford the subscription were excluded. Government, however, stepped in to address the problem. Legislation introduced in the second half of the eighteenth century provided for the courts to pay the prosecutor's expenses in all felony cases where the accused was convicted. Some courts paid even after an acquittal, if the case had been a reasonable one. Sir Robert Peel's Criminal Justice Act of 1826 extended the provision of expenses to witnesses, and during the 1820s and 1830s the number of capital offences was reduced from over two hundred to twelve. And yet there remained a distinct reluctance on the part of the victims of crime to prosecute offenders, so much so that many politicians came to the conclusion that the only way forward was to establish a system of public prosecution. This idea took nearly eighty years to come to fruition. While legislators argued its merits, the 'new police' stepped in to fill the breach.

We have no detailed information about how, when and why the police came to predominate as prosecutors, but it is clear that during the nineteenth century this became an increasingly important part of their public role. It seems likely that, given their key aim of preventing crime, arresting and ensuring the conviction of offenders was a logical step to take. So was bringing a prosecution in cases where the victim was too poor to do so himself, and similarly in cases where the victim was simply reluctant. From the late 1830s, as new laws encouraged (and from 1856 required) the establishment of police forces, officers began to take on the role of prosecutor.[24] Most of the victims of crime must have been only too happy to relinquish the responsibility.

Given the complexity of most poisoning cases (and hence their potential cost), and the fact that many poisoners and their victims were among the poorest in society, it is unsurprising to find the police acting as prosecutors from the earliest days of the uniformed service. The first known examples date from 1839: in Cheshire, Robert Standring was prosecuted by Joseph Sadler, a superintendent of the Stockport police, while in Staffordshire the parish constable who had alerted the coroner to the sudden death of Susannah Perry's husband performed a similar task.[25] Subsequently, police prosecutions were usually undertaken by a senior officer of the county force, though occasionally by the junior officer who had investigated the case. Found in all parts of the country until the early years of the twentieth century, one of the last instances was a case in Gloucester in 1913: the depositions are marked 'Rex on the prosecution of William Harrison against Amy Evelyne Rowe. Murder'.[26] The example set by earlier cases suggests that Harrison was a senior police officer who had no direct knowledge of Amy Rowe (his name does not appear in the depositions).[27] Unless the clerks of assize included a specific name, like Harrison's, in the standardised label that they gave to each case file, and that name also appeared within the written case records, it is now difficult to identify the prosecutor. Those files that do give some identification show that, in cases of murder, private prosecutions continued until at least the last decades of the nineteenth century.[28] By then the office of the Director of Public Prosecutions had been established: created in 1879, for thirty years its role was essentially advisory. In 1908 the office was separated from that of the Solicitor to the Treasury and began to assume its modern form and function. There is little sign of its involvement in poisoning trials, as the office handled only a few hundred cases per year.[29] Private citizens and chief constables retained much of the responsibility for prosecution until after the First World War.[30]

English law was, in effect, divided into two categories, and an alleged criminal could only be prosecuted if he had committed an offence against the common law or against statute; members of the legal profession tended to view the latter as complementary to the former. The common law was of medieval origin. Originally the unwritten law of custom, it was derived from experience and precedent and comprised violations of the rights and duties due to the whole community. Crimes that were clearly in breach of the common law included murder, theft, rape, arson and nuisance. The common law was an adaptable entity whose power rested in the hands of judges; it had long been used to shape laws that kept pace with social change, as it has continued to do in recent times by addressing offences inextricably linked to the modern era of mass production and civil liability. But since the early nineteenth century its importance has been reduced by the concomitant rise in the number of statutes. Statute, or written law, corrects or supplies deficiencies in the common law; in the event of a conflict between the two, it is statute that prevails. As in the common law, the application of statute is dependent on the interpretation of judges, though the laws themselves are the creation of parliament and are therefore subject to political whim. Private acts of parliament made special rules for special groups, which was one reason for the explosion in the number of capital offences during the eighteenth century. During the course of the next hundred years, many obsolete statutes were repealed, while others on similar themes were consolidated. But efforts to construct an encompassing code of criminal law failed, partly because politicians and members of the legal profession feared that a single code would lack the flexibility of the common law. In fact, by the 1860s the criminal law was so detailed that judges had hardly any discretion.[31] They were, therefore, liable to find their hands tied when any particularly unusual case came along: on the occasions when the law was not sufficiently explicit to cover an alleged 'crime', judges were forced to accept that the prosecution had no legal standing. This point is clearly illustrated by several poisoning cases in which statute failed to address actions that seemed by any standard of logic to be illegal.

All poisoning crimes fell into one of six categories that can, broadly speaking, be ordered by the relative gravity with which they were viewed by the criminal justice system: murder; attempted murder; administering poison with intent; manslaughter; destroying animals; attempted poisoning. The penalties for these crimes ranged from death to just a few months in prison, but conviction and sentencing were very much dependent upon statute. A crime punishable by death in 1800 – destroying animals, for example – might merit a short gaol sentence in 1900; conversely, a crime not even recognised in 1800, such as administering poison with intent to do grievous bodily harm, might be treated very harshly a century later. Most poisonings that resulted in a person's death were relatively straightforward cases of murder or manslaughter, but problems of interpretation, usually centred on the notion of criminal intent, did arise. Legal difficulties were, however, most likely to occur in cases where the victim of a poisoning crime survived, as the exact wording of the law under which the offender was tried was crucial, yet not always equal to the task at hand.

Most poisoners were likely to benefit from inconsistencies in the law, but in the last years of the eighteenth century a servant girl in County

Durham fared rather less well. In 1798 Mary Nicholson was working for the family of farmer John Atkinson in Little Stainton. In April, something made her decide to murder him, so she mixed arsenic into flour, intending to serve her master a poisoned pudding. But her plan went awry when his mother, Elizabeth Atkinson, used the poisoned flour to make a loaf of bread. Four members of the household subsequently became ill, but only Elizabeth Atkinson died, after languishing for sixteen days. Evidently racked with guilt, Nicholson confessed to three people, saying that she had planned to poison John Atkinson in order to conceal 'bad deeds' that she had done. Apparently an open and shut case, she was tried at the Durham summer assizes at the end of July, but the indictment was phrased in such a way that made the case legally complex: Nicholson was charged with intentionally contriving to murder Elizabeth Atkinson. In fact, she had done no such thing: she had planned to poison the victim's son, and the older woman had died by accident. But the jury, understandably, shrugged aside the sophistry of mere words and found her guilty. The judge sentenced her to death, but the legal question had to be decided and she was reprieved while the case was referred to the highest authority in the land, the twelve judges of the common law courts at Westminster. At the next assizes, one year later, they delivered their judgement: the conviction and sentence were just. Unless the contrary was proved, the law assumed malice from the act of killing. Accordingly, after a year spent working as a prison servant, sometimes sent alone into the city on errands, Mary Nicholson was hanged in July 1799. To add to the distress of the occasion, the rope broke and she had to wait nearly an hour for a new one to be brought. During what must have seemed far too short a time, she was alert enough to converse with her relatives.[32]

Nicholson must have had every reason to hope that her conviction would be quashed, as it was by no means unusual for a prosecution to fail if the accused could point to a defect in the indictment on which he or she had been tried. Indictments, legally intricate documents, were prepared by court attorneys and presented to a grand jury to endorse or reject. Often working with no legal knowledge, grand jurors were expected to weed out weak or baseless cases, but could not foresee the consequences if the often lengthy and abstruse wording of an indictment contained an error of fact or a legal omission. Clever lawyers and determined prosecutors sought to get around this problem by indicting the accused on as many counts as possible, to improve the chances of a conviction, but even murderers escaped justice when an indictment failed to describe their alleged crime accurately, or to name the victim correctly. When this happened, it was not usual for a fresh indictment to be prepared, though this was an option. It was never, however, an extensive problem: before the mid nineteenth century few prisoners had a lawyer, and thus had no way of determining whether an indictment contained a hidden get-out clause. In 1851 the Criminal Procedure Act simplified the forms of indictment, particularly in relation to homicide, and gave courts the power to amend them as necessary before trial. This had the desired effect of greatly reducing the number of acquittals based on a faulty indictment.[33]

Yet an indictment was, after all, only a statement of fact in relation to a crime; the crimes themselves were defined by statute. Poisoning cases highlight many of the problems associated with defining a criminal offence since, as it does today, the law was constantly evolving in response to current events and public opinion. Under the severe guidance of Lord Ellenborough, Lord Chief Justice of England from 1802 to 1818, ten new capital felonies were created, among them two relating to poisoning. On 1 July 1803 it became a hanging offence to administer poison with intent to murder or to cause abortion.[34] It was under this law, known as Lord Ellenborough's Act, that Elizabeth Ward and a number of other early nineteenth-century poisoners were tried. Not surprisingly, some escaped capital conviction because of a faulty indictment. In 1826, for example, a Cornish gunsmith, Richard Sargent, was committed for trial under Lord Ellenborough's Act for attempting to poison a customs officer and his family, but the indictment was framed as a mere misdemeanour at common law: mixing poison (arsenic) with human food (sugar). The defendant was a man of means and hired a tenacious lawyer who, knowing that his client would not hang, fought for an acquittal: the trial took eleven hours, much longer than many murder trials of the time. Sargent was convicted, but his three-year prison sentence was a far cry from the fate that might have befallen him.[35] Most of those convicted under the 1803 Act went to the gallows, though Elizabeth Ward was not the only one to escape execution. In 1825 a twenty-six-year-old Welsh labourer named William

Cadman was found guilty of the attempted poisoning of Elizabeth Davies, the mother of his illegitimate daughter, to whom he had given a cake and some cherries laced with copper sulphate and arsenic. She noticed something odd and refused to eat them or to give them to her child, taking them instead straight to a doctor. Cadman was fortunate to have the services of a lawyer, probably one attached to the court and assigned to his case shortly before the trial (something like the modern court-appointed attorney). The shrewd lawyer pointed out that Cadman had been indicted for 'administering arsenic and blue-stone with intent to poison', but that the 'administering' had not been proved to the letter of the law. The judge allowed the case to go to the jury on the proviso that, if the defendant were found guilty, it would be referred to the twelve judges at Westminster. Cadman was advised to prepare himself for death, but the decision went in his favour and he was given a free pardon in December 1825. As the victim had not swallowed the poisoned cake, it was held that a mere delivery to her did not constitute an administering within the meaning of the Act. Confusion remained, however, as the judges seemed to think that swallowing was not essential, and apparently failed to point out that Cadman should have been indicted for an attempt to administer poison, a crime explicitly cited by the statute.[36]

Although the nation clearly needed laws against attempted poisoning, the time had come for a change: in 1828 Lord Ellenborough's Act was repealed, to be replaced by a law that maintained essentially the same provisions and, hence, the same flaws.[37] Several poisoners who should have been tried on lesser charges had to be acquitted, as the intent to murder could not be proved.[38] The Cadman case was essentially replayed in Suffolk ten years later, but the accused woman, Elizabeth Gooch, was unluckier: her death sentence was, however, reprieved to transportation for life.[39] In 1837 the death penalty was removed from a wide variety of crimes, but attempted murder remained a capital offence.[40] This fact apparently took the public by surprise when, in 1841, an old man convicted in Devon of administering poison with intent to murder was sentenced to death (but later transported).[41] This anomaly was noted when further legislation that same year abolished more capital crimes, leaving only seven. In 1861 the number was finally reduced to four: murder, arson in naval dockyards, piracy on the high seas and treason.

After 1838 for the rest of the century no one was executed for any crime other than murder.[42]

The legislation that brought in this final reduction in the number of hanging offences was notable in another way: it recognised a motive for poisoning previously all but immune to legal sanction. The Offences Against the Person Act of 1861 made it a felony to administer poison with the intention to inflict grievous bodily harm; to injure, aggrieve or annoy was a misdemeanour.[43] Previously, the law had been unable to punish such deeds unless the unfortunate victim died, when it became a case of manslaughter, or unless the motive was attempted murder or abortion. By the late 1850s, when two cases made legal headlines, the need for such legislation had become urgent. On 2 November 1859, five of the six maids who worked for Joseph Paget, a Derbyshire magistrate, suffered burning pains in their bowels. Two weeks later it happened again, this time affecting Paget and his family as well. The family doctor diagnosed poisoning by cantharides (or Spanish fly), the ground-up wings and body of a blister beetle. As an irritant, it acted on the parts of the body that it came into contact with; it was thought to be an aphrodisiac because it irritated the genitals when it passed out of the system. A police detective was called in: after interviewing all the servants, his suspicion fell upon the coachman, Thomas Spowage, who had bought cantharides from a druggist who identified him. Detective Barnes clearly thought he had a strong case when he gave evidence before magistrates at the end of the month. Spowage had been arrested on a charge of wilfully administering poison, but the presiding magistrate decided that there was 'no criminal law to meet the case', and Spowage was released.[44]

The lusty coachman intended to arouse desire in the maids, not to harm them, and it seemed that the law was powerless to prevent people from poisoning others for non-homicidal reasons. His case followed on the heels of another that had highlighted the law's ineffectual response to such dangerous actions, and which was instrumental in stimulating the new provisions enacted in 1861. In April 1858 a young man named Frederick Heppenstall was committed for trial on a charge of administering croton oil with intent to commit murder. The victim, Benjamin Fawcett, had replaced him as the manager of a grocer's shop in Silkstone, a village near Barnsley, taunting him with the accusation that he was incapable of managing the shop, after Heppenstall cursed him as a 'damned villain'. In a rage, Heppenstall left the shop but returned the next day; Fawcett saw him go into the cellar, where the employees stored sugar, tea and other foodstuffs. The next time Fawcett had a cup of tea with sugar, his throat began to burn and he vomited heavily. Suspecting that he had been poisoned, he took the sugar, which was discoloured, to a surgeon, who identified the presence of croton oil, a purgative squeezed from the seeds of a British plant. It was little comfort to be told that 'I think it will not kill you, but you will be very ill after it'. Confined to his bed for five days, Fawcett remained very weak for over a month. A police superintendent arrested Heppenstall, who made a statement admitting everything, and two surgeons, including an expert witness, Thomas Scattergood of Leeds, held that a dose of more than three drops was poisonous. Tried at York in July 1858, Heppenstall claimed that he had only intended to play a joke on Fawcett, but the jury did not accept this and convicted him. His lawyer, however, objected to the indictment on the grounds that the act of administering the poison was not felonious, since it had been done as a joke. The judge disagreed, but referred the case to the Court for Crown Cases Reserved, since 1848 the successor to the Westminster common law judges in deciding cases where a conviction was disputed on a point of law. The court acknowledged that it was an important case, intending to make a decision by December, but Heppenstall died suddenly on 5 December and they changed their minds, declaring that there was now no need to decide it. Scattergood, who kept detailed casebooks, made a caustic note: 'It must therefore be considered unsettled whether if you all but kill a man by poison you are punishable for it.' A few years later he amended his notes: 'Since this and in consequence of it an Act passed, 24 & 25 Victoria 1861.'[45]

Legal loopholes in the wording of the statute meant that the Offences Against the Person Act made it difficult, but not quite impossible, for men like Heppenstall and Spowage to escape justice: clever lawyers could argue that certain substances were incapable of causing injury. In March 1877 William Hannah was tried in Cornwall for administering cantharides to a female friend, with intent to injure or annoy her. But the amount that he gave her was so small that his lawyer successfully argued that, regardless of intent, the indictment could not succeed if what was given to the victim could not have harmed her. In a complete reversal of the stance taken by the judge at Elizabeth Ward's trial sixty years earlier, two judges (including the chief justice) agreed that both the ability to injure and the intent to do so had to be proved in order to satisfy the statute. As the cantharides did not constitute a noxious substance in the quantity administered, Hannah could not be guilty. An editorial in the *Pharmaceutical Journal* marvelled at 'the glorious uncertainty of law', noting that cantharides was formally recognised as a poison by the 1868 Pharmacy Act, and asking why Hannah was not guilty of the *intent* to injure or annoy, which was what he had been charged with.[46] Perhaps the outcome would have been different had the chief justice been more familiar with the poison schedule. Sixty years later, the 1861 Act was still on the statute books and still offered the same escape clause, but medical professionals seem to have viewed it more favourably. In 1936 a textbook of forensic medicine pointed out that, if noxious substances were too closely defined, offenders might escape justice 'on a technical interpretation of the definition of poison'.[47] William Hannah was, presumably, one of only a few poisoners who so benefited, or the writer would not have been so sanguine.

The fact that a relative handful of poisoners managed to avoid severe punishment does not detract from the seriousness with which cases of deliberate poisoning were regarded. As felonies – at common law, crimes for which conviction automatically resulted in loss of property or life – most of those that came to light were dealt with by one of the nation's highest criminal courts, the assizes. This system, which originated in the late thirteenth century, was at first created to allow for certain types of property litigation under provisions (assizes) of Henry II. The twelve judges of the three common law courts (Exchequer, King's Bench, and Common Pleas), based at Westminster, were sent (normally in pairs) on circuits that covered all the counties of England except London, Middlesex and the palatinates of Durham and Lancaster. The temporary courts of these travelling judges became known as the assizes, and by the fifteenth century their work had come to be dominated by criminal cases that came to them directly or that were referred by lower courts, the quarter and petty sessions.[48] There were originally six circuits (eight after nineteenth-century revisions), the regions designated by a number of counties in close proximity to one another.[49] Surrounded by medieval pageantry, the judges went 'on circuit' twice a year, in the spring and summer, during which the assizes were held in each county's main town (making prosecution an expensive business for those who had to travel to attend the court). But there were some variations. The four northern counties had only a summer assize until 1820.[50] Twelve towns (including Bristol, Canterbury and Exeter) had the same status as counties, and usually combined their assizes with that for the adjacent county. The court typically sat in the most imposing building in the town, the shire hall or castle, and occupied an allotted number of days. This meant that in the more populous counties sittings were long and some trials rushed. The judges could get through ten cases or more in a day that, in summer, began near dawn and continued until dark; many were prepared to sit until late into the night.

In London and Middlesex prisoners were tried at the Old Bailey Sessions, held eight times a year in the Sessions House adjoining Newgate prison; two common law judges and two city judges presided. Already subject to twelve-hour sittings in a four or five day session, the court's workload doubled between 1800 and 1820, leading to ten-day sessions, the building of a second courtroom and the addition of a third city judge. In 1834 the Central Criminal Court Act brought metropolitan Essex, Kent and Surrey within the court's jurisdiction, and increased the number of yearly sessions to twelve. Judges, jurors and lawyers endured cramped conditions until 1907, when the present Central Criminal Court building was opened. In Wales and Cheshire criminal business was dealt with by the Courts of Great Sessions, created in 1536. The judges were not of a high standard, being lawyers who took on the role unpaid and part time. In 1830 this court was abolished and Wales and Cheshire were brought into the assize system. The number of common law judges was increased from twelve to fifteen, to accommodate the increased volume of work.[51] Lastly, there were the two palatinates, Durham and Lancaster, counties that had since medieval times had privileges that permitted them to hold courts which were not within the assize system, so that they effectively comprised two mini-circuits.

A number of changes were made to the system during the nineteenth century, giving assize status to the great industrial towns of the north and adding a third assize where the workload justified it. Durham and Lancashire were brought into the system in 1876, when the circuits were revised. The common law judges were now known as High Court judges. Complaints surfaced at regular intervals and more work was devolved onto magistrates, but the London-based judges, most of whom specialised in civil, not criminal law, continued to go on circuit. The ancient structure remained in place until 1971, when the assizes were replaced by the crown courts.

The business of the assize courts followed a fixed procedure. When the judges arrived at an assize town, one would deal with civil cases, the other with the criminal cases. Poisoners and other murderers fell into the latter category, together with rapists, burglars and a host of other felons, all of whom had been sent for trial at the assizes by a magistrate. Those committed for trial were held in the local gaol until the next assize; bail for serious offences was rare or non-existent. This was why the number of assizes had to be increased: prisoners, some of them innocent, often had to wait many months before their case was tried. (Conversely, some people could find themselves on trial within days of committing a crime, if they happened to do so while the assizes were in session.) Unlike prisons, gaols were not places of punishment, merely sites for the short-term custody of anyone awaiting trial. Yet they were unpleasant, and most prisoners must have welcomed the commencement of the assizes, when they were at last released and brought to the court in carts or wagons. Only two poisoners out of more than five hundred died in gaol before trial.[52]

Meanwhile, a grand jury, normally made up of county magistrates and other local worthies, was sworn in, charged with finding bills of indictment for each case. Unless the prosecutor could afford to pay an independent solicitor, the indictments were drawn up by the clerk of assize (a court solicitor) and presented to the grand jurors along with the relevant depositions. The prosecution witnesses were also sworn in, and then examined by the grand jurors, who had to decide whether the evidence showed that there was a case to answer. If there was, the indictment was endorsed as a 'true bill' and sent into court to be tried before a judge and a petty jury. The defence played no part in this process. Five per cent of all poisoning cases were thrown out of court after a grand jury failed to find a true bill, but the majority of these occurred before 1880, when weaknesses in the grand jury system (inconsistency, secrecy, ignorance of legal matters and sheer bias) were rampant. Regularly subject to harsh criticism, especially after throwing out seemingly good cases for mysterious reasons, the grand jury's importance diminished as stipendiary magistrates, in conjunction with the police, took on more responsibility for committing alleged felons for trial. By the turn of the twentieth century grand juries were dismissing less than 1 per cent of bills, but true reform came only in 1933, when the grand jury was abolished.[53]

Once a bill had been endorsed by a grand jury, the accused faced trial in open court, before a judge and a petty (from the French for small, *petit*) jury of his equals and neighbours. This was something of a misnomer, since only men aged between twenty-one and sixty who owned land or occupied a fairly large house were eligible to serve on a petty jury. Poor defendants were doubly disadvantaged. Not only did they face a jury made of up men with whom they might have little in common, they often faced the prosecutor and his lawyer alone. Between 1750 and 1850, however, when there were at most a few hundred barristers who took on criminal work, most cases tried at the assizes and quarter sessions were characterised by a direct confrontation between the accused and the prosecutor, with no legal intermediary.[54] Local solicitors could instruct barristers but could not speak in court. Legal etiquette demanded that barristers attach themselves to one of the circuits, but there was little money to be made from it: most prosecution work rarely attracted a fee of more than two guineas. The same was true of defence work: wealthy clients could afford to pay a decent sum, but others could not. In capital cases judges could assign a barrister, who was obliged to give his services for free, to represent a poor defendant. The failings in this system were epitomised by the case of Hannah Russell and Daniel Leney, tried for murder in Lewes in July 1826. Their court-appointed solicitor had only two hours to prepare (the barrister had less time, and seems to have thought his clients guilty), and the pair were convicted. Leney, an innocent man, was hanged a week later; Russell escaped death by a narrow margin.[55] The practice of appointing one of the barristers present in court to defend a prisoner was still new in the 1820s, but became increasingly common during the following decades, so that by 1880 no one facing a capital charge did so without legal counsel.[56] Those who lacked a lawyer also lacked information about the case against them: stuck in gaol, denied access to the depositions (even had they been able to read them), they could hardly be expected to mount a qualified defence. Most said little or nothing other than to deny the charges. The trial system was supposed to address this inequality. In the absence of a lawyer on either side, which was long the established trial procedure, the burden of proof lay firmly on the prosecutor, while the judge was meant to assist the accused, as Mr Justice Bayley rather half-heartedly did at the trial of Elizabeth Ward. Many judges were, however, completely indifferent to a prisoner's plight.

Even where the prosecution and defence had engaged lawyers, they were not usually instructed until the assizes began. This meant that prosecution barristers read the depositions on the day of the trial, while defence counsel (where present) had at most a few hours to prepare to defend a person's life. Until 1836 prisoners were not entitled to see the depositions or the indictment against them, nor could their lawyers address the jury on their behalf, leaving the accused – most of whom were incapable of making a persuasive speech in their own defence – at a distinct disadvantage. The Prisoners' Counsel Act finally removed this limitation, though the poor were still likely to find themselves in court with no legal representation. Examining and cross-examining the witnesses ranged against them must have been a daunting task, but the evidence from non-capital trials shows that lawyers were viewed as non-essential until well into the nineteenth century.[57] When young Emma Elizabeth Hume was tried at Chelmsford in July 1847 for the attempted poisoning of her aged husband, the old man was named as the prosecutor. In the absence of counsel to argue for either side, the judge asked one of the circuit barristers to 'examine the witnesses from the depositions', but left Hume to defend herself.[58] Just over twenty years later, when Susannah Seaman was tried in Kent for attempting to poison her niece, she was prosecuted by two lawyers whose legal expertise probably left her confused and frightened. The *Times* report of her trial noted that she 'made observations on the evidence as it went on', but said nothing in her defence except to deny the charge.[59] In 1887 Eliza Foxall and Mary Ann Scrafton were tried in Durham for giving poison to Foxall's husband. She had a lawyer, but Scrafton was un-defended.[60] All four women were convicted.

Hume, Seaman and Scrafton did not have attorneys because they could not afford to; since they were not tried on capital charges, the

judges chose not to appoint a court lawyer. Although many poor
defendants managed to borrow the money to hire a lawyer, there was
no formal mechanism to provide what we now know as legal aid. This
lack of provision was long a subject of criticism, but, as with so many
aspects of the English legal system, the problem dragged on until the
twentieth century. In 1903 the Poor Prisoners' Defence Act allowed
magistrates and judges to certify prisoners in need of legal aid, so a
solicitor and barrister could be assigned at public expense. The first
poisoners to benefit from the new law were tried in June 1904.[61] But
the privilege did not extend to prisoners who withheld their defence,
or to those who had not yet been committed for trial. It was only in
1949, when the Legal Aid and Advice Act was passed, that a system that
closely resembles the one that we take for granted emerged.[62]

As if lack of legal representation was not enough of a problem,
prisoners faced another impediment: they were not entitled to give
evidence on their own behalf, but had to remain mute in court. The
guilty, those who were easily confused or angered, or prone to lying,
may not have suffered many ill consequences, but the innocent were
denied the opportunity to give any impression of themselves other than
as a criminal. When this restriction was lifted in 1898, legal professionals
realised that it would be a double-edged sword for defendants.[63] Exposed
to examination and cross-examination, many helped to convict themselves, most notoriously the poisoner Frederick Seddon, whose
calculating demeanour convinced a jury he was guilty of murder, despite
the lack of concrete evidence against him. The Criminal Evidence Act
of 1898 shaped modern courtroom practice: until 1994 the prosecution
was forbidden to comment on a defendant's failure to give evidence,
but juries have long drawn a negative inference from any such silence.
Defence lawyers must therefore coach their clients carefully, as trial
outcomes may hinge on the impression made in the witness box.

Trials for poisoning crimes could last for anywhere from a few hours
to several days; today's murder trials lasting weeks were unheard of, and
child witnesses were treated like adults, as indeed were many child
criminals. During the eighteenth century it was not unusual for several
people to be convicted on capital charges during the course of a single
day in a single courtroom. Although we might wonder at the brevity of

such proceedings, the absence of lawyers and experts meant that cases tended to rest on the testimony of a few first-hand witnesses who told their stories quickly and were not subjected to rigorous cross-examin- ation. Lengthy trials became a commonplace during the course of the nineteenth century, however, as the roles played by lawyers and expert witnesses grew; there were more individuals involved in a trial, and many more complicated medical and scientific elements to consider. Eventually, however, once the evidence had been presented, the judge was supposed to summarise it for the jury, highlighting both the facts of the case and any relevant points of law. But the quality of a judge's summing up was often perfunctory, particularly prior to 1850; many did not bother to do so at all. Even afterwards, when standards began to improve, it was not unusual to find judges abandoning all pretence at impartiality and advising juries to convict or acquit. The notorious Florence Maybrick was convicted of poisoning her husband largely on the strength of the judge's personal antipathy to her. She would probably have been acquitted under another judge.[64]

Jurors seem to have made their deliberations swiftly, often in the jury box itself or, if they needed to discuss a case further, in the jury room. There they were locked up (until the 1860s, without food or drink) until they agreed a verdict; judges were reluctant to discharge juries, even if one of their number died or went absent. Before lawyers began to dominate the proceedings, jurors had a more prominent role in criminal trials, asking questions of witnesses and using their local knowledge of prosecutors and defendants to guide them in their decisions. As local men, jurors were prey to bias either for or against a defendant, and the problem of pre-trial publicity was one that grew with the developing news media from the 1780s onward. It was finally tackled head-on in 1856, during the case of the Rugeley Poisoner, the surgeon William Palmer. Local prejudice against Palmer led the Attorney General to move his trial to London, a decision that required a special Act of Parliament known as Palmer's Act. Invoked only in the most extreme circumstances, it allowed for indictments found elsewhere to be tried at the Central Criminal Court. Despite occasional shocking breaches of trust, the legal system relied on the media to regulate itself, and to abstain from publishing inflammatory material about defendants awaiting trial.[65]

The object of trial by jury is not to ascertain the truth, per se, but to obtain the highest amount of certainty and to reach a just verdict. The question that jurors had to determine was therefore not whether a defendant was guilty, but whether they had any reasonable doubt that he was guilty. Theorists held that more guilty people went free than innocent people were convicted, but accepted that there might sometimes be no reasonable doubt of the guilt of a perfectly innocent man.[66] Circumstantial evidence, always so crucial in poisoning cases from 1750 onward, could be highly persuasive even when the accused person was innocent, as in the case of Hannah Russell and Daniel Leney. Incomplete or inaccurate evidence also led to miscarriages of justice, most famously the execution of Eliza Fenning in 1815. What might seem like reasonable doubt to some did not seem so to the juries in question, and the innocent undoubtedly suffered unfairly. Yet, an examination of poisoning cases over a long period suggests that there were relatively few individuals who were victims of unsound convictions or who, though they may have been guilty, should probably have been acquitted for lack of direct proof. On the whole, the English trial system was favourable to accused poisoners, as less than half were convicted.

During the early nineteenth century conviction rates for all crimes tried at the assizes and quarter sessions were around 60 per cent, rising to about 70 per cent after the 1850s.[67] The vast majority of these convictions were for offences against property; violence against the person accounted for just over 10 per cent of all recorded crimes. Homicide was never a statistically significant offence, as levels rarely reached more than 1.5 cases per 100,000 population – in real numbers, only a few hundred reported murders per year.[68] Poisonings formed a small proportion of the annual total of crimes against the person: 164 people were tried for murder or attempted murder by poison during the poisoner's heyday, the 1840s. The results from half these cases show that 44 per cent were convicted and 54 per cent acquitted; grand juries refused to indict the remaining 2 per cent.

Over the second half of the eighteenth century and the whole of the nineteenth, conviction rates for all poisoning crimes averaged 46 per cent (including those found guilty but insane). Five per cent of cases were rejected by grand juries, the remainder resulting in acquittal or no trial at all due to the lack of a prosecutor or the insanity of the defendant. Of those convicted, 63 per cent were sentenced to death, but only two thirds of these were actually hanged,[69] the rest being reprieved to prison sentences or transportation to the colonies. Whether or not a convicted poisoner was likely to hang depended on the date. Before 1838, almost every poisoner under sentence of death was executed. After that year, only murderers were ever hanged, and over 40 per cent of poisoners had their death sentences commuted.[70] From 1837 to 1868 inclusive, 347 murderers were executed in England and Wales:[71] around 10 per cent were poisoners, more than half of whom committed their crimes during the 1840s. Between 1859 and 1880 the figure dropped to 314 executions, less than 5 per cent involving a poisoner.[72] This reflected a drop in the incidence of poisoning, as well as the courts' increasing use of alternative punishments for those found guilty.

The courts had two principal alternatives to execution for those convicted of serious crimes: transportation and prison. An Act of 1717 empowered judges to send such convicts to the American colonies for a period of at least seven years, where they were sold into employment as virtual slaves. About a thousand people were transported each year until the outbreak of the American War of Independence forced the system to change. From 1787 convicts were sent to penal colonies in Australia, where most settled after they had served their sentences. The practice was finally abolished in 1868, when penal servitude became the only option to execution. In May of the same year the last public execution took place in England, and seven months later a poisoner, Priscilla Biggadike, gained the dubious honour of becoming the first woman to be hanged inside a prison.

The use of imprisonment as the usual, rather than as a purely secondary, form of punishment dates from the mid nineteenth century. Local gaols were places for the temporary confinement of prisoners awaiting trial or for their sentences to be carried out; the barred rooms were big enough to hold a dozen or more people. Communities also built houses of correction, established during Tudor times and initially intended to provide work for people unwilling to find it for themselves. But they soon became the places to which minor offenders were sent, and by the eighteenth century it was common to find judges sentencing convicted felons to short terms in a house of correction. A Prisons Act passed in 1791 provided for the construction of prisons with cells, a first step towards making prison a longer-term punishment. During the 1830s

the government drastically reduced the number of capital crimes, recognising as it did so that, if convicts were not to be executed, some
other option had to be found. During the first half of the century over
fifty prisons were built, the prototype being Millbank, constructed in
1812–21. The prison regime was punitive, not reformatory: hard labour,
the tread-mill and the crank, silence and isolation made confinement a
physical and mental torment.[73] But the ticket of leave system, introduced
in 1853, offered prisoners the hope of early release, and in 1898 a regular
system for allowing prisoners to earn remission by good conduct was
introduced.[74] As transportation was phased out, and execution was used
only where there were absolutely no mitigating circumstances, the length
of prison sentences began to rise, to reflect the severity of the punishments it replaced. The sentences handed down around the country were
not uniform, but terms of ten or twenty years, or life in prison, awaited
convicted poisoners who, before the 1850s, would have been hanged or
transported for life.

9

Resolute for Killing

If they are resolute for killing, as they mostly are, and look the fact in the face, still it seems by no means so regular a murder as a blow or a stab, which leaves marks of blood and horror. Besides, poison shields the administrator from detection.

Household Words, 1851 [1]

In December 1851 the novelist Charles Dickens, proprietor and principal writer of the journal *Household Words*, surveyed with some alarm the many poisoning crimes that had been perpetrated in England during the preceding twelve months.[2] In Nottingham a young woman had sent her brother to buy the arsenic with which she and her lover had murdered her husband.[3] Other unhappy spouses, many having secret affairs, had also ended their marriages with poison. In the north of England, children of all ages had died so their parents could profit from the ubiquitous burial clubs. In the east of the country, an embittered servant resentful of the treatment meted out by her mistress had resorted to poison. An octogenarian had tried repeatedly to poison his daughter-in-law, seeking to regain control of property that her husband had given her as part of their wedding settlement. The aged assassin succeeded in killing her sister, yet it was only after he made another attempt on his intended victim that suspicion was aroused. When finally subjected to formal questioning, the ease and frequency with which he had purchased arsenic shocked the local magistrate and convinced Dickens that the new Arsenic Act was ineffective.[4] Then, for the fourth time in eighteen months, a woman convicted of husband poisoning was reprieved from execution. Law-abiding citizens began to wonder whether the precedent might not lead to an even more rapid increase in a burgeoning epidemic of crime.[5] It appeared that Victorian England had become a nation of fiendish poisoners, each possessed of a steely resolve and a manifest lack of pity.

Dickens was writing with justifiable anxiety at what proved to be the height of a relatively short-lived spate of poison murders, his article hinting at a trend that had elsewhere been noted more openly. In his report of the trial of William Chadwick, a twenty-three-year-old potter accused of poisoning his wife's great-uncle at a small town in Stafford-shire, a newspaper correspondent observed that 'the case was curious, as affording a proof of the scientific manner in which plain and appar-ently ignorant people can now poison each other ...'[6] Middle- and upper-class readers had grown accustomed to a steady succession of news articles that had shown that a poisoner did not need much money or intelligence to commit a murder. Given that, there was a very real fear that detected cases represented only a small proportion of the overall incidence of the crime. Moreover, it was evidently the native cunning and inherent depravity of the poorest and least educated members of English society that produced the most resolute criminals.

There are two strands of thought here, each with some basis in fact. Although criminal poisoning was always rare in relation to other types of violence, the publicity that it attracted fostered the widespread belief that it was more common than it really was. People feared poisoning because, as a secretive crime, it was impossible to protect oneself against it, especially if the perpetrator lurked within one's own home. Although such fears were exaggerated, there is no doubt that the number of reported poisoning crimes had been rising steadily since the late 1820s, reaching a peak around 1850, and that some cases had undeniably spawned imitators. Furthermore, with the exception of Mary Blandy, John Donellan, Mary Reed, Thomas Griffiths Wainewright and a few others whose high social status attracted especial notoriety, the poisoners of the period between 1750 and 1855 were of relatively low birth. Many lived lives tainted by appalling poverty; by the hatred generated by unhappy marriages; by greed, jealousy, casual cruelty and lack of choice.

The first half of the nineteenth century witnessed a genuine increase in both the actual number of poisoning crimes and the rate at which they were detected. This was due to a combination of factors. Indus-trialisation had created an urban consumer society that favoured fixed shops, while lack of regulation meant that shopkeepers could sell all kinds of poison with no restrictions whatsoever. Arsenic was used for many legitimate purposes, and was cheap and widely available. Its symptoms could be mistaken for those of disease, making it easily the criminal poisoner's weapon of choice. Secondly, the economic situation was such that many people lived on the fringes of penury; the nation experienced its worst unemployment during the early 1840s. The Poor Law Amendment Act of 1834 raised the spectre of the workhouse, which most people would do anything to avoid because of the stigma associated with it. At the same time, the Act encouraged an explosion in the number of friendly and burial societies. The small sums paid out by these clubs offered a way for the poor to avoid the hated workhouse, but provided a financial incentive to murder. Thirdly, in 1833 the Woolwich chemist James Marsh testified for the prosecution at the trial of John Bodle, a youth acquitted of the arsenic murder of his grandfather for lack of direct evidence of poisoning. Marsh, determined to avoid a repetition of his failure, developed the sensitive test for arsenic that came to bear his name. An important step forward for chemical analysis, the Marsh test had its flaws, and the German chemist Hugo Reinsch introduced a much-needed alternative in 1841. By the early 1840s both were in use throughout England. In 1835, the year before Marsh published his test, William Herapath proved a case of arsenic poisoning fourteen months after the victim's burial, and Mary Ann Burdock was consequently hanged for murder. Legal officials began to recognise the value of medical and scientific evidence. Lastly, the Medical Witnesses Act of 1836 authorised coroners to ask a doctor to attend an inquest and, if necessary, to carry out an autopsy and toxicological analysis. The establishment of a number of provincial medical schools and laboratories from the 1820s onwards gave local officials a ready supply of skilled medical men and analysts on whom to call when faced with cases of poisoning. Thus, by the 1840s, there were more poisoners than ever before, spurred on by poverty, desperation, publicity and a ready supply of arsenic and other poisons; but more and more crimes were detected and the perpetrators brought to trial.

The preponderance of the very poor among poisoners as a whole began to give way during the 1850s, as the Arsenic Act and the new police, the increasing financial independence of coroners, improved systems of death investigation and a general rise in the standard of living began to take effect. Poisoning crimes became more difficult to hide, even among the middle and upper classes, while some of the economic factors that had led to such crimes among the poor began to ease. People continued to poison each other for love, money and revenge, but the profile of the typical poisoner began to change. No longer drawn purely from the lowest classes of society, more and more middle-class, educated men and women were accused of being poisoners. In 1855 a respectable Durham businessman named Joseph Wooler was acquitted of poisoning his wife slowly to death. A man who kept a carriage, he was many steps higher up the social ladder than the William Chadwicks of the world. At the end of the same year, William Palmer, a surgeon and member of local Staffordshire 'society', was arrested for the strychnine murder of his gambling companion, following many sudden deaths among members of his own family. In 1859 Thomas Smethurst, a medically qualified hydropath who ran a successful London practice, was convicted of the murder of the woman he had bigamously married, supposedly standing to gain over £1700. Found guilty, his murder conviction was quashed as a result of the scientific controversy that surrounded the case. In 1866, Dr Alfred Warder committed suicide just days after an inquest jury found him guilty of poisoning his third wife, and there was every reason to believe that her predecessors had met the same fate. In the 1880s and 1890s these sensational revelations were superseded by the poisoning crimes of two more doctors, George Lamson and Thomas Neill Cream. The indications were that the latter killed for the sake of power and excitement, rather then money. Among female poisoners of the last quarter of the nineteenth century, the most prolific was the underprivileged Mary Ann Cotton, but the most infamous were three highly respectable, even wealthy, women: Florence Bravo, Adelaide Bartlett and Florence Maybrick, all of whom were self-confessed adulteresses.[7]

This succession of scandalous cases overshadowed the mundane murders of the lower classes. They revealed, in the most explicit manner, the hidden underbelly of 'respectable' Victorian domestic life, astonishing contemporaries and spawning a fascination maintained to the present day by a host of books, articles, and television dramas. They also served to introduce a stereotype now firmly entrenched in popular opinion. At the turn of the twentieth century, the former prison inspector Arthur Griffiths published a three-volume survey of world crime in

which he stated that 'the most notorious poisoners of modern times ...
have been members of the medical profession, chemists, and females,
whether wives, nurses, companions, cooks or other servants'.[8] The media
furore that surrounded the 1990s cases of Beverly Allitt, Harold Shipman,
John Allan (an industrial chemist) and Zoora Shah (an abused wife)
has given his conclusion renewed appeal.

But the claim that most poisoners are (or were) women or doctors
is patently false. The evidence of 540 poisoning cases of the period
between 1750 and 1914 has shown that poisoners were evenly divided
between males and females. The main difference between these murderers was that, in absolute numbers, the women killed more victims
than the men did; furthermore, there were more female than male serial
poisoners. Although murder itself was, and remains, largely a male
crime, there was a much higher proportion of poisoners among female
murderers as a whole than there were among male murderers. These
statistics have changed only slightly since the end of the Great War.
Murder remains a relatively infrequent crime; about 90 per cent of the
perpetrators are young males, often from deprived backgrounds.[9] Poison
accounts for approximately 2 to 3 per cent of all homicides.[10] However,
it appears there may have been more male than female poisoners in
twentieth-century England. The major murder cases of the last century
show that for every female poisoner (Barber, Bryant, Conroy, Major,
Merrifield, Shah, Wilson), at least one man had committed a similar
crime (Allan, H. Armstrong, Barlow, Black, Burdett, Ford, Hinks, Va-
quier, Marymont, Young). For each woman acquitted of a poisoning
charge (Hearn, Pace), so was a man (J. Armstrong, Greenwood). The
known medical poisoners in post-1914 England (excluding physicians
charged with committing euthanasia) – nurses Allitt and Waddingham,
and doctors Bodkin Adams, Clements and Shipman – were significantly
outnumbered by their non-medical counterparts.

Griffiths correctly identified money as the main motive of medical
poisoners, men whose profession gave them a high social standing and
respectability. He could not have foreseen a criminal like Shipman,
however, now the most infamous of them all. The Cheshire GP was
unusual in that his primary motive was not money but the inner demon
that impels the modern serial killer, the overwhelming majority of whom
are male. (The term itself is usually used to describe people who murder

repeatedly for reasons that may seem undefined, but which are often linked to sex or childhood abuse.) His choice of profession enhanced his ability to remain undiscovered. It is ironic that Shipman was caught only after he allowed greed to modify his appallingly successful modus operandi, but this was perhaps because, like many serial killers, he either wanted his crimes to be publicly acknowledged, or simply became careless.[11] Today, serial homicide by doctors and nurses has been linked to issues of access and opportunity and, needless to say, the use of poisonous drugs is an obvious choice in a health-care environment. Many people may have the potential to murder, but those who exhibit a pathological interest in the power of life and death but engage in non-medical professions find it more difficult to satisfy their cravings. With the sole exception of Thomas Cream, killers like Shipman and Allitt bear little relation to their infamous Victorian forebears, men whose greed turned them into killers. Rather, they represent a compulsion to kill rooted in the desire to exercise power over others and, although uncommon, the horror that such cases engender stands testament to our fear that other doctors might similarly betray the trust we place in them.[12]

It is unsurprising that in 1900 Griffiths should have identified the stereotypical female poisoner as a person who killed without compunction until she was caught, as several women of this kind had been hanged during his lifetime. But he ignored the issue of class, consigning all 'females' to one category and singling out as especially fearsome those who killed from sheer love of the crime: the serial poisoners. He seems to have been intrigued primarily by quantity, rather than motive or background, and assumed that such women were 'at enmity with the whole human race'.[13] This has a familiar, if unexpected, overtone, hinting at what today would be associated with the outlook of a criminal sociopath. But Griffiths's one-dimensional judgement derived from his Victorian notion of what constituted normal, acceptable womanly behaviour, and was strongly influenced by a handful of unusual European cases in which it appeared that female killers had poisoned repeatedly for no apparent motive.[14] As an English equivalent, he cited the case of Catherine Wilson, a woman apprehended in 1862 after she attempted to poison a friend. Tried at the Old Bailey, she was acquitted for lack

of evidence but immediately rearrested: a police investigation had uncovered a series of sudden deaths from which she had profited by
hundreds of pounds. This, of course, was her principal motive. It would
be more appropriate to compare her to the English serial poisoners of
the 1840s than to the continentals Jegado, Schönleben and Van der
Linden, all of whom exhibited 'homicidal fury', appear to have derived
pleasure from the sufferings of their victims, and were of questionable
sanity. Although all four poisoned employers, friends and companions,
displaying the calculating demeanour considered characteristic of the
stereotypical poisoner, Wilson was more evidently driven by greed than
by a lust for killing. She was in many ways similar to a woman like
Mary Anne Geering, hanged in 1849 for poisoning three male members
of her family for about £5 each. Both were considered cold and indifferent to their fate, and may well have felt the same way about the people
around them. The main difference between them lay in their social class
and the amount of money involved. Geering's family was extremely
poor and thus of insignificant social standing, but Wilson and her
victims were members of the lower middle class and therefore situated
on a higher plane of respectability. This made her crimes all the more
shocking – she should have been a useful and industrious member of
society – and it was perhaps this aspect of her story that caught Griffiths's
attention. Convicted at her second trial of a poison murder carried out
six years earlier, Wilson, like Geering, met her end on the scaffold,
executed in October 1862.

The only known English female serial poisoner of the nineteenth
century who might possibly have been suffering from some kind of
mania was Mary Ann Cotton, but this interpretation is itself a product
of Victorian mores, which held that a woman who killed was unnatural.
Local newspapers of the day claimed that she was further proof, if more
were needed, that women 'had a natural turn for poisoning', one or
two successes leading them to kill for no reason other than to satisfy a
morbid fascination. This suggests the influence of some sort of mental
imbalance. Yet, at the same time, it was acknowledged that life insurance
among the very poor offered an inducement to neglect, and perhaps
murder.[15] Numerous case studies have shown that some women, faced
with extreme poverty and distress, would poison their own relatives for
money, or simply to save money. Some, including Cotton, may well

have become so intrigued by the ease with which they could kill that they would not or could not have stopped themselves,[16] but it is highly unlikely that, as one historian recently claimed, Cotton would be considered insane by any modern standards.[17] She, and the others of her kind, seem more akin to the modern psychopath, a person who displays amoral and antisocial behaviour but whose mental 'instability' is controlled. Many of today's multiple killers, both male and female, are psychopaths, often highly ordered and intelligent but lacking in conscience and unable to empathise with other people. They understand the difference between right and wrong but always seek to satisfy their own needs; their actions carry no burden of guilt or remorse. Current medical thinking holds that such people are not insane. Even this, though, risks placing too modern an interpretation on the actions of a woman who was solidly rooted in her own time and station in life.

Until Harold Shipman burst on to the criminal scene in the late 1990s, Mary Ann Cotton was the most prolific of all known British murderers. Born Mary Ann Robson in the tiny village of Low Moorsley, County Durham, in late October 1832, she was the daughter of a teenaged coal-miner and his wife. Shortly after her birth the family moved to East Rainton, a mile away, and then to Murton, another pit village; people who knew her there thought her an exceptionally pretty child. Throughout her life she was to find that men were quickly drawn to her. Her childhood was relatively happy and untroubled, despite the early death of her father in a pit accident and her mother's remarriage. Mary Ann became a teacher at a Wesleyan Sunday school, and took a position as nursemaid to the large family of a colliery manager. Then, on 18 July 1852 she married William Mowbray, a miner, probably because he had made her pregnant. The couple moved to Cornwall, where she gave birth to four babies, all but one of whom had died – almost certainly of natural causes – by the time the family returned to Murton in 1856.[18] As a young woman Mary Ann Mowbray was regularly exposed to death and loss, but this was not unusual at a time when infant mortality was high and accidental death was common; the risk of both was highest in mining and quarrying areas of the country.[19]

By 1863 the Mowbrays had moved to Sunderland, where William took a job on a steamship and insured himself and three of his children with the Prudential. His wife had given birth to four more children, two of whom died within a year of birth. The first was not insured, but it is likely that they collected a small sum on the death of their son in September 1864.[20] The girl who had been born in Cornwall had died at the age of four in 1860; a colliery doctor certified death from gastric fever. Then, in January 1865 William Mowbray died within a few hours of the onset of an attack of violent diarrhoea. His death, also certified by a doctor, was supposedly due to gastric fever. It is now thought that his wife may have poisoned him with arsenic because their standard of living had deteriorated: he was in ill health, and they were no longer living in a community where they could count on family support. She is alleged to have had a horror of poverty, and, though there is no proof one way or the other, the insurance money of £35 paid by the Prudential may have tipped the balance. Or, if Mowbray died of natural causes, the insurance payment may have given her a motive to insure future husbands. The children's deaths in 1860 and 1864 were possibly her earliest murders, the first carried out for unknown reasons and the second for money, but there is no proof that they were murdered. Having by now endured the natural deaths of so many of her children, however, Mary Ann may well have found it difficult to form any strong maternal bonds with subsequent offspring.

Shortly after Mowbray's death Mary Ann met Joseph Nattrass and had a brief affair; then the younger of her two surviving children died of gastric fever. This may have been a poison murder: a widow's best chance of survival lay in remarriage, but many men would have been unwilling to take on another man's child. Her mother took the remaining child while the new widow went to work at the Sunderland infirmary, by all accounts a dedicated nurse to fever patients who died at the rate of one in five. It was there she met George Ward, an engineer aged thirty-two; the pair were married on 28 August 1865. Following a bout with fever, however, Ward was either too weak to work or unable to find a job, and by November the only money he brought in to the household was parish relief of 4s. a week. Then he became ill with a mysterious wasting disease, of which he died in October 1866. He had probably been a victim of slow arsenical poisoning by his wife, who resented the state of poverty to which his unemployment had reduced them. The fact that she bore him no children suggests that the union was not a happy one. Although two doctors attended him, neither suspected poison.

By Christmas 1866 the twice-widowed Mary Ann Ward had moved into the Sunderland home of recent widower James Robinson, a ship-building foreman, to act as housekeeper to him and his five small children. The youngest of these died within eight days of her arrival. A doctor who arrived after death certified gastric fever as the cause. In March 1867, by now pregnant by Robinson, Mary Ann went to look after her mother, who died only nine days later. She too was probably a victim of poison, her case marking the first time that Mary Ann predicted a death, though it is not clear why she was killed. There was no insurance money, and all her daughter gained from it was some clothing and bedding. She now had to resume the care of her remaining child, who returned with her to Robinson's house, and this may have been the reason she killed her mother. In April two more of the Robinson children died, and, in early May, so did the Mowbray girl. All were insured, and all had similar symptoms; their deaths were due to gastric fever, according to the same unsuspecting doctor as before. It was then that Robinson's three sisters seem to have become the first to suppose that Mary Ann was a poisoner.[21]

Her motive was by now clearly financial: Robinson had a good job and some savings, and was buying his own house. The fewer children he had to care for, the more cash there would be for his wife. Mary Ann Ward married James Robinson in August 1867, when both were aged thirty-four. Their child, a girl, was born at the end of November, but died of gastric fever three months later. A second child born to the couple survived. Although now part of a relatively well off family, Mary Ann began to steal from her husband's savings accounts when Robinson refused to have himself insured. She appears to have become something of a spendthrift who never had quite enough to pay for little luxuries. When the fraud was discovered, the marriage ended: Mary Ann left him in the autumn of 1869, taking her surviving child. By April 1870 she had held two jobs, in which she impressed her employers, had deserted her child (whom a friend returned to Robinson), and was pregnant once again, this time to the man by whose name history remembers her.

Early in 1870 Frederick Cotton's sister Margaret introduced him to Mary Ann, whom she had known since her teens; neither realised that she had had two husbands after Mowbray. Cotton's wife and two of their children had recently died, leaving him with two sons, so his sister had moved in to help with their care. Margaret Cotton died on 25 March, following severe stomach pains, her death proving to be fortuitous for Mary Ann, who became Cotton's lover and then his bigamous wife. They married in September and their son was born in January 1871, scandalously soon after the wedding, in the opinion of the neighbours. A few weeks after the marriage Mary Ann Cotton insured her husband's two boys with the Prudential, and in the spring of 1871 the family moved to West Auckland, County Durham. There they lived in the same street as Mary Ann's former lover, Joseph Nattrass who, like Cotton, worked at the local colliery.

A year and two days after his marriage, Frederick Cotton died suddenly at the age of thirty-nine. His doctor certified death due to gastric fever. Three months later Nattrass moved into the Cotton house as a lodger, expecting to marry Mary Ann. But she had taken a job as nurse to a brewery excise officer, a man much higher up the social scale than Nattrass or Cotton herself, and she began to clear a path for marriage to him. In March 1872 two of the Cotton boys (including her own son) and Nattrass died, apparently of natural causes, and Mary Ann was pregnant by the excise officer. She received insurance money of £5 15s. for the elder Cotton boy from the Prudential, but still had little money, as neither Cotton nor Nattrass had had much to leave to her. She relied on parish relief of 1s. 6d. per week for the remaining child, seven-year-old Charles Edward Cotton. She tried to send the boy to his uncle, or into the workhouse, but failed, and then predicted his early death to the assistant parish overseer. A week later, on 12 July, when this man heard that the apparently healthy child was suddenly dead, he went to the police, urged the doctor not to certify the death, and succeeded in having the case reported to the coroner. Without a certificate, Mary Ann Cotton was unable to claim the £4 10s. insurance money for the boy.[22]

A local doctor performed an autopsy on a table in the Cotton house, only an hour before the inquest. He was unable to state with certainty that death had not been due to natural causes and, in the absence of a chemical analysis, the jury found their verdict accordingly. But local opinion held that Mrs Cotton was a poisoner, and since Dr Kilburn had kept the stomach, its contents and other viscera, he did a Reinsch test after the inquest, finding the unmistakable signs of arsenic. Local rumour had spurred him into taking an action that other physicians

who had had dealings with Mary Ann had not dreamed necessary. On
18 July Mary Ann Cotton was charged with murder, and a week later
the body of Charles Edward Cotton was exhumed. Samples from it
were taken to Thomas Scattergood at Leeds, who confirmed the
presence of arsenic in many of the internal organs. His case notebook
shows in detail the tests that he did on these and on later samples as
Nattrass (September) and then two more Cotton children (October)
were exhumed; arsenic was found in all three bodies.[23]

In August 1872 magistrates ordered Mary Ann Cotton to stand trial
in December for the murder of Charles Edward Cotton. The magnitude
of the further possible charges against her, however, as well as her
advancing state of pregnancy, led legal officials to postpone the trial. In
early January 1873 she gave birth to her twelfth child, a girl, who
remained with her in gaol until the Durham spring assizes commenced
in March. In February three more charges of murder were added to the
counts against her; she had no lawyer at these committal hearings. A
few days before the trial the judge asked an experienced member of the
Northern circuit to take on her defence, while she was prosecuted by
the barrister who later defended Florence Maybrick.

The trial took nearly three days. Although the sole charge was that
of the murder of Charles Edward Cotton, the judge permitted the
prosecution to introduce evidence of the three other deaths, to prove
that the boy's had not been accidental. The trials of Mary Anne Geering
and another poisoner were cited as a legal precedent for such a move,
normally considered prejudicial to the defendant. After deliberating for
only an hour, the jury found her guilty. (Had she been acquitted, the
prosecution was ready to try her for the murder of Joseph Nattrass.)
The judge sentenced her to death, claiming that poison always left
'complete and incontestable traces of guilt'.[24] By the early 1870s this was
true of any arsenic poisoning, but the Cotton case shows how easily
unwary doctors working in areas of high mortality and unsanitary living
conditions could overlook those traces. The same mistakes were to be
made again in Liverpool in the early 1880s, as Catherine Flanagan and
Margaret Higgins exploited the carelessness of doctors and weaknesses
in the insurance industry. As Dickens had pointed out twenty years
earlier, poison could shield the administrator from detection for quite
some considerable time.

Mary Ann Cotton was hanged in Durham gaol on 24 March 1873, following the rule of allowing three clear Sundays to pass between sentence and death. She gave her infant up for adoption five days before the end, to a childless couple who assured her they would bring the girl up in the fear of God. Petitions to secure a reprieve on the grounds that there was very little direct evidence against her, and that her poverty meant she could not call upon an expert to challenge Scattergood, failed. The *Lancet* pointed out that her highly suspicious history had probably swayed the jury. With hindsight, it seems likely that her habit of moving from place to place long deflected attention from the pattern of deaths that followed in her wake. Cotton made no confession of guilt before she died, but her life story shows every indication that she poisoned at least twelve people, perhaps seventeen: all those close to her who died after 1860. The actual number is probably fourteen or fifteen: question marks hang over the deaths of William Mowbray and two of their offspring, while four more of their eight children probably died of natural causes. The motive for these killings seems to have been in each case related to money or the lack of it: children and adults were killed so that she could attract a better husband, be free of an idle one, or collect cash. In her quest for financial security she came to view children as commodities, a character flaw that was not especially unusual at a time when it was freely acknowledged that life insurance could have detrimental effects on children's welfare. Cotton was an extreme example of a type of killer first seen during the hungry 1840s, and only her chilling 'success' sets her apart from other female serial poisoners of the nineteenth century. No one was particularly surprised when children, particularly poor children, died young.

A woman driven by the same needs and weaknesses as Mary Ann Cotton is unlikely to appear in modern England, since many of the stimuli to murder experienced by the Victorian poor have been removed. Divorce is readily available, female employment opportunities have expanded, infant mortality rates are low, child deaths are investigated aggressively, insurance companies use sophisticated techniques to root out fraud, and national social welfare systems offer a safety net to those who fall upon hard times. The citizens of twenty-first century England, blessed with a high standard of living and an extensive range of personal freedoms, still commit murder by poison, but it is no longer a crime of the poor and underprivileged. Poison murders for profit are now associated with the middle classes. It is usually men who plot to inherit large amounts of money or obtain big insurance payments on the death of a spouse.[25] In March 2000, an unemployed chemist, John Allan, was sentenced to life imprisonment for poisoning his girlfriend with sodium cyanide in an attempt to inherit her £460,000 estate. He had forged her will, and when arrested in February 1999 had already set his sights on another wealthy woman.[26] Modern criminologists recognise a type of female serial murderer called the 'Black Widow', who usually uses poison to kill husbands or relatives for financial gain. Closely allied to these criminals are women who, normally using poison, kill people to whom they are not related, also for money, after creating a relationship with them (typically as nurse or housekeeper).[27] They are the modern successors of Catherine Wilson, but the last known English case was that of Dorothea Waddingham in the 1930s. Then there are the poisoners who suffer from Münchausen syndrome by proxy, a condition first noted in Leeds in 1977. Normally associated with women, the illness remained a medical oddity until Beverly Allitt came to the public's attention. In January 2003, a woman from west Cumbria was convicted of slowly poisoning her young son to death with a cocktail of prescription drugs.[28] An attention seeking disorder, Münchausen syndrome by proxy may lead women to poison their own children, but the murky psychological motives with which it is associated means that such crimes bear little relation to the child poisonings of the nineteenth century. Infants remain at the greatest risk of homicide in England, but they are rarely killed by poison.[29]

Although the public profile of the typical poisoner has changed over the years, poisoners of all centuries share one thing in common: nearly all are resolute in their determination to kill. Poison is rarely used in a moment of passion. Instead, the perpetrator carefully plans his or her crime, hoping or assuming that a lack of visible trauma will hide the fact that a murder has occurred. Always a relatively rare aspect of English criminal behaviour, the most obvious difference between modern poisoning crimes and their Georgian and Victorian predecessors lies in the poisoners and their victims. It is difficult to feel pity for a middle-class killer who has enough yet wants more. It is difficult to understand the bizarre motives of the modern serial killer, or the mentally ill. But it is perhaps more difficult to imagine the conditions in which many poisoners of the eighteenth and nineteenth centuries existed. Each society breeds its own criminals. The poisoners of the past – the wretched poor, servants, those who had little hope and few options, the depressed and disaffected, ordinary people neglected by society until they did or became something that could not be ignored – they were all of their time. The remarkable lives of some of England's long forgotten denizens, as well as some of its most notorious, offer us a glimpse of society as it once was.

Notes

Notes to Introduction

1. Public Record Office (PRO), ASSI 45/64, box 2 (Yorkshire), *Regina* v. *Rebecca Stevenson*, 1837. Deposition of George Gorell.
2. Ibid., depositions of Benjamin Stevenson, Joseph Stevenson and Jane Coates.
3. 'Statistics of Poisoning in England', *Lancet*, 1 (1839–40), pp. 597–99.
4. See, for example, M. S. Hartman, *Victorian Murderesses: A True History of Thirteen Respectable French and English Women Accused of Unspeakable Crimes* (paperback edn, London, 1985); T. Boyle, *Black Swine in the Sewers of Hampstead* (London, 1989); I. A. Burney, 'A Poisoning of No Substance: The Trials of Medico-Legal Proof in Mid-Victorian England', *Journal of British Studies*, 38 (1999), pp. 59–92; I. A. Burney, 'Testing Testimony: Toxicology and the Law of Evidence in Early Nineteenth-Century England', *Studies in History and Philosophy of Science*, 33 (2002), pp. 289–314.

Notes to Chapter 1: Victims

1. W. Roughead, ed., *Trial of Mary Blandy* (Edinburgh, 1914), p. 81.
2. Ibid., p. 35. The author is quoting from C. A. Mitchell, *Science and the Criminal* (1911).
3. S. Landsman, 'One Hundred Years of Rectitude: Medical Witnesses at the Old Bailey, 1717–1817', *Law and History Review*, 16 (1998), pp. 445–94.
4. T. R. Forbes, *Surgeons at the Bailey: English Forensic Medicine to 1878* (New Haven, 1985), pp. 21, 128 (three cases). The online Old Bailey Proceedings reveal four: www.oldbaileyonline.org.uk.
5. Forbes, *Surgeons at the Bailey*, p. 132.
6. Ibid., pp. 132–33.
7. Ibid., p. 133.
8. Roughead, *Trial of Mary Blandy*, pp. 80–86.
9. Ibid., pp. 83–84.

10. A. S. Taylor, *On Poisons in Relation to Medical Jurisprudence and Medicine* (London, 1848), p. 140.

11. Ibid., pp. 132–33.

12. D. J. A. Kerr, *Forensic Medicine: A Textbook for Students and a Guide for the Practitioner* (London, 1936), p. 247.

13. M. Farrell, *Poisons and Poisoners: An Encyclopedia of Homicidal Poisonings* (London, 1992), p. 29.

14. Kerr, *Forensic Medicine*, pp. 249–50.

15. See, for example, PRO, ASSI 45/51 (Yorkshire), *Rex* v. *William Bailey otherwise Knightson*, 1818. Deposition of Ann Dodsworth.

16. Ibid., p. 249.

17. See, for example, PRO, ASSI 52/8 (Lancashire), *Regina* v. *Mary Ann Britland*, 1886. Deposition of Dr Thomas Harris: 'Arsenic preserves a body after death'.

18. G. E. Male, *An Epitome of Judicial or Forensic Medicine: For the Use of Medical Men, Coroners and Barristers* (London, 1816), p. 59.

19. G. S. Rousseau and D. B. Haycock, 'Coleridge's Choleras: Cholera Morbus, Asiatic Cholera and Dysentery in Nineteenth-Century England', *Bulletin of the History of Medicine*, 77 (2003), pp. 298–328.

20. Ibid. See also C. Creighton, *A History of Epidemics in Britain*, ii (London, 1965), pp. 747–92.

21. M. Pelling, *Cholera, Fever and English Medicine, 1825–1865* (Oxford, 1978), pp. 1–3.

22. H. Letheby, 'On the Probability of Confounding Cases of Arsenical Poisoning with Those of Cholera', *Pharmaceutical Journal*, 8 (1848–49), pp. 237–40 (p. 239).

23. Ibid., pp. 239–40.

24. Kerr, *Forensic Medicine*, pp. 254–55.

25. Ibid., pp. 256–58; R. A. Witthaus, *Manual of Toxicology* (London, 1911), pp. 756–62, 768–71.

26. Kerr, *Forensic Medicine*, pp. 258–60; W. A. Brend, *A Handbook of Medical Jurisprudence and Toxicology* (6th edn, London, 1928), pp. 254–56; Witthaus, *Manual of Toxicology*, p. 719.

27. Witthaus, *Manual of Toxicology*, pp. 228–97.

28. PRO, DURH 18/1 (Durham), *Regina* v. *William Turnbull*, 1863. Deposition of John Evans.

29. PRO, ASSI 6/7 (Gloucestershire), *Regina* v. *Emanuel Barnett*, 1849. Inquest on Elizabeth Gregory, deposition of Diana Gregory. The boy was Elizabeth's illegitimate son, aged two. See also *The Times*, 9 April 1850, p. 7e.

30. Ibid., deposition of William Hatch.

31. Ibid., deposition of Dr William Philpot Brookes.

32. Ibid., deposition of Emanuel Barnett.

33. Ibid., deposition of Caroline Gregory.

34. J. Knelman, *Twisting in the Wind: The Murderess and the English Press* (Toronto, 1998), p. 215.

35. *Regina* v. *Emanuel Barnett*. Inquest on Elizabeth Gregory, deposition of Dr William Philpot Brookes.

36. Ibid., deposition of William Herapath.

37. Ibid., deposition of Caroline Gregory.

38. See, for example, S. Farr, *Elements of Medical Jurisprudence* (London, 1788), p. 96.

39. See, for example, J. G. Smith, *The Principles of Forensic Medicine, Systematically Arranged and Applied to British Practice* (2nd edn, London, 1824), p. 103. His work drew heavily on the writings of M. J. B. Orfila (1787–1853), the Spanish-born but Paris-based father of toxicology.

40. Male, *Judicial or Forensic Medicine*, pp. 55–58.

41. Witthaus, *Manual of Toxicology*, pp. 598–623.

42. W. T. Vincent, *The Records of the Woolwich District*, i (Woolwich, 1888), pp. 534–42.

43. J. Marsh, 'Account of a Method of Separating Small Quantities of Arsenic from Substances with Which it May be Mixed', *Edinburgh New Philosophical Journal*, 21 (1836), pp. 229–36.

44. Witthaus, *Manual of Toxicology*, pp. 604–5.

45. W. A. Campbell, 'Some Landmarks in the History of Arsenic Testing', *Chemistry in Britain*, 1 (1965), pp. 198–202.

46. See, for example, the cases of Robert and Ann Sandys, and Ann Edge (Cheshire, 1841), Hannah Roberts (Flintshire, 1842), Sarah Dazley (Bedfordshire, 1843), Betty Eccles (Lancashire, 1843).

47. H. Reinsch, 'On the Action of Metallic Copper on Solutions of Certain Metals, Particularly with Reference to the Detection of Arsenic', *Philosophical Magazine*, 19 (1841), pp. 480–83. First published in the *Journal für Praktische Chemie*, 19 (1841).

48. L. A. Parry, *Some Famous Medical Trials* (New York, 1928; reprint 1976), pp. 193–207.

49. R. J. Flanagan, B. Widdop, J. D. Ramsey and M. Loveland, 'Analytical Toxicology', *Human Toxicology*, 7 (1988), pp. 489–502.

50. Male, *Judicial or Forensic Medicine*, pp. 79–80; Brend, *Medical Jurisprudence and Toxicology*, pp. 234–38.

51. Taylor, *On Poisons*, p. 226; Witthaus, *Manual of Toxicology*, p. 299.

52. M. J. B. Orfila, *A General System of Toxicology: or A Treatise on Poisons*,

Drawn from the Mineral, Vegetable and Animal Kingdoms (Paris, 1814–15; translated by J. A. Waller, London, 1816–17).

53. N. G. Coley, 'Forensic Chemistry in Nineteenth-Century Britain', *Endeavour*, 22 (1998), pp. 143–47.

54. Brend, *Medical Jurisprudence and Toxicology*, pp. 250–58.

55. PRO, ASSI 65/14 (Montgomeryshire), *Regina v. William Samuel*, 1886. Deposition of Francis Ernest Marston.

56. Ibid., deposition of Thomas Porter Blunt.

57. Ibid., depositions of George Ellis, George Morris, John Pugh, George Davies.

58. PRO, ASSI 61/22, Crown Minute Book, North Wales Division, Montgomeryshire summer assizes at Newtown, 1886.

59. Kerr, *Forensic Medicine*, p. 276.

60. Witthaus, *Manual of Toxicology*, pp. 1040–41, 1044–46.

61. Ibid., p. 1050.

62. I. A. Burney, 'A Poisoning of No Substance: The Trials of Medico-Legal Proof in Mid-Victorian England', *Journal of British Studies*, 38 (1999), pp. 59–92, on p. 82.

63. PRO, ASSI 6/41 (Staffordshire), *Rex v. Martha Bowyer*, 1906.

64. 'Statistics of Poisoning in England', *Lancet*, 1 (1839–40), pp. 597–99; Witthaus, *Manual of Toxicology*, p. 948.

65. PRO, PCOM 1/73, Old Bailey Sessions Papers, *Regina v. Bridget Kavanagh*, 1857, pp. 756–60. Testimony of Jane Hart, p. 757.

66. Kerr, *Forensic Medicine*, pp. 272–75; Brend, *Medical Jurisprudence and Toxicology*, pp. 290–91, 299–301.

67. Ibid.

68. Parry, *Famous Medical Trials*, pp. 88–103.

69. J. S. Stas, 'Considérations sur une méthode générale propre a déceler les alcalis organiques dans le cas d'empoissonnement', *Bulletin de l'Académie Royale de Médecine Belgique*, 11 (1851), pp. 304–12.

70. M. Hall, 'Note on the Detection of Strychnia', *Lancet*, 1 (1856), pp. 36, 623.

71. Witthaus, *Manual of Toxicology*, pp. 792–95, 800.

72. 'Poisoning by Prussic Acid', *Pharmaceutical Journal*, third series, 7 (1876–77), p. 167.

Notes to Chapter 2: Poisons and Poisoners

1. C. Dickens, 'Household Crime', *Household Words*, 4 (1851), pp. 277–81 (p. 277).

2. This aphorism is attributed to Paracelsus (1493–1541): K. D. Watson, 'Highlights in the History of Toxicology', in Philip Wexler, ed., *Information Resources in Toxicology* (3rd edn, San Diego, 2000), pp. 1–13.

3. One grain has a mass of 65 mg. There are 437.5 grains per ounce.

4. Figures for Yorkshire are for the years 1783 to 1821. Those for Cheshire, Lancashire and Warwickshire relate to, respectively, 1863, 1834 and 1885.

5. Retail prices (per ounce) for other common poisons were as follows. In Lancashire (1808) savin oil cost 5s. In London in the 1850s, potassium sulphate and concentrated sulphuric acid sold for 3d. Pure opium and prussic acid were about 2s. across England, while laudanum ranged between 4d. and 6d. Lead acetate and oxalic acid were relatively cheap at 2d. In Montgomeryshire in 1886, pure strychnine cost over 7s. Prices did not vary much between different regions of the country.

6. G. Best, *Mid-Victorian Britain, 1851–75* (London, 1971), pp. 111–19. Figures refer to 1867.

7. T. McLaughlin, *The Coward's Weapon* (London, 1980), pp. 161–77.

8. M. S. Hartman, *Victorian Murderesses: A True History of Thirteen Respectable French and English Women Accused of Unspeakable Crimes* (paperback edn, London, 1985), p. 41.

9. 'Poisoning by Arsenic', *Pharmaceutical Journal*, second series, 2 (1860–61), pp. 191, 386.

10. B. Ryan, *The Poisoned Life of Mrs Maybrick* (London, 1977), pp. 177, 230, 238.

11. PRO, ASSI 52/95 (Lancashire), *Rex* v. *Ellen Burndred*, 1904. Deposition of John Hayes.

12. P. Bartrip, 'A "Pennurth of Arsenic for Rat Poison": The Arsenic Act, 1851 and the Prevention of Secret Poisoning', *Medical History*, 36 (1992), pp. 53–69, on p. 55.

13. *Cartoons From 'Punch'*, 4 vols (London, 1906), i, p. 205: 'Fatal Facility; or Poisons for the Asking', 8 September 1849.

14. PRO, ASSI 45/35/2/13 (Yorkshire), *Rex* v. *Ellen Bayston*, 1785.

15. P. H. Holland, *A Report of the Trial and Acquittal of Mary Hunter* (Manchester, 1843), pp. 7–9.

16. PRO, ASSI 52/3 (Lancashire), *Regina* v. *Mary Whiteside*, 1879. Deposition of Robert Chumley.

17. A. H. Allen, 'Vermin-Killers Containing Strychnine', *Pharmaceutical Journal*, third series, 20 (1889–90), pp. 296–99.

18. PRO, ASSI 45/73 (Yorkshire), *Regina* v. *Jane Torkington*, 1861. Deposition of William Steele.

19. V. Berridge and G. Edwards, *Opium and the People: Opiate Use in Nineteenth-Century England* (London, 1987).

20. PRO, ASSI 36/3 (Kent), *Regina* v. *Elizabeth Pettit*, 1838.

21. Berridge and Edwards, *Opium and the People*, pp. 226–29.

22. W. A. Brend, *A Handbook of Medical Jurisprudence and Toxicology* (6th edn, London, 1928), p. 288.

23. *The Trial of Michael Whiting for Administering Poison to George and Joseph Langman* (Cambridge, 1812).

24. PRO, PL 27/9, box 2 (Lancashire), *Rex* v. *Henry Scholfield*, 1817. Deposition of Isaac Woolfenden.

25. J. G. L. Burnby, *A Study of the English Apothecary from 1660 to 1760* (London, 1983), pp. 24–27, 53–61. A. Digby, *Making a Medical Living: Doctors and Patients in the English Market for Medicine, 1720–1911* (Cambridge, 1994), pp. 28–35.

26. Burnby, *A Study of the English Apothecary*, pp. 47, 53.

27. J. Langton and R. J. Morris (eds), *Atlas of Industrializing Britain, 1780–1914* (London, 1986), pp. 180–84; N. Cox, *The Complete Tradesman: A Study of Retailing, 1550–1820* (Aldershot, 2000), p. 224.

28. 'The Statistics of Poisoning', *Pharmaceutical Journal*, 17 (1857–58), pp. 249–51. This article reported that in England about 15,000 people sold medicines and drugs.

29. Bartrip, 'The Arsenic Act 1851', p. 57.

30. 'The Definition of the Term Chemist and Druggist', *Pharmaceutical Journal*, 1 (1841–42), pp. 329–31.

31. 'Mysterious Affair at Putney', *The Times*, 28 February 1831, p. 6a; 1 March 1831, p. 4b; 'Attempted Suicide', *The Times*, 7 March 1831, p. 7a.

32. See, for example, 'Parliamentary and Law Proceedings', *Pharmaceutical Journal*, third series, 3 (1872–73), pp. 574–75.

33. M. J. Clarke, 'The History of Suicide in England and Wales, 1850–1961: With Special Reference to Suicide by Poisoning' (unpublished D.Phil. thesis, Oxford University, 1993), p. 361.

34. PRO, ASSI 52/170 (Lancashire), *Rex* v. *Edith Agnes Bingham*, 1911. Deposition of William Henry Roberts.

35. G. L. Browne and C. G. Stewart, *Reports of Trials for Murder by Poisoning* (London, 1883), pp. 233–68. See ibid., pp. 235–36, for the suggestion that Dove was inspired by the Palmer case.

36. PRO, ASSI 13/31 (Northamptonshire), *Re. Johnson Deceased* [*Rex* v. *Octavius Edwards Trezise*], 1901.

37. J. H. H. Gaute and R. Odell, *Murder 'Whatdunit': An Illustrated Account of the Methods of Murder* (London, 1982), pp. 330–31.

38. B. R. Mitchell, *British Historical Statistics* (Cambridge, 1988), p. 9.

39. C. Emsley, *Crime and Society in England, 1750–1900* (2nd edn, London, 1996), pp. 42, 156.

40. D. J. V. Jones, *Crime in Nineteenth-Century Wales* (Cardiff, 1992), pp. 72–75.

41. *The Times*, 25 March 1826, p. 3a.
42. Emsley, *Crime and Society in England*, pp. 42–44.
43. J. Knelman, *Twisting in the Wind: The Murderess and the English Press* (Toronto, 1998), pp. 213–15.
44. F. Young, ed., *Trial of the Seddons* (2nd edn, Edinburgh, 1925).
45. This table notes the ages of accused poisoners, 1750–1914.

Age	Female	Male
10–19	37	15
20–29	62	46
30–39	38	30
40–49	23	28
50–59	14	10
60–69	2	6
>69	1	6
Unknown	100	122
Total	277	263

46. P. Jalland, *Death in the Victorian Family* (Oxford, 1996), pp. 143–45.
47. Emsley, *Crime and Society in England*, pp. 68–69.
48. C. A. Conley, *The Unwritten Law: Criminal Justice in Victorian Kent* (Oxford, 1991), p. 188.
49. See Chapter 4.
50. Eleven and nineteen cases, respectively, out of the total of 540.
51. 'Murder by Poisoning in Leicester', *The Times*, 15 April 1842, p. 6b.
52. *The Times*, 30 July 1889, p. 11f. For an account of the case against Winters and Frost, see *The Times*, 23 April 1889, p. 9d; 31 May 1889, p. 10f; 4 June 1889, p. 12c; 10 July 1889, p. 8c; 24 October 1889, p. 12e; 26 October 1889, p. 10c.
53. *The Times*, 26 April 1830, p. 2c. For the verdict see PRO, HO 27/39, Buckinghamshire Calendar of Prisoners, 1830.
54. PRO, PCOM 1/77, Old Bailey Sessions Papers, *Regina* v. *James Turner and Edward Keefe*, 1859, pp. 836–37.
55. A. Appleton, *Mary Ann Cotton: Her Story and Trial* (London, 1973), p. 135.
56. Poison cases involving multiple victims of a single perpetrator:

Perpetrator	Number of Victims				
	2	3	4	5	>5
Male	18	5	1	1	1
Female	14	13	4	1	5

Notes to Chapter 3: Reasons of the Heart

1. PRO, ASSI 36/5 (Suffolk), *Regina* v. *Catherine Foster*, 1846. Deposition of Maria Woodgate.
2. A. Macfarlane, *Marriage and Love in England, 1300–1840* (Oxford, 1986), pp. 321–31.
3. L. Davidoff, 'The Family in Britain', in F. M. L. Thompson, ed., *The Cambridge Social History of Britain, 1750–1950*, ii (Cambridge, 1990), pp. 71–129, on p. 105.
4. O. R. McGregor, *Divorce in England: A Centenary Study* (London, 1957), p. 84; M. Anderson, 'The Social Implications of Demographic Change', in Thompson, ed., *Cambridge Social History of Britain*, pp. 1–70, on p. 28.
5. The Matrimonial Causes Act of 1857.
6. McGregor, *Divorce in England*, pp. 17–22.
7. Anderson, 'Social Implications of Demographic Change', p. 31.
8. McGregor, *Divorce in England*, pp. 23–34.
9. G. Best, *Mid-Victorian Britain, 1851–75* (London, 1971), p. 302; Macfarlane, *Marriage and Love in England*, p. 230; J. Perkin, *Victorian Women* (London, 1993), pp. 115–18, 154.
10. See below, Chapter 5. We might note here the names of the medical murderers, Palmer, Smethurst and Lamson, as well as Seddon, as early examples of the sort of middle-class murderer found today.
11. Perkin, *Victorian Women*, p. 184.
12. Davidoff, 'The Family in Britain', p. 90.
13. L. Stone, *Road to Divorce: England, 1530–1987* (Oxford, 1990), pp. 143–48; Macfarlane, *Marriage and Love in England*, pp. 226–27.
14. Anderson, 'Social Implications of Demographic Change', p. 29.
15. Macfarlane, *Marriage and Love in England*, pp. 231–34; M. Abbott, *Family Ties: English Families, 1540–1920* (London, 1993), pp. 66–68, 92–94.
16. Anderson, 'Social Implications of Demographic Change', pp. 28–32.
17. PRO, ASSI 6/24 (Gloucestershire), *Regina* v. *Hannah Curtis*, 1850.
18. PRO, ASSI 45/82, box 1 (Durham), *Regina* v. *Mary Ann Scrafton and Eliza Foxall*, 1887.
19. G. Robb, 'Circe in Crinoline: Domestic Poisonings in Victorian England', *Journal of Family History*, 22 (1997), pp. 176–90, on pp. 178–79.
20. J. Knelman, *Twisting in the Wind: The Murderess and the English Press* (Toronto, 1998), p. 66.
21. Robb, 'Circe in Crinoline', pp. 176–77.
22. Knelman, *Twisting in the Wind*, p. 86.

23. C. Emsley, *Crime and Society in England, 1750–1900* (2nd edn, London, 1996), pp. 46–49.
24. Knelman, *Twisting in the Wind*, pp. 86–87.
25. *Regina* v. *Catherine Foster*, deposition of Robert Jones.
26. Ibid., deposition of Maria Woodgate.
27. Ibid., depositions of George Pook and William Edmund Image.
28. P. Wilson, *Murderess: A Study of Women Executed in Britain since 1843* (London, 1971), pp. 52–53.
29. He was probably Thomas Spraggons; see Knelman, *Twisting in the Wind*, pp. 96–97, 288.
30. *Regina* v. *Catherine Foster*, deposition of Maria Morley.
31. PRO, ASSI 45/35/2/13 (Yorkshire), *Rex* v. *Ellen Bayston*, 1785. Depositions of Ralph Dunn and James Cariss and confession of Ellen Bayston.
32. PRO, ASSI 45/65 (Cumberland), *Regina* v. *John Graham*, 1839.
33. Macfarlane, *Marriage and Love in England*, pp. 211–17.
34. PRO, PCOM 1/77, Central Criminal Court Sessions Papers, *Regina* v. *James Turner and Edward Keefe*, 1859, pp. 836–37.
35. D. G. Browne and E. V. Tullett, *Bernard Spilsbury: His Life and Cases* (London, 1951), pp. 38–54; on p. 38.
36. For a detailed summary of the case see F. Young, 'Hawley Harvey Crippen', in H. Hodge (ed.), *Famous Trials*, i (London, 1941), pp. 111–38.
37. Precisely why is unclear: she may have used his affair as an excuse for leaving a marriage she no longer had any use for.
38. M. Farrell, *Poisons and Poisoners: An Encyclopedia of Homicidal Poisonings* (London, 1992), pp. 67–68.
39. L. A. Parry, *Some Famous Medical Trials* (New York, 1928; reprint 1976), pp. 170–85.
40. PRO, ASSI 45/54 (Yorkshire), *Rex* v. *Ann Barber*, 1821. See also Knelman, *Twisting in the Wind*, pp. 93–94.
41. Most were under thirty-five; 72 per cent were single.
42. Anderson, 'Social Implications of Demographic Change', pp. 64–65.
43. PRO, ASSI 36/6 (Cambridgeshire), *Regina* v. *Elias Lucas and Mary Reeder*, 1850; Wilson, *Murderess*, pp. 85–89.
44. *An Account of the Trial, Execution, etc of William and John Curren, for the Wilful Murder of Thomas Raven, of Barrow-upon-Soar, and of William Barnett, for the Poisoning of his Wife* (Leicester, 1822).
45. PRO, ASSI 36/22 (Cambridgeshire), *Regina* v. *Samuel Shotliffe*, 1877; 'Poisoning by Strychnine', *Pharmaceutical Journal*, third series, 8 (1877–78), p. 579.
46. G. L. Browne and C. G. Stewart, *Reports of Trials for Murder by Poisoning* (London, 1883), pp. 16–49.

47. 'Charge of Wife Poisoning', *The Times*, 25 May 1878, p. 12e.
48. PRO, ASSI 36/2 (Norfolk), *Rex* v. *Frances Billing and Catherine Frarey*, 1835, and PRO, ASSI 36/3 (Norfolk), *Rex* v. *Peter Taylor*, 1836.
49. *The Times*, 17 August 1829, p. 2e.
50. PRO, ASSI 45/69 (Yorkshire), *Regina* v. *James Holdsworth*, 1849; 'Murder Near Bradford', *The Times*, 23 December 1848, p. 3f.
51. 'Poisoning by Arsenic', *The Times*, 14 August 1860, p. 10a, and *Pharmaceutical Journal*, second series, 2 (1860–61), pp. 191, 386.
52. *The Times*, 1 August 1835, p. 7b.
53. *The Times*, 31 July 1869, p. 11c.
54. PRO, PL 27/9, box 1 (Lancashire), *Rex* v. *Cecilia Collier*, 1813. Depositions of Maria Oxenbould, Elizabeth Oxenbould and Samuel Mee.
55. Emsley, *Crime and Society in England*, p. 47.
56. PRO, PL 27/11, box 1 (Lancashire), *Rex* v. *Betty Rowland*, 1836. Depositions of James Sawley and Joseph Saddler Thomas; *The Times*, 9 April 1836, p. 6c.

Notes to Chapter 4: Suffer the Little Children

1. PRO, ASSI 36/6 (Essex), *Regina* v. *Sarah Bright and David Gray*, 1847. Deposition of Emanuel Bright.
2. G. K. Behlmer, *Child Abuse and Moral Reform in England, 1870–1908* (Stanford, California, 1982), p. 18.
3. L. Rose, *The Massacre of the Innocents: Infanticide in Britain, 1800–1939* (London, 1986), pp. 6–8.
4. J. Langton and R. J. Morris (eds), *Atlas of Industrializing Britain, 1780–1914* (London, 1986), p. 19.
5. M. May, 'Violence in the Family: An Historical Perspective', in J. P. Martin, ed., *Violence and the Family* (Chichester, 1978), pp. 135–68, on pp. 150, 152.
6. Rose, *Massacre of the Innocents*, pp. 7–8, 12.
7. PRO, ASSI 6/15 (Gloucestershire), *Regina* v. *Edwin Bailey and Anne Barrey*, 1873; P. Wilson, *Murderess: A Study of Women Executed in Britain since 1843* (London, 1971), pp. 173–75.
8. Rose, *Massacre of the Innocents*, p. 60.
9. Ibid., p. 10.
10. M. J. Daunton, *Progress and Poverty: An Economic and Social History of Britain, 1700–1850* (Oxford, 1995), pp. 448–50.
11. Rose, *Massacre of the Innocents*, p. 24.
12. PRO, ASSI 45/62, box 1 (Yorkshire), *Rex* v. *Martin Slack*, 1829; *The Times*, 30 March 1829, p. 3d.

13. Rose, *Massacre of the Innocents*, pp. 22–34. The absolute number of illegitimate births corresponded to a rate of 7 to 8 per cent around mid century.

14. PRO, ASSI 36/6 (Essex), *Regina v. Sarah Bright and David Gray*, 1847.

15. Behlmer, *Child Abuse and Moral Reform*, p. 40. This law remained the basis for dealing with the financial maintenance of illegitimate children until 1957.

16. *Central Criminal Court Sessions Papers*, vol. 119, *Regina v. Emily Newber*, 1894, pp. 304–15.

17. Behlmer, *Child Abuse and Moral Reform*, pp. 72, 95.

18. A. Kidd, *State, Society and the Poor in Nineteenth-Century England* (London, 1999), p. 14.

19. E. P. Thompson, *The Making of the English Working Class*, reprint (London, 1980), pp. 269–79.

20. J. D. Chambers and G. E. Mingay, *The Agricultural Revolution, 1750–1880* (London, 1966), pp. 109–46.

21. Ibid., pp. 150–55.

22. C. Emsley, *Crime and Society in England, 1750–1900* (2nd edn, London, 1996), p. 37.

23. Chambers and Mingay, *Agricultural Revolution*, p. 151.

24. Thompson, *English Working Class*, p. 296.

25. Income tax was first imposed as a wartime measure by William Pitt the Younger in 1799, and continued at varying rates until 1816, when it was abandoned.

26. G. Best, *Mid-Victorian Britain, 1851–75* (London, 1971), pp. 140–53.

27. Wilson, *Murderess*, pp. 69–72.

28. Ibid.

29. *The Times*, 2 August 1849, p. 6f.

30. Wilson, *Murderess*, pp. 72–75.

31. *The Times*, 21 July 1849, p. 7f; 18 August 1849, p. 5b; 20 August 1849, p. 7c.

32. Wilson, *Murderess*, pp. 32–33; *The Times*, 17 September 1844, p. 4d.

33. PRO, PL 27/11, box 2 (Lancashire), *Regina v. Betty Eccles*; Wilson, *Murderess*, pp. 15–17; J. Knelman, *Twisting in the Wind: The Murderess and the English Press* (Toronto, 1998), pp. 55–56.

34. Behlmer, *Child Abuse and Moral Reform*, p. 120.

35. Rose, *Massacre of the Innocents*, p. 137.

36. PRO, ASSI 65/1 (Cheshire), *Regina v. Robert Standring*, 1839.

37. PRO, ASSI 65/2 (Cheshire), untitled copy of inquest testimony into the deaths of Elizabeth, Mary Ann and Catherine Sandys, 1840; Rose, *Massacre of the Innocents*, pp. 139–41.

38. Rose, *Massacre of the Innocents*, pp. 140–41; PRO, ASSI 61/9 (Cheshire), Summer Assizes 1841 and ASSI 61/11 (Cheshire), Spring Assizes 1842.

39. Rose, *Massacre of the Innocents*, pp. 136–58.

40. PRO, ASSI 65/10 (Cheshire), *Regina v. Edward and Ellen Heesom*, 1878; Rose, *Massacre of the Innocents*, pp. 150–51.

41. PRO, ASSI 52/8 (Lancashire), *Regina v. Mary Ann Britland*, 1886; Wilson, *Murderess*, pp. 217–19.

42. PRO, ASSI 52/9 (Lancashire), *Regina v. Elizabeth Berry*, 1887; Knelman, *Twisting in the Wind*, pp. 80–82.

43. PRO, ASSI 45/82, box 1 (Yorkshire), *Regina v. William Dawson Holgate*, 1888.

44. PRO, ASSI 13/19 (Derbyshire), *Regina v. George Horton*, 1889. Deposition of Annie Elizabeth Horton.

45. Ibid., deposition of David Cowlishaw. It is not clear who the other child was, as this comment was made two months before Kate's death.

46. Rose, *Massacre of the Innocents*, pp. 154–58.

47. Behlmer, *Child Abuse and Moral Reform*, pp. 108–9, 173.

48. PRO, ASSI 52/95 (Lancashire), *Rex v. Ellen Burndred*, 1904.

49. *Central Criminal Court Sessions Papers*, vol. 142, *Rex v. Arthur Devereux*, 1905, pp. 1359–99; on p. 1359.

50. Ibid., p. 1376.

51. C. Wilson and P. Pitman, *Encyclopaedia of Murder* (London, 1984), pp. 207–8.

52. PRO, PL 27/9, box 2 (Lancashire), *Rex v. Henry Scholfield*, 1817.

53. PRO, PL 27/9, box 2 (Lancashire), *Murder, Sarah Holroyd* (sic), 1816.

54. L. Stone, *The Past and the Present Revisited* (London, 1987), pp. 322–23.

Notes to Chapter 5: The Root of All Evil

1. *Lancet*, 23 February 1884, p. 351.

2. PRO, ASSI 52/6 (Lancashire), *Regina v. Catherine Flanagan and Another*, 1884. Deposition of Richard Jones.

3. J. Knelman, *Twisting in the Wind: The Murderess and the English Press* (Toronto, 1998), p. 78.

4. G. K. Behlmer, *Child Abuse and Moral Reform in England, 1870–1908* (Stanford, California, 1982), p. 49.

5. A. Brabin, 'The Black Widows of Liverpool', *History Today*, 52 (October 2002), pp. 40–46.

6. J. Adams, *Double Indemnity: Murder for Insurance* (London, 1994), pp. 2–3.

7. Dorothea Waddingham (morphine, 1936); Dr Robert George Clements (morphine, 1947); Dr John Bodkin Adams (morphine and heroin, 1957).

Waddingham was convicted and executed, Clements committed suicide before he could be brought to trial, and Adams was tried and acquitted.

8. S. Butler, *Erewhon* (London, 1872; reprint 1970), p. 170.
9. Rather than inferring something that may be incorrect, I have chosen to leave these cases out of this analysis, trusting that their exclusion will not affect the trends identified.
10. Joseph and Mary Pimblet, Cheshire, 1846; William and Ann Chadwick, Staffordshire, 1850.
11. Thomas Baker, Yorkshire, 1837; Catherine Wilson, London, 1862.
12. These figures do not allow for the several cases in which a second individual may well have had a hand in planning the crime – as in the Britland affair – but was never charged. It is clear, however, from the background information available for many of the crimes for which a sole individual was tried that a second person – always of the opposite gender – was involved, morally if not directly.
13. PRO, ASSI 65/5 (Cheshire), *Regina v. Jonathan Barcroft*, 1851.
14. PRO, PL 27/10, box 1 (Lancashire), *Rex v. Jane Scott*, 1827. See also Knelman, *Twisting in the Wind*, p. 54.
15. *Central Criminal Court Sessions Papers*, vol. 107, *Regina v. Henry Bowles*, 1888, pp. 438–73.
16. *The Times*, 23 January 1844, p. 3f; 27 January 1844, p. 6e.
17. C. Wilson and P. Pitman, *Encyclopaedia of Murder* (London, 1984), pp. 497–500; M. Farrell, *Poisons and Poisoners: An Encyclopedia of Homicidal Poisonings* (London, 1992), pp. 157–59; G. St Aubyn, *Infamous Victorians: Lamson and Palmer, Two Notorious Poisoners* (London, 1971), pp. 3–152; L. A. Parry, *Some Famous Medical Trials* (New York, 1928; reprint 1976), pp. 235–58.
18. B. Capp, 'Serial Killers in Seventeenth-Century England', *History Today*, 46 (March 1996), pp. 21–26.
19. H. A. L. Cockerell and E. Green, *The British Insurance Business: A Guide to its History and Records* (2nd edn, Sheffield, 1994), p. 57.
20. H. E. Raynes, *A History of British Insurance* (2nd edn, London, 1964), pp. 113–14.
21. G. Clark, *Betting on Lives: The Culture of Life Insurance in England, 1695–1775* (Manchester, 1999), p. 13.
22. Cockerell and Green, *British Insurance Business*, p. 58.
23. Clark, *Betting on Lives*, p. 27.
24. Cockerell and Green, *British Insurance Business*, p. 64.
25. R. Pearson, 'Thrift or Dissipation? The Business of Life Assurance in the Early Nineteenth Century', *Economic History Review*, 43 (1990), pp. 236–54.

26. P. H. J. H. Gosden, *The Friendly Societies in England, 1815–1875* (reprint, Aldershot, 1993), pp. 2–25.

27. R. Richardson, *Death, Dissection and the Destitute* (London, 1987), pp. 272–80.

28. Gosden, *Friendly Societies in England*, pp. 205–10.

29. Cockerell and Green, *British Insurance Business*, pp. 67–69.

30. PRO, ASSI 52/95 (Lancashire), *Rex* v. *Ellen Burndred*, 1904. Deposition of Ellen Burndred.

31. Clark, *Betting on Lives*, p. 51.

32. *The Trial of Mrs Mary Reed for Petit Treason in Poisoning her Husband William Reed* (Gloucester, 1796).

33. Wilson and Pitman, *Encyclopaedia of Murder*, pp. 624–25; A. Motion, *Wainewright the Poisoner* (London, 2000).

34. PRO, ASSI 62/7, Crown Minute Book, North Wales Division (Cheshire), 3 December 1863.

35. J. D. J. Havard, *The Detection of Secret Homicide* (London, 1960), pp. 70–73.

36. PRO, ASSI 65/3 (Cheshire), *Depositions James Edge: Wilful Murder against Ann Edge*, 1841.

37. PRO, ASSI 45/51 (Yorkshire), *Rex* v. *William Bailey otherwise Knightson*, 1818.

38. *The Trial of John Donellan for the Murder of Sir Theodosius Boughton* (Exeter, 1781); W. R. Grove, 'Rex v. Donellan, Warwick Assizes, 1781', *Medico-Legal and Criminological Review*, 2 (1934), pp. 314–39; Farrell, *Poisons and Poisoners*, pp. 82–85.

39. 'Murder at Plumstead', *The Times*, 11 November 1833, p. 3f.

40. See, for example, Motion, *Wainewright the Poisoner*; St Aubyn, *Infamous Victorians*.

41. *Murder by Poison! The Trial at Large of Elizabeth Woolterton* (Bury St Edmunds, 1815).

42. PRO, ASSI 13/40, box 2 (Warwickshire), *Rex* v. *John White*, 1910.

43. M. Huggins, *Flat Racing and British Society, 1790–1914: A Social and Economic History* (London, 2000), p. 193.

44. W. Vamplew, *The Turf: A Social and Economic History of Horse Racing* (London, 1976), pp. 103–4.

45. PRO, ASSI 45/33/3/139 (Yorkshire), untitled testimony on the death of Miss Nightingale taken before a local magistrate, 15 October 1778.

46. *The Extraordinary Trial of Daniel Dawson* (Newmarket, 1812).

47. *The Second Trial and Capital Conviction of Daniel Dawson for Poisoning Horses* (London, 1812).

48. R. Onslow, *Headquarters: A History of Newmarket and its Racing* (Cambridge, 1983), pp. 32–33; Huggins, *Flat Racing and British Society*, p. 186.

49. R. Huson, ed., *Sixty Famous Trials* (London, 1938), pp. 695–706, on p. 695.

50. Ibid., p. 700.

51. PRO, ASSI 45/44, box 1 (Yorkshire), *Rex* v. *Mary Bateman*, 1808. Depositions of William Perrigo and Rose Howgate.

52. Huson, *Sixty Famous Trials*, p. 706.

53. PRO, HO 140/113, *Calendar of Prisoners*. County of Lancaster, Calendar of Prisoners Tried at the Assizes Held at Liverpool on Saturday 9 March 1889.

54. J. Caminada, *The Crime Buster* (new edition, London, 1996), pp. 205–32. Caminada was the senior detective on the case.

55. PRO, ASSI 52/10 (Lancashire), *Regina* v. *Charles Parton*, 1889. Depositions of John Hampton Barker, Edward Phillips, Samuel Oldfield, John Parkey, Charles Bromley.

56. F. Young, ed., *Trial of the Seddons* (2nd edn, Edinburgh, 1925), p. xiii.

57. Ibid., pp. xiii–xv; Farrell, *Poisons and Poisoners*, pp. 180–83.

Notes to Chapter 6: Fear and Loathing

1. 'The Murder Near Morpeth', *The Times*, 2 March 1846, p. 7f.

2. Ibid.

3. PRO, ASSI 45/67 (Northumberland), Depositions of Witnesses ... Touching the Death of Robert Joicey, 1845, deposition of Ann Richardson.

4. Ibid., and *The Times*, 2 March 1846, p. 7f, testimony of Arthur Hedley.

5. *The Times*, 2 March 1846, testimony of Hannah Brown.

6. Inquest on Robert Joicey, deposition of Walter Weallens.

7. Ibid., testimony of John Whigham.

8. 'Execution of a Parricide', *The Times*, 20 March 1846, p. 8c.

9. PRO, PL 27/16, box 1 (Lancashire), *Regina* v. *William Robert Taylor and Martha Ann Taylor*, 1862.

10. PRO, PCOM 1/104, Central Criminal Court Sessions Papers, *Regina* v. *Ann Dickson*, 1873, pp. 477–78.

11. See Chapter 5.

12. PRO, ASSI 45/36/3/211 (Yorkshire), *Rex* v. *Hannah Whitley*, 1789.

13. 'Poisoning Bullocks at Ashbocking', *The Times*, 1 January 1839, p. 7a.

14. B. Hill, *Servants: English Domestics in the Eighteenth Century* (Oxford, 1996), p. 6.

15. P. Horn, *The Rise and Fall of the Victorian Servant* (Stroud, 1996), pp. 231–32.

16. J. Pink, *'Country Girls Preferred': Victorian Domestic Servants in the Suburbs* (Surbiton, 1998), p. 2; F. V. Dawes, *Not in Front of the Servants: A True Portrait of Upstairs, Downstairs Life* (revised edition, London, 1984), p. 15.

17. Horn, *The Rise and Fall of the Victorian Servant*, p. 146.

18. Ibid., p. 30; Pink, *Country Girls Preferred*, p. 83.

19. Pink, *Country Girls Preferred*, p. 25.

20. Horn, *The Rise and Fall of the Victorian Servant*, pp. 158–63.

21. D. Marshall, *The English Domestic Servant in History* (London, 1949), p. 12.

22. See above, Chapter 4.

23. 'Professor Alfred S. Taylor's Report on Poisoning, and the Dispensing, Vending, and Keeping of Poisons', *Pharmaceutical Journal*, second series, 6 (1864–65), pp. 172–84, on p. 179.

24. *The Genuine Trial and Affecting Case of Eliza Fenning* (2nd edn, London, 1815), p. 6.

25. J. Knelman, *Twisting in the Wind: The Murderess and the English Press* (Toronto, 1998), pp. 182–88.

26. *Trial of Elizabeth Miller at Kingston Assizes, April 5, 1816* (London, 1816); *The Times*, 18 September 1815, p. 3e.

27. In a later chapter we will consider how changes in legal procedure helped to prevent the worst failings of the Fenning case from recurring.

28. 'Attempt to Poison', *The Times*, 1 June 1859, p. 9c.

29. *The Times*, 21 December 1891, p. 10e.

30. 'Attempt to Poison with a Sheep Dipping Powder', *Pharmaceutical Journal*, third series, 7 (1876–77), p. 546.

31. *The Times*, 12 April 1838, p. 5e; 10 August 1838, p. 5c.

32. Between 1881 and 1911, the proportion of all domestic servants aged fifteen to twenty fell from over a third to 28 per cent; the number of male indoor domestics declined by over 20 per cent. In the same period, female domestics aged between twenty-five and forty-five increased their share from 24 to about 32 per cent. See Horn, *The Rise and Fall of the Victorian Servant*, pp. 28, 232.

33. 'Arsenic Poisoning', *The Times*, 6 April 1899, p. 4f.

34. W. H. Willcox, 'A Fatal Case of Bichromate of Potash Poisoning', *Transactions of the Medico-Legal Society*, 7 (1909–10), pp. 69–71.

35. M. MacDonald, 'Suicidal Behaviour', in G. E. Berrios and R. Porter (eds), *A History of Clinical Psychiatry: The Origin and History of Psychiatric Disorders* (London, 1995), pp. 625–32.

36. Ibid., p. 628.

37. Ibid.

38. M. Halbwachs, *The Causes of Suicide*, translated by Harold Goldblatt (London, 1978), pp. xix–xxv, 10.

39. O. Anderson, *Suicide in Victorian and Edwardian England* (Oxford, 1987), pp. 13–15.

40. Ibid., pp. 418–19.

41. Ibid., pp. 19–20, 35, 361.

42. Ibid., pp. 144–45, 156–57, 179. It would almost certainly be possible to challenge the assumption about poisoning if a wider sample was studied.

43. P. Wilson, *Murderess: A Study of Women Executed in Britain since 1843* (London, 1971), pp. 26–29.

44. *The Times*, 25 August 1848, p. 7d (case of Hannah Leath). See also the cases of James Brain (Bedfordshire, 1841) and Ann Rothwell (Lancashire, 1844).

45. I. Loudon, 'Puerperal Insanity in the Nineteenth Century', *Journal of the Royal Society of Medicine*, 81 (1988), pp. 76–79, on p. 76.

46. I. Loudon, *Death in Childbirth: An International Study of Maternal Care and Maternal Mortality, 1800–1950* (Oxford, 1992), pp. 143–45.

47. K. Dalton, *Depression after Childbirth* (4th edn, Oxford, 2001), p. 2.

48. PRO, ASSI 52/148 (Lancashire), *Rex* v. *Alice Lucas*, 1909.

49. H. Marland, 'Getting Away with Murder? Puerperal Insanity, Infanticide and the Defence Plea', in M. Jackson (ed.), *Infanticide: Historical Perspectives on Child Murder and Concealment, 1550–2000* (Aldershot, 2002), pp. 168–92.

50. PRO, ASSI 13/3 (Yorkshire), *Regina* v. *Catherine Groocock*, 1872.

51. *Pharmaceutical Journal*, third series, 7 (1876–77), pp. 1034–35, 1053.

52. H. R. Fedden, *Suicide: A Social and Historical Study* (London, 1938), p. 262.

53. PRO, ASSI 13/17 (Nottinghamshire). Depositions against John Jessop for Murder, 1887; deposition of PC Samuel Titchmarsh.

Notes to Chapter 7: Inquests Duly Held

1. PRO, ASSI 6/1, box 1 (Herefordshire), *Rex* v. *Luke Mapp*, 1772.

2. *The Times*, 25 May 1876, p. 10c.

3. Clerical assistance had become fairly common by 1900.

4. J. Smith, *Death Disguised.* Part 1 of the Official Inquiry into the Crimes of Dr Harold Shipman (July 2002). See www.channel4.com/news for the full report. It is estimated that Shipman murdered 215 of his patients. Forty-five others died in suspicious circumstances, and there was insufficient evidence in a further thirty-eight deaths.

5. See, for example, the cases of Harriet Thomley (Cheshire, 1853) and Amy Rowe (Gloucestershire, 1913).

6. The often secondary role played by the police will be discussed in the following chapter.

7. See above, Chapters 1 and 4, respectively.

8. *Rex* v. *Luke Mapp*, deposition of Zacheus Wyke; PRO, ASSI 2/22, Crown Minute Book, Hereford lent assizes 1772.

9. A. K. Mant, 'Milestones in the Development of the British Medicolegal System', *Medicine, Science and the Law*, 17 (1977), pp. 155–63; p. 155.

10. R. F. Hunnisett, ed., *Wiltshire Coroners' Bills, 1752–1796* (Devizes, 1981), p. xxix. Coroners were elected officials until 1888.

11. Mant, 'Milestones', pp. 155–56; J. D. J. Havard, *The Detection of Secret Homicide* (London, 1960), p. 35.

12. T. R. Forbes, 'Crowner's Quest', *Transactions of the American Philosophical Society*, 68 (1978), pp. 3–52; p. 6.

13. Ibid., pp. 6–7; Mant, 'Milestones', p. 158.

14. Havard, *Detection of Secret Homicide*, p. 36.

15. Forbes, 'Crowner's Quest', pp. 6–7; Mant, 'Milestones', p. 158; Havard, *Detection of Secret Homicide*, p. 37.

16. I. A. Burney, *Bodies of Evidence: Medicine and the Politics of the English Inquest, 1830–1926* (Baltimore and London, 2000), pp. 16–51.

17. Hunnisett, *Wiltshire Coroners' Bills*, pp. xlviii-l.

18. Burney, *Bodies of Evidence*, pp. 4, 174.

19. G. I. Greenwald and M. W. Greenwald, 'Medicolegal Progress in Inquests of Felonious Deaths', *Journal of Legal Medicine*, 2 (1981), pp. 193–264.

20. Ibid., pp. 197–98; Havard, *Detection of Secret Homicide*, p. 38; Forbes, 'Crowner's Quest, p. 6.

21. C. Crawford, 'Legalizing Medicine: Early Modern Legal Systems and the Growth of Medico-Legal Knowledge', in M. Clark and C. Crawford (eds), *Legal Medicine in History* (Cambridge, 1994), pp. 89–116.

22. J. Briggs, C. Harrison, A. McInnes and D. Vincent, *Crime and Punishment in England: An Introductory History* (London, 1996), pp. 26–28; A. H. Manchester, *A Modern Legal History of England and Wales, 1750–1950* (London, 1980), pp. 74–79.

23. Havard, *Detection of Secret Homicide*, pp. 42–59.

24. Borough coroners were excluded until 1882. The Local Government Act of 1888 broke the last link, as it transferred all financial responsibility for coroners to county councils.

25. Havard, *Detection of Secret Homicide*, pp. 60–65; Greenwald and Greenwald, 'Medicolegal Progress', pp. 197–98.

26. Burney, *Bodies of Evidence*, p. 4.

27. Havard, *Detection of Secret Homicide*, pp. 37–38; Forbes, 'Crowner's Quest', p. 8; Greenwald and Greenwald, 'Medicolegal Progress in Inquests', p. 218.

28. Havard, *Detection of Secret Homicide*, pp. 44–48, 68–73; Greenwald and Greenwald, 'Medicolegal Progress in Inquests', pp. 220–22.

29. Mant, 'Milestones', p. 157.

30. Burney, *Bodies of Evidence*, p. 208; Forbes, 'Crowner's Quest', p. 6. See also I. A. Burney, 'Viewing Bodies: Medicine, Public Order, and English Inquest Practice', *Configurations*, 2 (1994), pp. 33–46.

31. Havard, *Detection of Secret Homicide*, pp. 4, 37; T. R. Forbes, *Surgeons at the Bailey: English Forensic Medicine to 1878* (New Haven, 1985), pp. 46–48.

32. E. Sherrington, 'Thomas Wakley and Reform, 1823–62' (unpublished D.Phil. thesis, Oxford University, 1974), p. 204.

33. S. Landsman, 'One Hundred Years of Rectitude: Medical Witnesses at the Old Bailey, 1717–1817', *Law and History Review*, 16 (1998), pp. 445–94; p. 449.

34. Greenwald and Greenwald, 'Medicolegal Progess in Inquests', p. 206; Forbes, 'Crowner's Quest', p. 42; T. R. Forbes, 'Coroner's Inquisitions from the County of Cheshire, England, 1817–39 and 1877–78', *Bulletin of the History of Medicine*, 59 (1985), pp. 481–94.

35. T. Golan, 'The History of Scientific Expert Testimony in the English Courtroom', *Science in Context*, 12 (1999), pp. 7–32; on pp. 14–15.

36. *Rex* v. *Luke Mapp*, deposition of Zacheus Wyke.

37. S. Spokes, 'A Case of Circumstantial Evidence', *Sussex County Magazine*, 11 (1937), pp. 118–22.

38. Landsman, 'One Hundred Years of Rectitude', pp. 456–70.

39. Mant, 'Milestones', p. 159.

40. Forbes, 'Crowner's Quest', p. 43; Havard, *Detection of Secret Homicide*, pp. 48–49.

41. PRO, ASSI 65/10 (Cheshire), *Regina* v. *Edward Heesom and Ellen Heesom*, 1878, deposition of Thomas Starkey Smith.

42. G. Lathom Browne and C. G. Stewart, *Reports of Trials for Murder by Poisoning* (London, 1883), pp. 107–9.

43. Havard, *Detection of Secret Homicide*, pp. 152–53.

44. Based on the sample of 540 cases collected for this study.

45. The table has been compiled by frequency of consultation, but a similar list based on location would include many more academics, each involved in a handful of cases during the mid nineteenth century.

46. He performed the autopsy in one case; the other was an attempted murder.

47. PRO, ASSI 45/38/2/84B (Yorkshire), *Rex* v. *Ann Scalbird*, 1794.

48. PRO, ASSI 45/41 (Yorkshire), *Rex* v. *Alvera Newsome*, 1802.

49. See, for example, Herapath's testimony in these cases: PRO, ASSI 72/1 (Breconshire), *Regina* v. *Margaret Michael*, 1849; PRO, ASSI 72/1 (Pembrokeshire), *Regina* v. *Jane Thomas and Anne Thomas*, 1863.

50. R. O. Myers, 'Famous Forensic Scientists, 6. Alfred Swaine Taylor (1806–1880)', *Medicine, Science and the Law*, 2 (1962), pp. 233–40, p. 237;

N. G. Coley, 'Alfred Swaine Taylor, MD, FRS (1806–1880): Forensic Toxicologist', *Medical History*, 35 (1991), pp. 409–27.

51. 'The Late Extraordinary Case of Poisoning at Hackney', *The Times*, 13 November 1847, p. 8e.

52. PRO, ASSI 6/5 (Monmouthshire), *Regina v. Mary Howells and James Price*, 1848.

53. 'Action for Recovery of Fees for Chemical Analyses; Implied Contracts', *Pharmaceutical Journal*, 11 (1851–52), pp. 185–88.

54. *Great Burdon Slow Poisoning Case* (Darlington, 1855), p. 8.

55. 'Alleged Poisoning at Bath', *The Times*, 30 April 1849, p. 8b. This was the case of Charlotte Harris.

56. Burney, *Bodies of Evidence*, p. 4.

57. B. Dyer and C. A. Mitchell, *The Society of Public Analysts and Other Analytical Chemists: Some Reminiscences of its First Fifty Years and a Review of its Activities* (Cambridge, 1932), pp. 1–3.

58. 'Meeting of Public Analysts' *Pharmaceutical Journal*, third series, 5 (1874–75), pp. 121–32.

59. R. O. Myers, 'Famous Forensic Scientists, 5. Sir Thomas Stevenson (1838–1908)', *Medicine, Science and the Law*, 2 (1962), pp. 165–68; C.E.G., 'Thomas Stevenson', *Journal of the Chemical Society*, 95 (1909), pp. 2213–15; S.B.A., 'Sir Thomas Stevenson, MD, FRCP', *Transactions of the Medico-Legal Society*, 5 (1907–8), pp. 186–88.

60. Sherrington, 'Thomas Wakley and Reform', p. 203.

61. Of 376 cases of murder and manslaughter, over twice as many (256) were dealt with primarily by a coroner as by a magistrate (120).

Notes to Chapter 8: The Rule of Law

1. *The Times*, 6 August 1816, p. 3b.

2. *The Times*, 15 August 1816, p. 3b.

3. PRO, ASSI 45/49 (Yorkshire), no title, 1816.

4. *The Times*, 15 August 1816, p. 3b. Poskitt was more confident when he testified against Ann Barber five years later.

5. 43 George III c. 58, from 1 July 1803. For more on this Act, see below.

6. *The Times*, 15 August 1816, p. 3b.

7. *The Times*, 28 September 1816, p. 3b.

8. 'Further Respite of Elizabeth Ward', *The Times*, 18 September 1816, p. 3a.

9. J. Briggs, C. Harrison, A. McInnes and D. Vincent, *Crime and Punishment in England: An Introductory History* (London, 1996), pp. 47–54.

10. G. Morgan and P. Rushton, 'The Magistrate, the Community and the

Maintenance of an Orderly Society in Eighteenth-Century England', *Historical Research*, 76 (2003), pp. 54–77.

11. Briggs et al., *Crime and Punishment in England*, pp. 61–71.

12. PRO, PL 27/9, box 1 (Lancashire), *Rex* v. *Cecilia Collier*, 1813. Deposition of Samuel Mee. See also Chapter 3.

13. Briggs et al., *Crime and Punishment in England*, pp. 141–49; A. H. Manchester, *A Modern Legal History of England and Wales, 1750–1950* (London, 1980), pp. 220–25.

14. Ibid., D. Taylor, *Crime, Policing and Punishment in England, 1750–1914* (Basingstoke, 1998), pp. 71, 78.

15. C. Emsley, *Crime and Society in England, 1750–1900* (2nd edn, London, 1996), p. 234.

16. D. Taylor, *The New Police in Nineteenth-Century England: Crime, Conflict and Control* (Manchester, 1997), pp. 44–88; Taylor, *Crime, Policing and Punishment in England*, pp. 88–105; H. Shpayer-Makov, *The Making of a Policeman: A Social History of a Labour Force in Metropolitan London, 1829–1914* (Aldershot, 2002).

17. PRO, PL 27/10, box 1 (Lancashire), *Rex* v. *Jane Scott*, murder, 1827. See also above, Chapter 5.

18. PRO, ASSI 6/1, box 1 (Staffordshire), 'Elizabeth Nixon and Elizabeth Davis charged with murder of male bastard child', 1825. Nixon was either a servant or a lodger in the Davis house, which explains why William Davis was almost certainly the father of her child.

19. See, for example, the cases of Joseph Walters (1838) and Flanagan and Higgins (1883).

20. See, for example, the cases of Stanley Hickling (1872) and Edwin Bailey and Anne Barrey (1873).

21. PRO, ASSI 65/4 (Flintshire), *Regina* v. *Hannah Roberts*, murder, 1842; deposition of Sarah Cowpland. In 1878 police sergeant Levi Bebbington was living in a Cheshire police station with his wife, who brought the serial poisoner Ellen Heesom, then a prisoner at the station, from a cell to the parlour when she wanted to make a statement.

22. This was Isaac Philipson. See the cases of Mary Hunter and Francis Bradley, both 1842.

23. See the following cases: Benjamin Whiteley (Yorkshire, 1765): witnesses £20, prosecutor £40; John Winship (Durham, 1785): prosecutor £40; Mary Nicholson (Durham, 1798): witnesses £40, prosecutor £50; Mary Bateman (Yorkshire, 1809): £50 each; Joseph William Hodgson (Durham, 1824): witnesses £10, prosecutor £40; Elizabeth Pettit (Kent, 1838): £20 each.

24. Emsley, *Crime and Society in England*, pp. 189–93.

25. PRO, ASSI 65/1 (Cheshire), *Regina* v. *Standring* for murder, 1839; PRO, ASSI 6/4 (Staffordshire), *Regina* v. *Susannah Perry* for murder, 1839.
26. PRO, ASSI 6/48 (Gloucestershire), 1913.
27. He was not a chief constable: M. Stallion and D. S. Wall, *The British Police: Police Forces and Chief Officers, 1829–2000* (Hook, Hampshire, 1999).
28. PRO, ASSI 26/23 (Bristol), Regina on the prosecution of *Albert Sloman* v. *Sarah Ellen Joseph*, charged with murder, 1887. The girl, a nursemaid, had deliberately overdosed Sloman's infant son.
29. The DPP, via the Treasury Solicitor, prosecuted a case in Worcester in 1888: PRO, ASSI 6/21 (City of Worcester), Regina on the prosecution of the Solicitor to the Treasury against Mary Eleanor Powell and James Henry Keatley, 1888.
30. Manchester, *Modern Legal History*, pp. 227–28. In 1912 a cotton weaver was prosecuted by the DPP: PRO, ASSI 52/195 (Lancashire), Rex on the prosecution of the Director of Public Prosecutions against James Stezaker for murder, 1912. Stezaker was charged with suffocating his wife and daughter and attempting suicide with carbon monoxide.
31. Ibid., pp. 22–49.
32. PRO, DURH 17/38 (Durham), no title (case of Mary Nicholson), 1798; DURH 16/2, Palatinate of Durham, Crown Minute Book, Tuesday 31 July 1798; *The Times*, 31 July 1799, p. 3c. See also A. Appleton, *Mary Ann Cotton: Her Story and Trial* (London, 1973), p. 129.
33. D. Bentley, *English Criminal Justice in the Nineteenth Century* (London, 1998), pp. 134–37.
34. 43 George III, c. 58.
35. *The Times*, 25 March 1826, p. 3a.
36. *The Times*, 16 August 1825, p. 3c. See also J. Jervis, *Archbold's Summary of the Law Relative to Pleading and Evidence in Criminal Cases* (4th edn, London, 1831), pp. 336, 339.
37. 9 George IV, c. 31.
38. See the cases of Jane Coleman (Devon, 1829), Hannah Kingston (Bedfordshire, 1830), and William Kimber (Surrey, 1832).
39. *The Times*, 1 August 1835, p. 7b. This article refers to the statute as Lord Lansdowne's Act.
40. V. A. C. Gatrell, *The Hanging Tree: Execution and the English People, 1770–1868* (Oxford, 1994), pp. 618–19.
41. This was the case of William Major, aged seventy-four. See *The Times*, 2 August 1841, p. 6e, and PRO, HO 27/63, County of Devon. Calendar of Prisoners 1841.
42. Bentley, *English Criminal Justice in the Nineteenth Century*, p. 12.

43. 24 & 25 Victoria, c. 100. See D. J. A. Kerr, *Forensic Medicine: A Textbook for Students and a Guide for the Practitioner* (London, 1936), pp. 211–13.

44. *The Times*, 28 November 1859, p. 5b; 30 November 1859, p. 9d.

45. University of Leeds, Brotherton Library, Department of Manuscripts and Special Collections: Thomas Scattergood, Case Notes 1846–97, MS 534/1–3, volume 1, pp. 10–13; on p. 13. See also PRO, ASSI 41/21, Crown Minute Book, North Eastern Circuit, 13 December 1858.

46. *Pharmaceutical Journal*, third series, 7 (1876–77), pp. 757, 766–67.

47. Kerr, *Forensic Medicine*, p. 211.

48. At quarter sessions cases were tried by part-time judges or magistrates, with juries; at petty sessions, by magistrates with no jury.

49. The six original circuits were Home, Midland, Norfolk, Northern, Oxford and Western. Changes in 1876 revised and expanded the number to eight: Midland, Oxford, South Eastern, North Wales, South Wales, Northern, North Eastern, Western. Only the Oxford and Western circuits remained unchanged throughout the period covered by this study.

50. Cumberland, Durham, Northumberland and Westmoreland.

51. Bentley, *English Criminal Justice in the Nineteenth Century*, pp. 51–57.

52. Hannah Roberts, aged sixty-nine (Yorkshire, 1834), and Ann Thomason, in her twenties (Buckinghamshire, 1839).

53. Bentley, *English Criminal Justice in the Nineteenth Century*, pp. 131–34; Manchester, *Modern Legal History*, pp. 95–99.

54. Emsley, *Crime and Society in England*, p. 193.

55. S. Spokes, 'A Case of Circumstantial Evidence', *Sussex County Magazine*, 11 (1937), pp. 118–22. See also above, Chapter 7.

56. Bentley, *English Criminal Justice in the Nineteenth Century*, pp. 98, 110–15.

57. Taylor, *Crime, Policing and Punishment in England*, p. 114; Bentley, *English Criminal Justice in the Nineteenth Century*, p. 113.

58. *The Times*, 28 April 1847, p. 8e; 14 July 1847, p. 7c.

59. *The Times*, 31 July 1869, p. 11c.

60. *The Times*, 7 November 1887, p. 10d.

61. PRO, ASSI 52/101 (Westmoreland), *Rex* v. *Elizabeth Nicholson and Thomas Medcalf*, 1904.

62. Manchester, *Modern Legal History*, pp. 100–2.

63. Taylor, *Crime, Policing and Punishment in England*, p. 115; Bentley, *English Criminal Justice in the Nineteenth Century*, pp. 173–74, 185–204. In 1885 those charged with sexual offences were given the right to testify; alleged murderers had to wait another thirteen years to gain the same privilege.

64. B. Ryan, *The Poisoned Life of Mrs Maybrick* (London, 1977), pp. 201–23.

65. Bentley, *English Criminal Justice in the Nineteenth Century*, pp. 43–49.

66. J. F. Stephen, 'On Trial by Jury, and the Evidence of Experts', *Papers Read before the Juridical Society*, ii, *1858–1863* (London, 1863), pp. 236–49; on p. 238.

67. Taylor, *Crime, Policing and Punishment*, p. 20; C. A. Conley, *The Unwritten Law: Criminal Justice in Victorian Kent* (Oxford, 1991), p. 17.

68. Emsley, *Crime and Society in England*, pp. 41–42, 46.

69. Of 155 death sentences, there were two suicides before execution, 108 executions, and forty-five reprieves.

70. There were five reprieves, out of sixty-two death sentences, to 1837, but forty out of ninety-three after that date.

71. Gatrell, *The Hanging Tree*, p. 619.

72. Seven women and four men.

73. P. Priestley, *Victorian Prison Lives: English Prison Biography, 1830–1914* (paperback edn, London, 1999), pp. 121–47.

74. Manchester, *Modern Legal History*, pp. 253–57.

Notes to Chapter 9: Resolute for Killing

1. C. Dickens, 'Household Crime', *Household Words*, 4 (1851), pp. 277–81; on p. 277.

2. Ibid.

3. Sarah Barber and Robert Ingram, tried at Nottingham in July 1851. Ingram was acquitted, while Barber was convicted and sentenced to death (later commuted to transportation for life).

4. William Rollinson, tried at Bury St Edmunds in March 1852. Convicted and sentenced to death, he was reprieved on account of his great age.

5. *The Times*, 22 August 1851, p. 8e.

6. *The Times*, 29 July 1850, p. 7c.

7. A. Appleton, *Mary Ann Cotton: Her Story and Trial* (London, 1973); J. Ruddick, *Death at the Priory: Love, Sex and Murder in Victorian England* (London, 2001); M. S. Hartman, *Victorian Murderesses: A True History of Thirteen Respectable French and English Women Accused of Unspeakable Crimes* (paperback edn, London, 1985).

8. A. Griffiths, *Mysteries of Police and Crime*, 3 vols (London, 1903), vol. 3, p. 87.

9. E. Leyton, *Men of Blood: Murder in Modern England* (London, 1995), pp. 127–30, 260.

10. C. Rooney and T. Devis, 'Recent Trends in Deaths from Homicide in England and Wales', *Health Statistics Quarterly*, 3 (1999), pp. 5–13; on p. 12.

11. B. Whittle and J. Ritchie, *Prescription for Murder: The True Story of Mass Murderer Dr Harold Frederick Shipman* (London, 2000), pp. 332–34.

12. H. G. Kinnell, 'Serial Homicide by Doctors: Shipman in Perspective', *British Medical Journal*, 321 (2000), pp. 1594–97; C. Stark, B. Paterson and B. Kidd, 'Opportunity May Be More Important than Profession in Serial Homicide', *British Medical Journal*, 322 (2001), p. 993. See also M. D. Kelleher and C. L. Kelleher, *Murder Most Rare: The Female Serial Killer* (New York, 1998), pp. 89–104.

13. Griffiths, *Mysteries of Police and Crime*, p. 54.

14. Hélène Jegado (France, 1833–51); Anna Schönleben, also known as Zwanziger (Germany, 1810s); Mrs Van der Linden (Holland, 1869–85).

15. Appleton, *Mary Ann Cotton*, p. 104.

16. This is what Betty Eccles claimed of herself in 1843.

17. J. Knelman, *Twisting in the Wind: The Murderess and the English Press* (Toronto, 1998), p. 77.

18. Appleton, *Mary Ann Cotton*, pp. 47–52.

19. R. Woods and M. Shelton, *An Atlas of Victorian Mortality* (Liverpool, 1997), pp. 47–64, 131, 133.

20. R. S. Lambert, *When Justice Faltered: A Study of Nine Peculiar Murder Trials* (London, 1935), pp. 108–37, on pp. 116–17.

21. Appleton, *Mary Ann Cotton*, pp. 58–60.

22. Ibid., pp. 13–15.

23. University of Leeds, Brotherton Library, Department of Manuscripts and Special Collections: Thomas Scattergood, Case Notes 1846–97, MS 534/1–3, volume 1, pp. 179–206.

24. Appleton, *Mary Ann Cotton*, p. 100.

25. J. Adams, *Double Indemnity: Murder for Insurance* (London, 1994), pp. 2–3.

26. *The Guardian*, 18 January 2000, 7 March 2000, 8 March 2000. See www.guardian.co.uk.

27. Kelleher and Kelleher, *Murder Most Rare*, pp. 89–104, 131–50.

28. Michelle Dickinson, aged thirty-one. 'Life Jail Term for Poison Mother', *The Guardian*, 14 January 2003. See www.guardian.co.uk.

29. Rooney and Devis, 'Recent Trends in Deaths from Homicide', pp. 8–9.

Bibliography

MANUSCRIPTS

Public Record Office, London

Assizes Records:
Oxford:

      ASSI 2/22–49 (Crown Books, 1770–1914)

      ASSI 4/32, 34 (Miscellaneous Books – Costs, 1850s)

      ASSI 6/1–48 (Depositions, 1719–1914)

Midland:

      ASSI 11/5–39 (Crown Minute Books, 1832–1911)

      ASSI 13/1–40 (Depositions, 1862–1914)

      ASSI 81/22, 45, 97 (Pardons)

Western:

      ASSI 21/57–84 (Crown Minute Books, 1829–1917)

      ASSI 26/1–42 (Depositions, 1861–1917)

South Eastern:

      ASSI 31/22–37 (Agenda Books, 1816–1867)

      ASSI 32/13–14 (Minute Books, 1864–1871)

      ASSI 33/11–15 (Gaol Books, 1830–60)

      ASSI 36/1–28 (Depositions, 1813–1914)

      ASSI 40/1 (Index, 1860s)

North Eastern:

      ASSI 41/5–31 (Minute Books, 1765–1888)

      ASSI 42/7–8 (Gaol Books, 1759–1768)

      ASSI 44/80–82, 104, 117 (Indictments, 1765–1802)

      ASSI 45/26–82 (Depositions, 1759–1890)

Northern:

    ASSI 51/10–127(Indictments, 1879–1914)

    ASSI 52/1–214 (Depositions, 1877–1914)

    ASSI 53/1–3 (Order Books, 1879–1890, 1910–1914)

North Wales Division:

    ASSI 61/6–22 (Crown Minute Books, 1836–1887)

    ASSI 62/3–9 (Crown Books, 1842–1879)

    ASSI 65/1–15 (Depositions, 1831–1891, 1909–1914)

South Wales Division:

    ASSI 72/1 (Depositions, 1837–1914)

    ASSI 76/2–4 (Crown Minute Books, 1849–1863)

Palatinate of Durham:

    DURH 16/2–7 (Crown Books, 1780–1858)

    DURH 17/20–106 (Indictments, 1780–1842)

    DURH 18/1–2 (Depositions, 1843–1876)

Palatinate of Lancaster:

    PL 27/6–17 (Depositions, 1781–1867)

    PL 28/3–12 (Miscellanea – Minute Books, 1780–1876)

HO 27 (Home Office, Criminal Registers, 1805–1892)

HO 140 (Home Office, Calendar of Prisoners, 1868–1914)

PCOM 1 (Old Bailey Sessions Papers, 1801–1912 (printed))

University of Leeds, Brotherton Library

Thomas Scattergood, Case Notes, 1846–1897, MS 534/1–3

PRIMARY SOURCES

Periodicals and Newspapers

Central Criminal Court Sessions Papers
Lancet (from 1823)
Pharmaceutical Journal (from 1841)
The Guardian
The Times

Books, Pamphlets and Articles

Allen, A. H., 'Vermin-Killers Containing Strychnine', *Pharmaceutical Journal*, third series, 20 (1889–90), pp. 296–99.

An Account of the Trial, Execution, etc of William and John Curren, for the Wilful Murder of Thomas Raven, of Barrow-upon-Soar, and of William Barnett, for the Poisoning of his Wife (Leicester, 1822).

Brend, W. A., *A Handbook of Medical Jurisprudence and Toxicology* (6th edn, London, 1928).

Browne, G. L. and Stewart, C. G., *Reports of Trials for Murder by Poisoning* (London, 1883).

Butler, S., *Erewhon* (London, 1872; reprint 1970).

Caminada, J., *The Crime Buster* (new edition, London, 1996).

Cartoons from 'Punch', 4 vols (London, 1906).

Dickens, C., 'Household Crime', *Household Words*, 4 (1851), pp. 277–81.

Farr, S., *Elements of Medical Jurisprudence* (London, 1788).

Great Burdon Slow Poisoning Case (Darlington, 1855).

Hall, M., 'Note on the Detection of Strychnia', *Lancet*, 1 (1856), pp. 36, 623.

Holland, P. H., *A Report of the Trial and Acquittal of Mary Hunter* (Manchester, 1843).

Jervis, J., *Archbold's Summary of the Law Relative to Pleading and Evidence in Criminal Cases* (4th edn, London, 1831).

Kerr, D. J. A., *Forensic Medicine: A Textbook for Students and a Guide for the Practitioner* (London, 1936).

Letheby, H., 'On the Probability of Confounding Cases of Arsenical Poisoning with Those of Cholera', *Pharmaceutical Journal*, 8 (1848–49), pp. 237–40.

Male, G. E., *An Epitome of Judicial or Forensic Medicine: For the Use of Medical Men, Coroners and Barristers* (London, 1816).

Marsh, J., 'Account of a Method of Separating Small Quantities of Arsenic from Substances with which it may be Mixed', *Edinburgh New Philosophical Journal*, 21 (1836), pp. 229–36.

Murder by Poison! The Trial at Large of Elizabeth Woolterton (Bury St Edmunds, 1815).

Orfila, M. J. B., *A General System of Toxicology: or a Treatise on Poisons, Drawn from the Mineral, Vegetable and Animal Kingdoms* (Paris, 1814–15; translated by J. A. Waller, London, 1816–17).

Reinsch, H., 'On the Action of Metallic Copper on Solutions of Certain Metals,

Particularly with Reference to the Detection of Arsenic', *Philosophical Magazine*, 19 (1841), pp. 480–83.

Smith, J. G., *The Principles of Forensic Medicine, Systematically Arranged and Applied to British Practice* (2nd edn, London, 1824).

Stas, J. S., 'Considérations sur une méthode générale propre a déceler les alcalis organiques dans le cas d'empoissonnement', *Bulletin de l'Académie Royale de Médicine Belgique*, 11 (1851), pp. 304–12.

Stephen, J. F., 'On Trial by Jury, and the Evidence of Experts', *Papers Read Before the Juridical Society*, ii, *1858–1863* (London, 1863), pp. 236–49.

Taylor, A. S., *On Poisons in Relation to Medical Jurisprudence and Medicine* (London, 1848).

The Extraordinary Trial of Daniel Dawson (Newmarket, 1812).

The Genuine Trial and Affecting Case of Eliza Fenning (2nd edn, London, 1815).

The Second Trial and Capital Conviction of Daniel Dawson for Poisoning Horses (London, 1812).

The Trial of John Donellan for the Murder of Sir Theodosius Boughton (Exeter, 1781).

The Trial of Michael Whiting for Administering Poison to George and Joseph Langman (Cambridge, 1812).

The Trial of Mrs Mary Reed for Petit Treason in Poisoning her Husband William Reed (Gloucester, 1796).

The Trial of Robert Sawle Donnall (Falmouth, 1817).

Trial of Elizabeth Miller at Kingston Assizes, April 5, 1816 (London, 1816).

Vincent, W. T., *The Records of the Woolwich District*, i (Woolwich, 1888).

Willcox, W. H., 'A Fatal Case of Bichromate of Potash Poisoning', *Transactions of the Medico-Legal Society*, 7 (1909–10), pp. 69–71.

Witthaus, R. A., *Manual of Toxicology* (London, 1911).

SECONDARY SOURCES

Abbott, M., *Family Ties: English Families, 1540–1920* (London, 1993).

Adams, J., *Double Indemnity: Murder for Insurance* (London, 1994).

Anderson, M., 'The Social Implications of Demographic Change', in F. M. L. Thompson (ed.), *The Cambridge Social History of Britain, 1750–1950*, ii (Cambridge, 1990), pp. 1–70.

Anderson, O., *Suicide in Victorian and Edwardian England* (Oxford, 1987).

Appleton, A., *Mary Ann Cotton: Her Story and Trial* (London, 1973).

Bartrip, P., 'A "Pennurth of Arsenic for Rat Poison": The Arsenic Act, 1851 and the Prevention of Secret Poisoning', *Medical History*, 36 (1992), pp. 53–69.

Behlmer, G. K., *Child Abuse and Moral Reform in England, 1870–1908* (Stanford, California, 1982).

Bentley, D., *English Criminal Justice in the Nineteenth Century* (London, 1998).

Berridge, V. and Edwards, G., *Opium and the People: Opiate Use in Nineteenth-Century England* (London, 1987).

Best, G., *Mid-Victorian Britain, 1851–75* (London, 1971).

Boyle, T., *Black Swine in the Sewers of Hampstead* (London, 1989).

Brabin, A., 'The Black Widows of Liverpool', *History Today*, 52 (October 2002), pp. 40–46.

Briggs, J., Harrison, C., McInnes, A. and Vincent, D., *Crime and Punishment in England: An Introductory History* (London, 1996).

Browne, D. G. and Tullett, E. V., *Bernard Spilsbury: His Life and Cases* (London, 1951).

Burnby, J. G. L., *A Study of the English Apothecary from 1660 to 1760* (London, 1983).

Burney, I. A., 'Viewing Bodies: Medicine, Public Order, and English Inquest Practice', *Configurations*, 2 (1994), pp. 33–46.

Burney, I. A., 'A Poisoning of No Substance: The Trials of Medico-Legal Proof in Mid-Victorian England', *Journal of British Studies*, 38 (1999), pp. 59–92.

Burney, I. A., *Bodies of Evidence: Medicine and the Politics of the English Inquest, 1830–1926* (Baltimore and London, 2000).

Burney, I. A., 'Testing Testimony: Toxicology and the Law of Evidence in Early Nineteenth-Century England', *Studies in History and Philosophy of Science*, 33 (2002), pp. 289–314.

Campbell, W. A., 'Some Landmarks in the History of Arsenic Testing', *Chemistry in Britain*, 1 (1965), pp. 198–202.

Capp, B., 'Serial Killers in Seventeenth-Century England', *History Today*, 46 (March 1996), pp. 21–26.

C. E. G., 'Thomas Stevenson', *Journal of the Chemical Society*, 95 (1909), pp. 2213–15.

Chambers, J. D. and Mingay, G. E., *The Agricultural Revolution, 1750–1880* (London, 1966).

Clark, G., *Betting on Lives: The Culture of Life Insurance in England, 1695–1775* (Manchester, 1999).

Clarke, M. J., 'The History of Suicide in England and Wales 1850–1961, with Special Reference to Suicide by Poisoning' (unpublished D.Phil. thesis, Oxford, 1993).

Cockerell, H. A. L. and Green, E., *The British Insurance Business: A Guide to its History and Records* (2nd edn, Sheffield, 1994).

Coley, N. G., 'Alfred Swaine Taylor, MD, FRS (1806–1880): Forensic Toxicologist', *Medical History*, 35 (1991), pp. 409–27.

Coley, N. G., 'Forensic Chemistry in Nineteenth-Century Britain', *Endeavour*, 22 (1998), pp. 143–47.

Conley, C. A., *The Unwritten Law: Criminal Justice in Victorian Kent* (Oxford, 1991).

Cox, N., *The Complete Tradesman: A Study of Retailing, 1550–1820* (Aldershot, 2000).

Crawford, C., 'Legalizing Medicine: Early Modern Legal Systems and the Growth of Medico-Legal Knowledge', in M. Clark and C. Crawford (eds), *Legal Medicine in History* (Cambridge, 1994), pp. 89–116.

Creighton, C., *A History of Epidemics in Britain*, ii (London, 1965).

Dalton, K., *Depression after Childbirth* (4th edn, Oxford, 2001).

Daunton, M. J., *Progress and Poverty: An Economic and Social History of Britain, 1700–1850* (Oxford, 1995).

Davidoff, L., 'The Family in Britain', in F. M. L. Thompson (ed.), *The Cambridge Social History of Britain, 1750–1950*, ii (Cambridge, 1990), pp. 71–129.

Dawes, F. V., *Not in Front of the Servants: A True Portrait of Upstairs, Downstairs Life* (revised edition, London, 1984).

Digby, A., *Making a Medical Living: Doctors and Patients in the English Market for Medicine, 1720–1911* (Cambridge, 1994).

Dyer, B. and Mitchell, C. A., *The Society of Public Analysts and other Analytical Chemists: Some Reminiscences of its First Fifty Years and a Review of its Activities* (Cambridge, 1932).

Emsley, C., *Crime and Society in England, 1750–1900* (2nd edn, London, 1996).

Farrell, M., *Poisons and Poisoners: An Encyclopedia of Homicidal Poisonings* (London, 1992).

Fedden, H. R., *Suicide: A Social and Historical Study* (London, 1938).

Flanagan, R. J., Widdop, B., Ramsey, J. D. and Loveland, M., 'Analytical Toxicology', *Human Toxicology*, 7 (1988), pp. 489–502.

Forbes, T. R., 'Crowner's Quest', *Transactions of the American Philosophical Society*, 68 (1978), pp. 3–52.

Forbes, T. R., 'Coroner's Inquisitions from the County of Cheshire, England, 1817–39 and 1877–78', *Bulletin of the History of Medicine*, 59 (1985), pp. 481–94.

Forbes, T. R., *Surgeons at the Bailey: English Forensic Medicine to 1878* (New Haven, 1985).

Gatrell, V. A. C., *The Hanging Tree: Execution and the English People, 1770–1868* (Oxford, 1994).

Gaute, J. H. H. and Odell, R., *Murder 'Whatdunit': An Illustrated Account of the Methods of Murder* (London, 1982).

Golan, T., 'The History of Scientific Expert Testimony in the English Courtroom', *Science in Context*, 12 (1999), pp. 7–32.

Gosden, P. H. J. H., *The Friendly Societies in England, 1815–1875* (reprint, Aldershot, 1993).

Greenwald, G. I. and Greenwald, M. W., 'Medicolegal Progress in Inquests of Felonious Deaths', *Journal of Legal Medicine*, 2 (1981), pp. 193–264.

Griffiths, A., *Mysteries of Police and Crime*, 3 vols (London, 1903).

Grove, W. R., 'Rex v. Donellan, Warwick Assizes, 1781', *Medico-Legal and Criminological Review*, 2 (1934), pp. 314–39.

Halbwachs, M., *The Causes of Suicide*, translated by Harold Goldblatt (London, 1978).

Hartman, M. S., *Victorian Murderesses: A True History of Thirteen Respectable French and English Women Accused of Unspeakable Crimes* (paperback edn, London, 1985).

Havard, J. D. J., *The Detection of Secret Homicide* (London, 1960).

Hill, B., *Servants: English Domestics in the Eighteenth Century* (Oxford, 1996).

Horn, P., *The Rise and Fall of the Victorian Servant* (reprint, Stroud, 1996).

Huggins, M., *Flat Racing and British Society, 1790–1914: A Social and Economic History* (London, 2000).

Hunnisett, R. F. (ed.), *Wiltshire Coroners' Bills, 1752–1796* (Devizes, 1981).

Huson, R. (ed.), *Sixty Famous Trials* (London, 1938).

Jalland, P., *Death in the Victorian Family* (Oxford, 1996).

Jones, D. J. V., *Crime in Nineteenth-Century Wales* (Cardiff, 1992).

Kelleher, M. D. and Kelleher, C. L., *Murder Most Rare: The Female Serial Killer* (New York, 1998).

Kidd, A., *State, Society and the Poor in Nineteenth-Century England* (London, 1999).

Kinnell, H. G., 'Serial Homicide by Doctors: Shipman in Perspective', *British Medical Journal*, 321 (2000), pp. 1594–97.

Knelman, J., *Twisting in the Wind: The Murderess and the English Press* (Toronto, 1998).

Lambert, R. S., *When Justice Faltered: A Study of Nine Peculiar Murder Trials* (London, 1935).

Landsman, S., 'One Hundred Years of Rectitude: Medical Witnesses at the Old Bailey, 1717–1817', *Law and History Review*, 16 (1998), pp. 445–94.

Langton, J. and Morris, R. J. (eds), *Atlas of Industrializing Britain, 1780–1914* (London, 1986).

Leyton, E., *Men of Blood: Murder in Modern England* (London, 1995).

Loudon, I., 'Puerperal Insanity in the Nineteenth Century', *Journal of the Royal Society of Medicine*, 81 (1988), pp. 76–79.

Loudon, I., *Death in Childbirth: An International Study of Maternal Care and Maternal Mortality, 1800–1950* (Oxford, 1992).

MacDonald, M., 'Suicidal Behaviour', in G. E. Berrios and R. Porter (eds), *A History of Clinical Psychiatry: The Origin and History of Psychiatric Disorders* (London, 1995), pp. 625–32.

Macfarlane, A., *Marriage and Love in England, 1300–1840* (Oxford, 1986).

Manchester, A. H., *A Modern Legal History of England and Wales, 1750–1950* (London, 1980).

Mant, A. K., 'Milestones in the Development of the British Medicolegal System', *Medicine, Science and the Law*, 17 (1977), pp. 155–63.

Marland, H., 'Getting Away with Murder? Puerperal Insanity, Infanticide and the Defence Plea', in M. Jackson (ed.), *Infanticide: Historical Perspectives on Child Murder and Concealment, 1550–2000* (Aldershot, 2002), pp. 168–92.

Marshall, D., *The English Domestic Servant in History* (London, 1949).

May, M., 'Violence in the Family: An Historical Perspective', in J. P. Martin (ed.), *Violence and the Family* (Chichester, 1978), pp. 135–68.

McGregor, O. R., *Divorce in England: A Centenary Study* (London, 1957).

McLaughlin, T., *The Coward's Weapon* (London, 1980).

Mitchell, B. R., *British Historical Statistics* (Cambridge, 1988).

Mitchell, C. A., *Science and the Criminal* (London, 1911).

Morgan, G. and Rushton, P., 'The Magistrate, the Community and the Maintenance of an Orderly Society in Eighteenth-Century England', *Historical Research*, 76 (2003), pp. 54–77.

Motion, A., *Wainewright the Poisoner* (London, 2000).

Myers, R. O., 'Famous Forensic Scientists, 5. Sir Thomas Stevenson (1838–1908)', *Medicine, Science and the Law*, 2 (1962), pp. 165–68.

Myers, R. O., 'Famous Forensic Scientists, 6. Alfred Swaine Taylor (1806–1880)', *Medicine, Science and the Law*, 2 (1962), pp. 233–40.

Onslow, R., *Headquarters: A History of Newmarket and its Racing* (Cambridge, 1983).

Parry, L. A., *Some Famous Medical Trials* (New York, 1928; reprint 1976).

Pearson, R., 'Thrift or Dissipation? The Business of Life Assurance in the Early Nineteenth Century', *Economic History Review*, 43 (1990), pp. 236–54.

Pelling, M., *Cholera, Fever and English Medicine, 1825–1865* (Oxford, 1978).

Perkin, J., *Victorian Women* (London, 1993).

Pink, J., *'Country Girls Preferred': Victorian Domestic Servants in the Suburbs* (Surbiton, 1998).

Priestley, P., *Victorian Prison Lives: English Prison Biography, 1830–1914* (paperback edn, London, 1999).

Raynes, H. E., *A History of British Insurance* (2nd edn, London, 1964).

Richardson, R., *Death, Dissection and the Destitute* (London, 1987).

Robb, G., 'Circe in Crinoline: Domestic Poisonings in Victorian England', *Journal of Family History*, 22 (1997), pp. 176–90.

Rooney, C. and Devis, T., 'Recent Trends in Deaths from Homicide in England and Wales', *Health Statistics Quarterly*, 3 (1999), pp. 5–13.

Rose, L., *The Massacre of the Innocents: Infanticide in Britain, 1800–1939* (London, 1986).

Roughead, W. (ed.), *Trial of Mary Blandy* (Edinburgh, 1914).

Rousseau, G. S. and Haycock, D. B., 'Coleridge's Choleras: Cholera Morbus, Asiatic Cholera and Dysentery in Nineteenth-Century England', *Bulletin of the History of Medicine*, 77 (2003), pp. 298–328.

Ruddick, J., *Death at the Priory: Love, Sex and Murder in Victorian England* (London, 2001).

Ryan, B., *The Poisoned Life of Mrs Maybrick* (London, 1977).

S. B. A., 'Sir Thomas Stevenson, MD, FRCP', *Transactions of the Medico-Legal Society*, 5 (1907–8), pp. 186–88.

Sherrington, E., 'Thomas Wakley and Reform, 1823–62' (unpublished D.Phil. thesis, Oxford, 1974).

Shpayer-Makov, H., *The Making of a Policeman: A Social History of a Labour Force in Metropolitan London, 1829–1914* (Aldershot, 2002).

Smith, J., *Death Disguised.* Part 1 of the Official Inquiry into the Crimes of Dr Harold Shipman (London, 2002).

Spokes, S., 'A Case of Circumstantial Evidence', *Sussex County Magazine*, 11 (1937), pp. 118–22.

St Aubyn, G., *Infamous Victorians: Lamson and Palmer, Two Notorious Poisoners* (London, 1971).

Stallion, M. and Wall, D. S., *The British Police: Police Forces and Chief Officers, 1829–2000* (Hook, Hampshire, 1999).

Stark, C., Paterson, B. and Kidd, B., 'Opportunity May Be More Important than Profession in Serial Homicide', *British Medical Journal*, 322 (2001), p. 993.

Stone, L., *The Past and the Present Revisited* (London, 1987).

Stone, L., *Road to Divorce: England, 1530–1987* (Oxford, 1990).

Taylor, D., *The New Police in Nineteenth-Century England: Crime, Conflict and Control* (Manchester, 1997).

Taylor, D., *Crime, Policing and Punishment in England, 1750–1914* (Basingstoke, 1998).

Thompson, E. P., *The Making of the English Working Class* (reprint, London, 1980).

Vamplew, W., *The Turf: A Social and Economic History of Horse Racing* (London, 1976).

Watson, K. D., 'Highlights in the History of Toxicology', in P. Wexler (ed.), *Information Resources in Toxicology* (3rd edn, San Diego, 2000), pp. 1–13.

Whittle, B. and Ritchie, J., *Prescription for Murder: The True Story of Mass Murderer Dr Harold Frederick Shipman* (London, 2000).

Wilson, C. and Pitman, P., *Encyclopaedia of Murder* (London, 1984).

Wilson, P., *Murderess: A Study of Women Executed in Britain since 1843* (London, 1971).

Woods, R. and Shelton, M., *An Atlas of Victorian Mortality* (Liverpool, 1997).

Young, F. (ed.), *Trial of the Seddons* (2nd edn, Edinburgh, 1925).

Young, F., 'Hawley Harvey Crippen', in H. Hodge (ed.), *Famous Trials*, i (London, 1941), pp. 111–38.

Index